RIPOFF: HOW TO SPOT IT, HOW TO AVOID IT

PETER T. MAIKEN

Ripoff:
How to Spot It
How to Avoid It

ANDREWS AND McMEEL, INC.
A Universal Press Syndicate Company
KANSAS CITY

To all the people who had the interest, the kindness, and, sometimes, the courage to contribute to this book.

Portions of this book appeared originally in the *Chicago Tribune Magazine*.

Library of Congress Cataloging in Publication Data

Maiken, Peter T   1934-
    Ripoff.

    1. Fraud—United States—Case studies. I. Title.
HV6695.M34   364.1'63'0973   79-10086
ISBN 0-8362-6203-4
ISBN: 0-8362-6204-2 (pbk.)

CONTENTS

PREFACE

"How cynical," was one of the first reactions I got to my announcement that I was researching a subject for a book by asking people in a variety of occupations how ripoffs occur in their fields. Perhaps there was an element of cynicism present because my own experience as a ripoff victim was my original inspiration to undertake the project. Maybe there was some weird planetary action going on at the time—at least it seemed to me that I was somehow the target of more than a normal share of activity that was benefiting other people at my expense. We are, of course, all ripped off in varying degrees by employers, employees, acquaintances, relatives, and the whole spectrum of people we deal with in our everyday market encounters. One message of the tax revolt is that a legitimate need to raise public revenue finally has become a ripoff of society at large. Ripoffs, in other words, certainly do abound.

Because it would seem that most of us have more to say about ripoffs from the victim's point of view, I thought that the most informative presentation would stem from my going to the persons *doing* the ripoffs and asking them how they are done. We've come to regard certain segments of the American work-force as being notorious for the ripoffs they perpetrate, but what of the many other occupations we don't so highly suspect—are they doing it too? Are we all in this together, each of us using our own particular method of screwing the people we deal with? To find out, I decided to go to the perpetrators for the supposed expert testimony they might offer.

My purpose, while it may be based upon a certain degree of cynicism, is entirely one of exposition: to present, in interview format, a journalist's look at action and thought as it exists in America at the end of the 1970s. But if there is a degree of cynicism, I would hope there is a greater element of meliorism, in the sense that knowing and understanding is better than merely ignoring or wishing a problem away. And while this book gives a definite nod to consumerism, I would also hope that what it presents goes beyond a mere recitation of *caveat emptor*. I hope it tells us all more about ourselves than we knew before.

Most of the people I interviewed showed a reaction to the ripoffs they recounted ranging from disapproval to total disgust. I would conclude that the majority of them are fundamentally honest people who saw in their interview an opportunity to expose wrong-doing that had bothered them for some time. On the other hand, a few smirked over their exploits in what I would consider to be expressions of egotism, as did several who professed to be profoundly embittered with the whole system and spoke of their activities as being a sort of revenge. Very rarely were those who perpetrated the ripoffs, however, proud of their actions. Mostly they acknowledged that they were doing wrong and regretted it and attempted to justify it in their own minds by reason of their being prisoners of the system. "What am I supposed to do when everyone else is doing it?" or "when someone tells me to do it?" or "when that's just the way things are done?" etc. Of course, some of the speakers were not the perpetrators, they were close witnesses. Within this group the sense of outrage was most pronounced. In slightly over half of the cases, the people no longer work in the jobs they describe, and some are in totally different fields altogether. None of the subjects are relatives of mine. Many of the young adults speak from the experience of low-rung employment they had in school or when they were first making their way into the labor market. A second major group consists of people who have spent 15 or more years in their field and at some point in middle age decided it was all a crock of baloney.

In an earlier, magazine version of this material, the editor received several letters of complaint that said, in effect, that I was smearing the good name of their occupational group by holding up unworthy examples that were not representative of the group as a whole. In no way do I mean to suggest that these people I interviewed are typical examples of their various groups. I'm sure there is no way of knowing how they fit into their particular groups other than by reading what they have to say and deciding for yourself. They are simply people, who, for their own reason (which, probably in many cases, was disenchantment), decided to respond to my solicitation and comment accordingly. Certainly the reputation of a class does not ride on the comments of an individual member.

I started out by interviewing people I knew, however casually. This circle of people, of course, was limited in number, and it became necessary to find more candidates willing to talk. Thus I had to leave the comfortable field of interview subjects who knew and trusted me enough to speak with candor and instead approach a group of new prospects unknown to me as I was to them. I began by running a classified ad in a Chicago newspaper. The ad was brief: "I'm writing a book on ripoffs in various occupations. Will you share your job experiences in confidential telephone interview?" Response was good, and in the beginning I got three or four solid interviews every week. And despite my earlier fears that respondents would be reluctant to talk openly with a stranger, this proved to be not the case at all. Furthermore, it opened up communications between me and a group of people often quite strongly motivated to share their grievances. After several months, when it became clear I might be depleting that particular supply of readers, I placed similar ads in other newspapers.

When people called, I explained the nature of my project, told them that real names would not be used, and that I hoped they would talk freely about their experiences. Most of the interviews were conducted over the telephone, and most of them were taped. In most cases the identity of the callers are unknown to me. All names of subjects in the book, accordingly, are fictitious, given by me in an alphabetically random pattern. If by some remote coincidence the name I gave a person happens to be his or her real name, it is purely unintentional on my part.

In a few cases, I have either omitted or changed the details that would serve to identify the subjects. None of this, however, alters the basic truth that I hope emerges. In cases where I tried to get the subject to make a quantitative assessment or an estimate of frequency, I would ask something to the effect of: "In what percentage of the cases does that happen?" So when a subject in this book says: "Twenty-five percent of our salesmen overcharge," the reader should not assume that such a statement is uttered in the spirit of statistical accuracy. Virtually none of us, at least in my area, could answer the question: "How often have you been rained on in the last year?" with anything more than an approximate guess.

Although the following assortment of interviews presents a fairly broad view of the American job establishment, it is by no means comprehensive, and I can think of several occupational categories I wish I had got but didn't. A project such as this, however, has to be contained at some point, and I preferred having the subjects' willingness to come to me and talk be the limiting factor rather than my forcing an effort to fill those gaps. Although there are some higher-echelon people included, most of those interviewed are in the great middle range of the labor market. Perhaps executive and professional people will be another project entirely.

Many subjects spoke of "wage ripoffs": how they were paid only the minimum wage, or the fact that they earned less than their counterparts at other companies. While there is no doubt that by certain standards many people are "underpaid" (not to mention "overpaid"), if one accepts and remains at a job at the wage rate offered, he is tacitly, no matter how reluctantly, agreeing to the terms, and there is no definable element of ripoff that I can see. Except, of course, one may be a "prisoner of the system," an attitude I suspect most of us voice at one time or another. Much of this sort of material I have eliminated, as well as personal-victim anecdotes that require a fuller understanding of the persons involved, the background, and the situation than time and space would allow. Nor did I use much material on commonly known office ripoffs like paper-clip theft, tardiness, etc.

I found probably the most common motivation for ripping off to be the desire for gain, in degrees ranging from simple betterment to examples of outright greed. There were other motivations, however, some locked deeply in the psyche of the speakers, and these I made no attempt to explore because they are beyond the competence of a journalist alone to deal with and require the attention of scientists who specialize in the study of the human mind. My intention, therefore, was to deal with the fact of the ripoff's existence, the "what" and the "how," and to leave the "why" to others. I did, however, frequently lead the people into giving clues to their behavior by asking their attitudes—how they felt about what they had done and whether they had any feelings of remorse. Such attitudes as these, I believe, are significant because they do shed light on actions—although in most cases I leave it to the reader to draw his or her own inferences.

There are statements in the book relating to racial and ethnic identity that I hope are not construed as being offered in the spirit of racism. When a subject made a comment as evidence of a certain racial group dominating a class of either victims or perpetrators, I sometimes included it for the sake of what it told. Beyond that, I did not set out to make a statement and "prove" that blacks and women are still discriminated against, or that little guys are always the victims of big guys, or any other such thing. The main point of view in this book is that ripoffs abound, and only by informing ourselves about them can we deal with them as the problems they are.

INTRODUCTION

The English language has a remarkable ability both to enrich and impoverish itself by absorbing new words and discarding old ones. Knowing this, I find it hard to imagine how, just a decade ago, we made do with such a meager assortment of words as: steal, pilfer, rob, swindle, cheat, exploit, and so on, when what we obviously needed to say all along was "rip off." Out of the U.S. street culture of the late 1960s came this expression, which is still classified as slang by those dictionaries that list it. It began appearing in print, according to one reference, in 1970. In a news story that summer, *Time* magazine held it at arm's length by putting it in quotes, explaining to its readers that it meant "to steal." Now we have "ripoff," the noun, and "rip off," the verb, and we use them endlessly, all the while giving them new meanings that the words soak up like thirsty sponges.

But all that is medieval history, and today you can advertise in the newspapers that you want to talk ripoffs, and even septuagenarians will know what you mean. Or do they? There is frequently a need for a new word that accurately labels the uniqueness of its subject. As matter and action become ever more fragmented, there is a continuing need to be more specific. So why, one might ask, should a word that is nothing more than an umbrella for many already precise and useful words gain such currency? And by the way, what the hell *does* ripoff mean? The dictionaries list all the definitions mentioned above and will probably increase their number as time passes. Meanwhile, the word ripoff continues to show the dynamic traits of a hunter's stew: You are never quite sure of the ingredients, but you know when it works. If I were to add the carcass I've snared to the seething cookpot—to attempt to define the common element that all cases in this book share—I would define ripoff as: The acquisition of something at someone else's expense.

When thieves steal goods from a deserted warehouse in the night, they are engaging in a transaction: They are the perpetrators of a ripoff, and there are victims—though not present—who will soon bear the cost of the crime. Every ripoff is a transaction that involves a perpetrator and a victim, whether singular or plural. In the following interviews, in which I have asked people about the ripoffs in their particular occupations, most of them usually spoke from the perpetrators' point of view. These classes of victims are certainly the most sizable:

- Consumers—Surprisingly, consumer awareness is even older than the expression rip off. Many consumer advocates today are giving the old *caveat emptor* (let the buyer beware) added thrust, and for good reason. Consumers frequently get sheared in basic market encounters by either getting less than expected or paying more for their purchase than it's worth.
- Employers—Or, "Don't you have a Xerox machine in your office?" As any worker knows, employers are often taken advantage of by those whose livelihood they provide.
- Employees—It works both ways. Workers are sometimes unfairly, even illegally, used by those who hire them.
- Government—Show remorse only if you wish, but government at all levels is cheated. And as this happens, individual citizens and taxpayers, as well as society at large, are also indirectly cheated.
- Stockholders—They, after all, *own* the company, although sometimes you'd never know it by watching the actions of the employees, including hired management.

There are other perpetrator-victim relationships that emerge as well. Fellow employees generally work in a cooperative situation, although that sometimes turns into competition, and, ultimately, even warfare. The buddy system, in other words, goes only so far. Directors and trustees oversee most of the key enterprises of American society, yet some are remarkably ignorant of the workings of their trust. Of course, many of those responsible for reporting to them would just as soon keep it that way.

Lower-echelon employees often represent their companies in many dealings, and they are not always treated justly by their counterparts in other firms, especially when goods and money change hands at loading docks, seaports, etc. Members of organizations, especially unions, are sometimes at the mercy of the whole or of their leadership. That keeps unions powerful. Consumers are rarely on an equal footing with professional and technical service people, and that state of dependency can be lucrative—though not for the consumer. And, of course, vendors can just as easily be victims as they can be perpetrators. That, after all, is how the word ripoff crept into the language, as a synonym for theft of goods.

We all know from our own experience as victims that ripoffs do exist and on occasion run rampant, but at what point does a seemingly harmless action become a ripoff? Is the theft of a ballpoint pen from your company a ripoff, or must you walk out the back door with twenty-five pounds of their salted nuts before you qualify? If you can photocopy your tax forms with impunity, is it okay to run off your novel? If they have a WATS line, does it matter if you call your old sorority sister in Boston—if you are, say, in Los Angeles? At some point, ripoffs that are routinely accepted—usually because it would cost more to prevent them—become intolerable, not just to those directly involved, but to the larger community as well.

Estimates of cost are imprecise, which helps explain why ripoffs flourish in the first place. The perpetrators can engage in their activities largely unobserved and unchallenged. If better figures were available, that would imply greater watchfulness and less chance for ripping off to occur. Nonetheless, some of the figures available are enormous. In September 1978, the General Accounting Office estimated that the cost of fraud and related white-collar crimes against the U.S. government could run as high as $25 billion. The Department of Commerce estimated that employee theft in American business amounted to $18 billion in 1977, compared to $3 billion a decade earlier. The National Council on Crime and Delinquency estimates that as much as 15 percent of the money Americans spend for goods and services goes to cover losses due to employee theft and the cost of insurance to protect against it. In the autumn of 1978, Robert Half, Inc., a management consulting firm in New York, estimated that "deliberate waste and misuse of on-the-job time" was an $80-billion drain on the U.S. economy. Though appalling, these figures are only part of the story.

There are forces at work that all of us collectively have created but which none of us has any significant voice in controlling. Our population in the twentieth century has changed from a mostly rural to a mostly urban society, which has brought a new dimension of rootlessness and impersonality into our dealings. This has given many of us a chance for higher pay, though at a cost of greatly increased uncertainty. We have become removed from the benign influences and support systems that smaller communities offer, with their extended families and networks of friends. We have searched for greatness and instead have found only bigness, and we find to our dismay that all our days are spent in encounters with unresponsive bureaucracies and their voluminous rules that govern the conduct of our affairs. We have created a technology that has at once liberated and enslaved us through our own impotence to gain mastery over it. Our commercial giants have outgrown the notion of doing business on a personal scale and, using the patois of a police officer writing up a rape report, speak mostly of market penetration. Some say the dollar is doomed.

In our new state of uneasiness, we have salved ourselves with the notion that despite the adversities, it's all worthwhile. As the wealthiest among nations, we take our materialism seriously, and we have a host of hedonistic men's magazines that confirm our persuasion that, indeed, comfort, pleasure, and wealth are truly the bottom line. If it feels good, do it. We have been told in the spirit of consciousness-raising to exalt overselves above all else and look out for No. 1. We have been told that there is nothing truly right or wrong, only varying shades of gray. In such a landscape of moral confusion as this, the ripoff struts most visibly and unchallenged.

It requires no great mental leap on the part of ordinary mortals who are exposed to news of the crooked schemes of politicians, businessmen, and labor leaders, to convince themselves that if those people are getting theirs, why shouldn't the little guy get his? If a Watergate is a reality, of what significance is a missing carton on a loading dock? As Camus said, even if one is prepared to admit one's guilt, one is invariably convinced of the presence of mitigating circumstances that excuse one's actions. Such rationalizations are easy to find when "everybody does it," or when "that's just the way the system works." Nor is it difficult for people who have little to contribute to the economic system—people who have a vivid awareness that crime does pay for many of their peers—to stoke the fires of their expectations with feelings of revenge and go out and tie the score in their own minds; now becoming the perpetrators, no longer the victims.

If ripoffs are a symptom of a declining civilization, however, then our lot has always been somewhere in an advanced state of decay. But for exceptional pockets of innocence and purity, much of history consists of the exploits of someone getting something at someone else's expense. From the conquests of the ancient world, through the age of exploration, through nineteenth-century imperialism in Africa (down to the Communist conquests of the twentieth century), the lands that hosted these ventures have been mightily ripped off—and the settlement of the Americas certainly deserves listing, too. The rulers, the nobility, and the church have all been prime exponents of this darker side of human nature. There is no point in suggesting that ripping off one's fellow men is a crisis peculiar to our time, because precedent is just too ample.

At one point it was suggested to me that this project was an attack on the free-enterprise system and that it would support the contentions of critics that capitalists are, after all, just a horde of predators. I don't agree with that judgment in the least; neither would I be inclined at this point to disparage the concept of the market economy. The classical economists knew well that rascals were afoot in the world and that they operate under any kind of economic system. Yet, these economists showed beyond doubt that, while scoundrels might prosper without challenge in an authoritarian system, they are most vulnerable to exposure where economic freedom is assured. When sellers must compete with other sellers and openly display their goods or services for all to see, the chance for deception is present but to a far lesser degree than in any other conceivable system. The question to be asked is: What constitutes a free-enterprise system, and how much do we want our own to be tampered with for the sake of special interests?

The free market is continuously challenged by factions that wish to direct its operation to their own advantage. People who rip off the system are, first of all, restricting the productive apparatus by not contributing to the supply of goods or services; and, second, they are cheating the distribution system by taking what they are not entitled to get. In other words, they are getting something at someone else's expense. This, however, is the ripoff, the villain of the piece. What about the heroes, the elements responsible for producing the wealth the ripoff so brazenly siphons off?

America today is virtually placing its economic trust in the hands of three large elements, two of which are productive, and the third of which is not: big business, big labor, and big government. And every member of this triad is putting the same pressure on the market economy as the small-time ripoff perpetrator employs: Each one, in its own way, seeks to restrict production and to restructure the distribution to its own advantage. Each does this by playing monopoly. Big business tends to conduct its affairs in such a manner as to ensure that it will reach a point where it can engage in monopoly pricing. Big labor achieves its goals by having the legalized privilege of monopolizing the supply of labor. And big government acts as both traffic cop and supreme arbiter by employing its naturally bestowed monopoly of the use of coercion.

Big business tries to restrict production by excluding foreign competitors for its markets through government-enacted trade barriers. If the laws do not allow one corporation to do in its domestic competitors, either by licking them or acquiring them, they will all seek to fix prices at a level of mutual comfort. But in the absence of any rules of the game, the natural thrust of each is to become *the* one and only, and, now in the era of conglomerates, not just in its own particular industry. As a monopoly, a corporation is thus in a position to charge monopoly prices, which are higher than market prices, and thereby assure itself of a bloated share of the distribution.

Most every goal of big labor in a negotiation situation is either to restrict production through limiting work time, or—assuming production is kept the same—increase the distribution to its union members. Sometimes, big labor goes for both, and it is frequently successful in getting all or many of its wishes, simply because it has the power to close the business if its demands for monopoly-price wages are not met.

Big government restricts production in many ways: Regulation adds to the cost of doing business and results in some things not being produced that otherwise would have been. Wage-protection legislation also increases the cost of doing business, resulting in fewer people being employed and fewer goods produced. In one of the greatest of all economic paradoxes, the government gives subsidies for *not* producing certain crops. On the other side of the copper-clad coin, most all government welfare activities—not to mention its taxation system—are directed toward redistribution of income. Moreover, the government is primarily responsible for one of the most insidious ripoffs of all, inflation of the currency, which, apart from all its other evils, directs an ever-increasing flow of revenue to the government through the progressive-tax system. As for the matter of waste in government, let the comments of the people I interviewed suffice.

What does one say of the small-time ripoff, when it is apparent that the three pillars of our modern economy work in much the same manner, albeit far more respectably, because they have legions of toadies to emit propaganda, prepare self-serving statistics, and write depositions to keep their sponsors out of jail? Oddly enough, all these activities the Big Triad engages in are commonly viewed as being entirely legitimate—actions that should be pursued for the good of all. This, of course, does not take cognizance of the plateau all members of this group have attained beyond the bounds of legitimacy.

Big business has virtually disenfranchised the very source of capital that made its productive enterprise possible: the stockholder. Hired management insulates itself from the dictates of the true owners of a corporation by ensuring that they exercise no function other than ratifying the selection of an accounting firm to audit the company's books. One chief executive of a large American corporation recently admitted that he found the meetings of the board of directors, who supposedly represent the interests of the company's stockholders and who should have been telling him what to do, time consuming and fruitless. And so he prefaced the meetings with a spread of strong drink and food. "At least one of the older directors," the *Chicago Tribune* quoted the executive as saying, "would fall asleep at the meeting, and the subsequent embarrassment would make everyone eager to get the whole mess over as soon as possible." This is how a corporation becomes, in effect, a private fiefdom of those hired to manage it, and when a stockholding gadfly dares to challenge the salaries and perks that management has lavished upon itself, not to mention their right or wrong decisions, he is sternly admonished as a meddler and shouted down as an enemy of free enterprise.

Nor have some of the leaders of big labor been content simply to strive for the betterment of the working man. Their unions have become rife with corruption through the squandering of union funds on poor investments and high living for the official élite and their cronies, as well as through neglect of their constituents' interest when defending it would upset the sweetheart relationship they enjoy with their corporate counterparts.

In addition to the frequent use of elected public office for private gain, big government has provided taxpayers with a new class of bureaucratic élite whose numbers dwarf anything previously imaginable. Useful or not, they endure, they proliferate, and they carry on as participating partners in assuring the workability of the Great American Dream. With "friends" of capitalism such as those found among the Big Triad, what further use is there for Karl Marx?

None of this is meant to condone the existence of ripoffs at any level of human action; it is merely to show that they are not the special province of a lawless minority. I do not think that ripoffs are in any sense a cancer unique to the corpus of American capitalism. Perhaps we suffer them to the degree we do because we have encouraged the growth of a system that in so many ways does not resemble in the least what a free-market economy is all about. And in doing so, we have unwittingly disposed of the best possible remedy we have.

ADVERTISING/MARKETING/PR

PUBLIC RELATIONS DIRECTOR

The first encounter Max J. had with ripoffs in the field of public relations was his introduction to the business itself. Applying for a job at a PR agency, he was asked, as all applicants were, to propose a public relations campaign for a mythical client. "Later," says Max, "I learned that it was not a mythical client at all. He was using my ideas on a real, live account." In the course of his career as a public relations director, Max supervised both external and internal communications and press relations for about ten major corporations. Despite his mandate to accentuate the positive, at least to the outside world, he emerged knowing that a goodly portion of his work consisted of whitewashing certain sets of facts. And he doesn't feel very sanguine about the sort of aura he was paid to generate. "Ripoffs in corporations," he says, alluding to a recent municipal exposé, "are on a higher plane, but they are every bit as extensive, widespread, and horrifying as ripoffs engineered by corrupt city inspectors."

I was often directed by management to lie to or deceive the news media, but usually management would back off. They would agree we didn't have to lie, but we just wouldn't tell the media everything. It's generally agreed that you're an honest press secretary if you don't lie. You can omit, you can avoid providing negative information on your client, you can emphasize favorable information, but you should never lie.

Once, our president gave an earnings estimate to the *Wall Street Journal*, which he and everyone else knew was untrue. When I told the reporter, he said I'd given the president a chance to correct it, but he didn't, so the story moved. On my own, I corrected it and sent a note to the president, and I never heard a word. This was a ripoff of the investing public—a deceitful earnings estimate that affected the price of the stock.

1

Top management views the news media as adversaries. Management believes the news media are as wild as Tiny Tim and that they'll tell any kind of lie to make a buck. Management wants you to fight with the media, stall them—don't tell them anything.

Business does as it pleases. Most companies do not take sincere action on complaints from consumers. Only if they're going to get in trouble with a federal regulatory body or because it's good PR do they heed a suggestion.

People are terribly naive to think major corporations are in business to make a good product or provide a good service at a reasonable price. This is not the idea at all. Making a profit is paramount. Yet, the only reason top management is mindful of stockholders is that traditionally they have been stockholders themselves. Because of their options, as their stock climbs, so does their wealth. They work hard to make money for stockholders, and by coincidence, they happen to be stockholders.

But if managers had to choose between saving their own necks and increasing the price of the stock, they are going to save their own necks first. The stockholders and the customers do not come first. I have represented a dozen major U.S. corporations, and I know they have a callous disregard for and lack of understanding of what the American public wants and needs.

Company directors are among the greatest rip-off artists of all time. Theoretically, board members are there to provide an independent look at a company and bring their own expertise to bear on its problems. One director at a meeting I attended napped, then ignored the debate on some important capital expenditure by reading the *New York Times*. My recollection is that directors got $1,000 a board meeting, plus expenses. By coincidence, their companies got to underwrite our new stock offerings, or they might be representatives of law firms that would profit from our business. I knew of a board member who would leave a meeting and call his friends and tell them a stock split would be announced in a few hours, so they could take advantage of it.

If the boards are made up of insiders—company officers who

owe their total allegiance to the president—then everything they do is phony. Everyone lines up and says the president's new grandson is beautiful—they tell him exactly what he wants to hear. They give him nothing but a stamp of approval, because they'll get fired if they don't.

One of my companies brought in outside auditors to brief the directors at board meetings. Then the auditors would meet with the president of the company and would repeat to him every question the board of directors had asked, so he was prepared in case the directors pursued any heated lines. That was all a sham. The implication was that the "independent" outside auditors had better remember who the hell their employer was: the management of the company, not the outside directors.

Another of my companies hired a site-search firm to make a study of where the company headquarters should be relocated. They studied all the cities in America, and by coincidence, they recommended locating the company in the city where the chairman had a wife and family and where he commuted to every weekend. The board of directors took fifteen seconds to approve the move. Also, by coincidence, that man is now divorced.

You're in a big club when you're on the board of directors. You get to go to New York and have meetings at the Pierre Hotel and dinners at the 21 Club. You celebrate the birthdays of seventy-five-year-old directors and the marriages of sixty-five-year-old directors. You go to Monaco and have dinner with Princess Grace in her castle.

Annual reports are the big BS documents of the year. A company must put out a full disclosure of certain things—such as a balance sheet—but it doesn't have to be an expensive, beautiful document. It's hard to justify companies spending more on the annual report than on dividends they pay stockholders. Ten years ago there were some annual reports like pieces of art—they cost $5 and $6 apiece. This is done for the same reason that presidents of companies travel in chauffeured limousines and belong to shiny-floored clubs—because it's prestige. It enables them to win awards and be heralded as titans of industry. Few stockholders complain; they just assume this is the way it's done in business. But every corporation in America produces an annual report that costs more than is necessary.

There's an adversary relationship between most companies and their employees. Most top management people believe that PR is a total frill, not even a necessary evil. They have to be told that employees have a right to be communicated to, that it's not an intrusion by an employee to want to know where the hell the company is going. When management has trouble with profits, the last thing they concern themselves with is communicating with the goddamned employees. Most internal communications programs are incomplete; there's neither sincerity nor continuity implicit to them.

Public relations agencies are superficial and can't possibly devote the amount of time the client pays for. They'll give you three accounts, then your executive vice president goes on vacation and her three accounts get apportioned, then somebody's ill and you have to handle that one, too, and pretty soon you don't even have time to return the phone calls let alone do the work. When I was preparing a presentation for a prospective client, I found the agency always had said it employed twenty-one professionals. I said, hell, we've got four. After a big argument, the boss agreed to strike the figure and talk about "the many" PR professionals on the staff. One trick this agency used when a client was going to pay a visit was to close all the office doors and put all the women account executives and bookkeepers, etc., on typewriters out front.

Agencies charge as much as they can get. I once competed with a firm on a design program for a state organization, and they beat me with a bid of $6,500. For a major corporation's program, charging what the market would bear, they won the design bid for, I think, $350,000. After buying that program, the chairman saw the same logo (only sideways) on the facade of a building a few streets away. Another designer told me he'd seen the same design, with slight changes, submitted to three or four other companies.

The only unethical newsman I know once did an interview with a PR man in the automotive field and planned a big story.

4

The PR man told me he had introduced his fiancée to the reporter. She told her fiancé that the reporter had called and made it very clear to her that if her boyfriend wanted the story in print, she ought to become a little bit friendlier. I told the PR man, who was then a novice, to tell the reporter where he could shove his story. The reporter's still at it. He gets lots and lots of presents.

Another news reporter does legitimate stories on companies, then when the company wants to reprint those stories, he says his firm has a policy of extracting an honorarium, which goes to him. He knows a company will want to reprint a story when it's favorable. I could be persuaded that that's unethical.

Probably the biggest ripoff concerns the subject of WORK. The difference between the unemployed and the worker is often very slight. In some corporations people come to work, then they make a cup of coffee, then they finish reading the *Wall Street Journal*, which they didn't finish reading on the train, or they read all the *Wall Street Journal* if they drove to work, then they make another cup of coffee, then they make a few personal phone calls to get a few things lined up, then they go to the bathroom for a very important activity, carrying the newspaper with them, then they start making rounds. For instance, I used to hit the various executive offices to find out what was going on, and inevitably what was going on included a recitation of what they did last night, inquiries about when were we going to see them and their spouses for dinner, etc. And when they get back to their desks, there are some business calls to return and a few memos to get approved, then they go out for an early lunch with their fellow executives or suppliers, and there's a long queue, then they come back and go to the toilet again, then they get their personal photocopying done, then they talk to their spouses a couple of times and their kids, and maybe call the school to find out why the hell their children are having problems, then they get a haircut, and they go to the dentist when necessary, then they go home, on time. Some workers really don't do that much work. The difference is basically one of appearance.

ADVERTISING MAN

In his long career in advertising, Bradley V. has worked as a senior executive for several department store and promotional department store chains. Along the way, he has worked in "borax houses," selling schlock furniture. Borax houses are high-priced operations that hawk their wares and services on late-night TV. His responsibilities were in both advertising and merchandising. In most of their dealings with large retailers, says Bradley, "customers are pretty much at the mercy of the system."

When I handled advertising for a leading furrier, I would run an ad in the newspapers featuring a number of items on sale, including, say, one mink coat at cost or below. In other words, I'd advertise a coat that normally sells for $4,000 for $2,000. We'd say we only had one, although, in fact, we made sure we had two, a small and a large size. When a big woman came in, they brought out the small coat. Then after they'd convinced her they couldn't fit her in the sale item, they would try to switch her into something they could make a normal profit on. That is one of the "bait and switch" methods.

Of the other sale items, they would bring out furs of inferior grades: A coat made out of bellies, which is not as fine a fur as the back, but it would still have a mink, or whatever, label on it. Maybe it would be a coat made from tiny pieces, or remnants, instead of full skins. Maybe the coats were made of improperly processed furs; there are reputable fur makers and schlocky ones. If a fur is not processed properly, the hair will fall out, or the dye will come off on your hands. Of course, we didn't make any of these distinctions in the advertising.

One of the greatest ripoffs in stores is the concealed stock, where the customer is strictly at the mercy of the salesperson. These stores keep only samples out, or maybe a rack of something on clearance, but everything else is behind the curtains. As a result, the customer does not necessarily get an opportunity to make a free choice. When merchandise doesn't move fast—it might be last year's, or a style that is sticky or inferior in some

6

way—the manager may pay the sales girl extra commission to move it. That gives her the incentive to show these things and limit the choice of the customer. Which is another thing a salesperson wants to do. When customers see too many things, they get confused, so you want to limit their choices. This tactic is used by fine stores all over the country.

The main ripoffs in the "borax" furniture houses are in the grades of the fabrics and the construction. In their advertising, the furniture stores rely mainly on the old bait and switch. They will advertise an item they have had made in a special way so that no one will buy it. Everything they say in the ad is true, but because of the styling and color, it looks like garbage. It's nylon, but it might be a manure brown. They purposely make it look like the devil so they can bait and switch.

In a borax house, the salesmen have plenty of margin—it's no 40 percent markup deal; it's probably what they call "a number and a half." When a store "makes a number," it means they have doubled the cost price. When they make a number and a half, they make the cost price plus one-and-a-half times that. If cost is $100, the sale price would be $250. On a typical price tag, the sale price will be marked, then there is a code, which is usually one of the stock numbers or factory numbers, and that tells the salesmen just how low they can go in price.

When customers show signs of walking, you call the assistant manager, who is usually nothing more than another salesman, and introduce him to the customer as Mr. Cutter or Mr. Turner or, sometimes Mr. Otto. This gives the second salesman the signal to keep the customer on the line by giving a little lower price. He knows the first salesman has quoted the regular price, and the code tells him how far he can go below that. If that doesn't work, the last person they introduce the customer to is "Mr. Burns." He knows the customer is not going to buy, so he's supposed to point out some defect and give the customer a fantastically low price on it for when the customer comes back. Of course, by that time it's long gone.

A lot of stores, particularly the borax houses, have two or three charts in different colors that show finance charges computed at different rates of interest. Either the salesmen or the credit man will determine which chart to use. If they think you will stand for it, they'll charge you at a higher rate. If customers look kind of rugged, they will go to the higher rate, because the ordinary finance company would not take them otherwise. In some cases, the store gets a kickback from the finance company. Over a period of time, the total cost of a purchase might be 20 or 30 percent higher than if the lower rate card were used. Some charts I've seen are a total cheat, because they are full of arithmetical errors—in favor of the store. Most people can't multiply in their head, and if the customer questions it, all the salesman has to do is point to the chart and say, "Here it is, right in the table."

Some stores don't even offer wood furniture anymore. Various wood-grain finishes are photographically applied to a sort of paper that is put onto a press-board. This is real crap that will not maintain its looks for very long and is easily damaged. I've even seen this stuff used in dressers, where sides were made out of corrugated board—like cardboard boxes. The bottoms of the drawers were made out of cardboard—just like artboard in weight—and the drawers were put together with staples.

In bedding, generally, the more coils, the better the mattress. But if the coils aren't fastened properly, the body will disrupt them too soon, and the mattress that looked beautiful when you bought it won't hold up. But even if you buy a name brand, there is no way to know whether a mattress will be sagging in six months, because all the coils are concealed. The greatest ripoff in bedding is boxed springs. They are not expensive to make, but they are priced the same as the mattress, even though there is a world of difference as to their contents. That's how the companies make their money. They will take a little closer profit on the mattress and will make it up on the boxed springs at the factory level. In couch-beds, the main ripoff is in the grading of the fabric, and there are no uniform standards in the industry. Even though the fabrics may be only a few cents higher a yard, the stores will charge $10 or $20 for a grade difference.

There are people in the furniture business who set up what

they call "stuffed flats," where they rent an apartment, fill it up with furniture, then run a want ad in the newspapers that says they are moving and willing to "sacrifice" their furniture. So the people who respond come in and think they are making a real deal when they are told, "I just paid $3,500 for all this at a department store, and I will give it to you for $2,500." Most people don't know if the things are priced right—they're only concerned with the total price. So the retailer makes the sale, clears out the apartment, and brings more in and starts over. Many times people who conduct those so-called house sales will have bought some line from a retailer that they add to what they're selling in the house.

Warehouse sales you hear so much about are largely gimmicks. People think they are getting a big price cut that they are not necessarily getting. They are entirely variable, and while one sofa may be a good buy, the one next to it may be a number and a half. The deck may be solid instead of being of coil springs, or the wood frame may be of inferior quality.

Even though stores try to do the best they can at the top-management level, there are people below them who are not too honest. They may not want to give back their commission, so they will, what we call, blow off the complaints. Or the buyer doesn't want to take the blame for buying an inferior line. Stores will teach buyers their methods, but they don't necessarily give buyers the opportunity to learn the details of the particular manufacturing effort with which they have become involved. So, they are a glorified monkey concerned only with price, and the factory is selling them whatever they want to.

A customer is paying extra for a label in most cases. These are name brands that a manufacturer wants customers to associate with quality, but that's not necessarily what customers are paying extra for. Usually, they are paying for the advertising. Designer fashions are a little more unusual, but the quality is probably about the same as any other clothing, and in some cases, it is not even as good.

When I was handling a store's advertising, sometimes management might give me suggested prices that were a little out of line, but everything else I put in the paper was true. The only thing was—I didn't necessarily tell the whole story. ↙

COMMERCIAL ARTIST

At various times in his career, Raymond I. has been both an art director and a working commercial artist who creates illustrations and visual material for advertising and editorial clients. His advice to artists who work free-lance: Get it in writing.

I got mad about a job I did for a small ad agency on a newspaper ad. I was told the job paid $300. I turned in the roughs (drawings), and they said go ahead and finish them. Well, I did the inking and turned them in, and they decided they weren't going to use them. They paid me $100 and said, well, the client didn't want to go that way. It was just an oral arrangement. I didn't have any purchase order or anything. I told the guy I didn't like it, but there wasn't an awful lot I could do about it.

This is the way I always worked as an art director: when artists come in with roughs, then you make the changes. If you don't like what they're doing, you have them change it. If you're sure you don't like what they do, you get another artist, but you pay the first artist a reject fee, probably about a third of what the finished job would be. But, if I approved the roughs and said go ahead with the finished drawings, then we were committed to pay the full amount when the artist delivered. If someone in our company or a client didn't like what an artist did, that was our problem.

The answer is to get a purchase order so that everything is understood. An artist gets a fee for rejection, but it has to come during the rough stage. If you go to a finish, you get paid the full price. ↙

10

PRINTING SHOP MARKET
REPRESENTATIVE

Most of the advertising that people call junk mail originates in printing shops that produce the materials specified by the advertising agencies. Lois T. works in sales for a printing shop, and one of her jobs consists of dealing with the establishments that handle the next phase of the operation, the actual mailing of the advertising material. These are called letter shops, and they receive the material, collate it, insert it into envelopes, and mail it according to predetermined address lists.

Very often the letter shop will take a portion of what we have printed and delivered to them and sell it for waste. They claim a shortage, which means we have to go back to press at our own expense and make up the run. We know we supplied them with enough material, because we've got our counts from the presses and folders, and we can also determine the quantity by weight.

If they have lost a skid of material, say 100,000 to 150,000 pieces—and it is easy to lose them in the big letter shops—instead of looking for it, they'll holler "shortage." They know that when they ultimately find the skid, they can sell it for waste. This used to be more prevalent. Now, there are just one or two places that do it a lot anymore.

We always print overruns to allow for spoilage, and we know from the piece and the package how much there's going to be. When a particular letter shop becomes suspect, when they yell "shortage" repeatedly, we deliberately send an extra 5 or 7 percent over the required count. If this doesn't work, we print one lift load—say we're doing cards for them—on a lighter and heavier weight stock, and intermingle them. Then when the stock goes through the machines that label the cards, the suction, which is geared for a regular weight stock, starts picking up doubles, etc. This slows down the whole business and increases production time. This lets them know we're onto what they're doing. They get the message, and they cool it.   ✒

AUTO MANUFACTURING
AND SERVICE

AUTO SERVICE MANAGER

For more than a quarter of a century, Leonard R. worked as a service manager in several garages and automobile dealerships. He was responsible for directing the staff of mechanics and body repairmen who worked for him. Leonard is now retired from the business, because "They made it increasingly hard to work honestly."

Just a few weeks ago, a relative began having problems with her car. When the engine was running, the torque would kick it from side to side and change the selection of gears, possibly into reverse or park. I crawled underneath the car and diagnosed it as a problem with the transmission linkage, which is a problem common to the particular year of her car. So I called a certain transmission company, because I thought it was a reputable place, and they offered free towing.

Well, initially they called me and said it was not the transmission and that the fault lay elsewhere. Then, when I protested, they called me back and said I was partially right, but that the problem was deeper than the linkage. They said they had pulled the transmission out and told me it would need a rear drum, a front drum, bands, clutch pack, all seals, plus cleaning of the valve body and checking the front pump and converter. It would cost from $350 to $400. Well, the transmission had run fine up to then, and I couldn't see any way it could be that much. I told them I'd call them back, then I jumped into my car and went over there.

When I introduced myself, they were quite jumpy about it, because they were aware of my past experience in automobile repairs. "We have a man working on the valve body," the guy told me, "and you can't see the car or the transmission, because it is a very delicate operation." I asked him who gave them permission to remove it, because I had not consented to that. He admitted that I was right, because he knew that I knew what I was talking about. "Now I demand to see my transmission," I told him, "or we are going to meet elsewhere." He knew what I meant, so he went back to talk to the repairman, and when he came back out, he said I could go look at it.

"There's your transmission," he said. It was off the car but not dismantled. "I thought you had it disassembled," I told him. "You have not even touched it—I can see the bolts haven't even been loosened—you have lied to me." There was no way he could have made that diagnosis without taking it apart. When I challenged him, he was willing to do whatever I wanted done. I said I'd pay him for replacing the linkage, the fluids, the transmission mount, and even the towing. Fine, he said, and he wrote me up a guarantee and charged me $68. I found at another transmission shop it could have been done for $18, because the transmission does not have to be removed to replace the linkage. My relative is driving the car now, and the transmission shifts beautifully, and there are no other problems. If *I* almost got burned *that* badly, think of what happens to a layman going in there. There is no law that can control this. The only thing you can do is expose these crooks, and let the public know who they are.

Not all franchised operations are bad. You just have to find the good ones on a trial-and-error basis. There are muffler shops where, whenever you have something done, it's invariably $90 or so, and that means a complete exhaust system. It is so easy for them just to take a cutting torch and drop everything and replace it with new parts, whether they're needed or not. That's where the money is. I always have three estimates made before I have any work like that done.

Today's mechanics are far from what they used to be. Back in the forties and fifties, it was difficult to get into a shop, and they'd all worked fifteen or twenty years at their trade. The shortcomings of today's mechanics show up most in their lack of knowledge of the electrical system and the carburetor. They can dismantle a carburetor and clean it, but they can't tell you about anything they're cleaning. Now they just rely on putting another one on, and you and I are paying for it. It's unheard of today to pull and repair starter motors for a fraction of what their replacement cost is. If I sell you one, for $70, I am making a 40 percent markup on it, so consequently I am making more money than if I would just stop and rebuild it. It is usually much cheaper to repair than to replace, even at today's wage rates.

Every repair shop has flat-rate manuals that set forth both the time a repair should take as well as its cost. The manufacturers put out their own manuals after doing time studies, and they consider everything, from getting the car off the lot and putting it on the rack, to drawing the required parts. Most automobile agencies follow these at first, but they completely disregard them after the warranty has expired. Then they switch to other flat-rate manuals put out by private publishers in which the rates have been inflated so they can make more money. If a customer challenges them on a repair cost, they can pull out these manuals and say, "Look, we are honest. We're sticking to the book."

I once applied for a job of service manager at a new-car dealership, and the man was very concerned about my honesty and integrity. After checking all my references, he wanted to hire me, and he wanted to pay me well, too. Then he asked me, "Are you capable of writing a thousand dollars worth of warranty over and above in a month?" This means making false warranty claims to the manufacturer. They have an address card that has all the data on it pertaining to a car owner's warranty. They'll get the guy's signature on a routine inspection, then write on all the copies except the customer's anything they want—falsifying warranty claims and sending them into the factory. What he was asking me for was smaller than what many of them are trying to get away with. And, of course, when you talk about $1,000 of labor, you're also talking about $1,000 in parts, which was pure gravy for them in terms of profit for the service department. If the factory had some kind of cross-checking between the customer's repair bills and what was claimed on warranty, you would be able to buy an automobile much cheaper. I told the dealer I did not want to work for anybody who was so worried about my own honesty, but whom I couldn't trust myself. I just walked out.

Earlier in my career, I worked in the parts department of a garage that had a fleet contract with a utility company to fix their trucks. If they had a transmission breakdown, the mechanic was told to put in maybe about three or four gears, and that was all. My manager would come in and hand me a repair order with a long list of parts—even though I'd only given the mechanic three or four—and tell me to price them. They invariably over-charged the large companies with whom they had fleet contracts. If customers want to see the old parts, how many do they want to see? There's no way they can prove they were theirs. I used to make a point of putting customers' old parts in what we'd call people bags, similar to doggy bags, to show them that we were being honest with them, but that is rare.

Even though garages advertise genuine replacement parts, many times they are not genuine. They will substitute inferior parts they've bought for a third of the price, and many times used parts are substituted. But the price the customer pays is for the factory-suggested retail. At one dealer I worked for, the parts manager started buying inferior ignition points, and a lot of our customers were bringing their cars back. When I found out what he was doing, I started sending to the purchasing department all the towing and repair bills from the cars that were coming back, and pretty soon I started getting my genuine parts back in. Most dealers will tell their service managers that any way they can make money is fine with them. They build these big shops on which they have to make mortgage payments, so they will steal any way they can.

The biggest ripoff is selling a customer work that is not required. Tire outfits are big on ball joints, which your wheels pivot and turn on. They will sell tires and then a front-end alignment; then when they're doing that they tell you they can't get the alignment to the correct specs, because your ball joints are worn. Replacement can run anywhere from $70 to $130. They make a lot of money on them, because they do them so

16

often they can break the flat-rate time. I would have many customers ask me to check their ball joints, and I'd find they were fine. I'd ask them who told them their ball joints were bad, and invariably it was a tire company.

Billing people for more parts than are used is prevalent on used cars, especially if they offer a fifty-fifty warranty, in which the customers pay half, and the dealer pays half for repairs. A repair bill might be $50 for labor and $50 for parts, but the dealers do not want to lose any money on this, so they will inflate the parts' prices, or maybe add some, so the total bill comes out to maybe $130, and they are sure of covering their parts' cost. Some dealers, too, will buy the cheapest oil they can get and pump it out of bulk. The only way you can know you're getting the specifications you want is by buying only canned, name-brand oil.

My state requires safety inspections of all used cars that are sold—it's about a forty-point check. The trouble is, all the inspectors are mechanics working for the dealers and garages. Everyone has a mechanic in the shop who is a safety inspector. For what little they pay them, the mechanics are not going to take the time to put the car up on the rack and go all over it. They are going to do it the fastest way they can and write it out and let it go. The idea is good, but the system stinks, because there is no one to enforce it.

In one body shop I worked with, the dishonesty involved the shop foreman, the customers, and the insurance companies. It was mandatory for my mechanics to write down on the back of the repair order any additional work the car might need, so we could inform the customer. One customer brought in a compact that had dents on every panel, every fender was bent, the bumpers were hanging, and it had a bad transmission, which he wanted an estimate on. As it turned out, he couldn't afford it, so he just paid us for our inspection. About six weeks later, the car showed up in the body shop, and an insurance adjuster came and asked me what it would cost to repair the transmission. I went to my file, and showed him the repair order we'd written up six weeks before. He asked me how I'd gotten it estimated so fast. "Look at the repair order," I said. "It's dated six weeks ago."

And he said, "But the car was just stolen, and whoever stole it did all this." I thought he was kidding. The dents and all were the same ones that had been there all along. The owner had even made out a police report. But rather than risking a big legal battle, the insurance company paid the claim. And because of this, you and I are paying higher insurance rates.

I've even had people coming in wanting to claim warranty work on things they had done themselves, like removing a wheel bearing with a chisel. They'd ask me to collect from the manufacturer for something they had butchered.

I never did things for dishonest insurance adjusters to get them to throw business my way, things like taking care of their family automobile for no charge. Some of these adjusters would tell dealers that if they wanted the job, they'd have to supply the adjuster with three different estimates. The dealers would make up the estimates using different letterheads, making sure that their's was the lowest so they would get the job.

I never paid off anybody—that's probably why I am not in the business anymore. After more than ten years at my last place, they eased me out and put in a man with a degree in business management. My shop was immaculate, and my people were honest. If they gave me a reason not to trust them, they did not work for me anymore. The new guy came in and immediately inflated the prices. It was not long before the customers realized that they were paying almost twice as much for repairs, and the shop lost all the people we had had for so many years as faithful customers. I'm sure the owner now realizes that instead of getting rid of me, it would have been a lot more profitable in the long run to have had an honest person running the operation. ✔

AUTO TRANSMISSION MECHANIC

Emil R. has never had any formal training as an automobile transmission mechanic. When he was in his early twenties, he simply

18

applied for a job in a transmission shop, was hired, and thereafter learned by doing. Although he has worked for five shops, he says, "They're pretty much the same. There are different prices and different names, but most of them are out to get you."

I would tell customers one price, and when they came back to pick up their cars, it would be $85 more. I got pissed off and quit transmissions for that reason. Everyone was told by the manager, "Nobody gets out the door for less than $50." Even if it was for nothing, like tightening up your wheel bearings, the linkage, the shock absorbers. The customers were getting away with a driveable car and the fundamental problem fixed, but it was just a stop-gap measure in a lot of cases. If they were under a guarantee, we would try to push them through that ninety-day period, kind of stall them until they came back and you could tell them their warranty was void. People would turn around and look at me and say I was a fucking thief. Or people whom the manager had billed for a part that I had really not replaced would come back saying they still had problems. When things got hot and heavy, the manager would point over to me and say, "There is the guy who did the work. That's the guy you're looking for."

I got tired of dealing with people like that. The guy I worked for the last time did it to family, did it to friends, did it to anybody. The managers of these shops started off the same way I did, at the bottom. They work up to the manager's job. If they learn a good line of shit, if they can sell a lot of transmissions, well, then they are going to become the manager.

If people only realized what's involved on an average transmission rebuilding job. They are paying whoever pulls the trans out of the car about $3.50 an hour. I can pull one in twenty-five minutes. Within a half-hour, I could have a transmission torn down, rebuilt, and washed up. It takes about twenty minutes to put it back in. In parts, you're talking a complete gasket set and new clutches, maybe $25 plus the fluid. This is the job people who go to their car dealers pay $400 for. We charge the dealer $200, and if the customer had come to us in the first place, we would have charged $250. That's a lot of markup.

I would say that maybe a third of our work was necessary and the other two-thirds were ripoffs, just minor things that needed fixing. They would con people into a whole transmission job, when the only problem was a blocked filter or a leaking gasket. I would tell people honestly what was wrong after I got it up on the rack, then the manager would come along and say, see, this is going to go bad, this is going bad, and just push them into a lot of extra stuff for whatever the traffic would bear. One built-in ripoff we used on most of our jobs was billing customers for exchanging their torque converters, when all we did was drain them and spray-paint them.

Invariably, when we installed a "new part," it was a used part we billed them for as new. I would say 95 percent of all the parts used in transmission shops are used, a lot of them out of junk-yards. Of course, they never tell the customer that. Even the car dealers we worked for knew we were using used parts, but they never did anything about it. We just hoped the parts would last for sixty or ninety days, whatever the guarantee was, so we could charge them again. You can look at a used part and estimate how long it will run and be pretty close to home.

It is essential that you replace *all* the fluid in the trans every 25,000 miles, otherwise the life of the transmission will be reduced. It was common practice in all my shops, however, not to replace it all. Nine times out of ten, a guy would go out paying for a lot of the same trans fluid he had in there originally. It takes thirteen quarts of fluid to flush a complete transmission system, but they would just replace the three quarts or the gallon that comes out in the pan and not the two or so gallons the converter and cooling system hold. Of course, they billed the customer for replacing the whole thing. All transmissions give off metal filings, and if you don't drain all the fluid and replace it, the filings eventually come back into the transmission and get all eaten up. In all my experience, I found that transmissions that were jammed with filings would go out at about 30,000 or 35,000 miles. Those that were serviced properly would last 70,000.

Transmissions in the new cars are really cheap, and they are not adequate to do the job. They are too small to pull the size of the cars. We had about seventy-five cars in for work, and only ten of them had any more than 8,000 miles on them. We did a couple of 1977 cars that only had 8,000 miles, and the work was not even covered under the warranty.

The average consumer has almost nowhere in the automotive trade to turn to for an honest transmission or any other type of repair job. There are little mechanics here and there who can do engine work, but I don't know of anyone who can do transmission work. You just have to go to the person who screws you a little bit less than anyone else. 🖛

AUTO MECHANIC

"I knew I was going to come out of this a sick, old man," says Kurt I., who, after seventeen years of exposure to concrete floors and petrochemicals, quit his business as a foreign auto mechanic to pursue a trade not so demanding on his health. He has a bleeding ulcer, arthritic knees, lungs sickened by polyurethane body finishes, and failing eyesight—all of which he traces to a garage mechanic's occupational hazards. He's not just sick; he's also embittered. He's angry that he couldn't operate profitably in his highly skilled trade charging customers $40 an hour; angry that there are only "two skilled professionals out of every 1,000 mechanics"; angry that virtually every foreign and domestic auto and parts manufacturer produces flawed products; angry that 98 percent of his customers listened to him with only half an ear, "because they really didn't care." As an auto mechanic, Kurt I. was a prideful perfectionist, who boasted that there was no car he couldn't fix and that his work was always done by the highest professional standards. He is highly opinionated and, in the strict sense of this project, was not a flagrant rip-off artist who worked in the sort of garages where motorists are routinely sheared; he was his own man. Yet, he does offer interesting insights into the auto repair field, and his remarks are presented in that spirit.

21

The easiest way to rip off customers is to do nothing at all and bill them for it. If they are decent drivers, they can often tell if a job hasn't been done, like a front-end alignment. Otherwise, only a professional mechanic can tell. My sister-in-law bought an eight-month-old car, and the previous owner had been billed by the dealer for a front-end alignment. I checked it, and it never had had one at all. The second most common thing to doing nothing at all is doing too much. I know a guy who took his car into a garage with a bad torsion bar, and the next thing he knew he had a full brake job and a full tune-up. What if a garage can't justify the work they did? What is the customer going to do about it?

Regardless of what garages tell you, three-quarters of them have no rate schedule. They don't charge you X number of dollars an hour. They do a job and say, "Well, this is what we should charge." They add a percentage here and a percentage there, and the numbers sound good, and the customer gets the bill. I used to jack up parts' prices to what I thought I could get. Occasionally, I'd zoom them up if I didn't like the guy. I'd buy used body parts—but I'd never buy used mechanical parts—and tell customers they were new. It didn't matter, because I'd back up the work. This sort of practice is widespread.

We have big, thick books that list various jobs—the parts, how long it's supposed to take you, the costs, etc.—that have price data fed in by the insurance companies. They're very poorly done, and the figures are arbitrary. Instead, I use service books put out by the manufacturer. They are solid and tell me what I need to know.

The insurance companies are at your throat and will shortchange you the best they can. The insurance company will generally write up an estimate for repairs 30 percent lower than the mechanic's, and the customer is screwed for the rest. If the customer doesn't pay, the mechanic either eats it, or he has to go repossess the car.

Good adjusters will either write a legitimate estimate that's in line with the real costs or else will take a payoff. They may tell the mechanic to write up the estimate and add $100 to it, and

22

they will split the $100. That's illegal and corrupt, but it's the only way you can do it 60 percent of the time.

Some insurance companies will stiff you completely. I'll get an okay on a job, fix the car, and give it back to the customer, and six months later, I still haven't heard from the insurance company. They'll say, "Who are you? We never heard of you." You can take them to court, but it isn't worth the time and money. For what it costs me to close up my shop for a day, go to court, and fight a corporation that buys people on a daily basis like raw meat, it isn't worth it. With the exception of a few of the big companies, the smaller the company you're dealing with, the worse it gets.

Repossessions are a joke. The state law allows you to repossess an automobile if your repair bills haven't been paid—but it doesn't tell you how to do it. So once you've got your repossession papers, you've literally got to steal the car to get it back into your hands. I got caught once on a repo breaking into a car. I showed the cop my papers, though, and he said, "Okay, go ahead." ✒

AUTO PLANT PRESS OPERATOR

The automobiles made and driven by Americans are produced on assembly lines where the work can be both dangerous and tedious. In the stamping plant where Helen C. works, the pieces are removed from the presses and stacked in piles awaiting further processing to rid them of sharp edges. Despite the hard work, Helen finds her job as a press operator fascinating and the pay ($7 an hour, plus lots of overtime) good. Now 48, she has worked in production jobs all her adult life, and she is able to step in wherever needed. Although she gets along well with her colleagues, she does see a difference between herself and some of the younger workers.

I go to work to do a day's work. A lot of people go there to get hurt so they can sue the company and get lots of money for damages. Some of them have been there for eight or ten years. One girl I rode to work with used to say, "If I ever get hurt, they're going to pay me a good dollar." At the time, she was hunting herself a car. One day, we were stamping some parts for under the hoods, and she was stacking the pieces after they came off the press. There were two stacks about eighteen inches apart, and all the pieces in the stack had jagged edges of metal. I told her not to walk through those stacks, or she would get cut. And she said, don't worry, they will pay for it, and so she walked through the stacks and deliberately cut herself—got six stitches, I think. They pay you so much a stitch automatically, and she got about $1,000. She made a down payment on a car with that money.

At least half the injuries are intentional. People would sit around at the breaks and talk about what they had gotten for injuries and what they were going to get. You can cut yourself very easily—there's sharp stuff sitting all around. Cutting is the most common injury, but some people might drop something on their foot. Another girl got into an argument with her boyfriend, and he flung her into a truck. She told the doctor she got bruised on the line, so she collected sick benefits from the company while she was off work. Others will purposely get hurt so they can stay home with pay—$170 a week. I've seen at least eight cases of this happening.

One guy was missing more days than he was there, so they fired him. He said okay, and then he headed downstairs to the washroom. A little later, someone else went downstairs and found the guy lying on the floor saying he'd fallen down the stairs. They called for help, but the doctor couldn't find anything wrong with him. The guy kept saying he was hurt, and finally they gave him his job back to keep him from suing the company. I heard some people talking about it with the inspector, and everyone felt he just went down there, doubled over, and lay down. A lot of times an inspector will talk to the guy's buddies, and they'll say, yes, we saw it happen, even though they didn't.

24

I've seen someone deliberately put a piece of scrap metal into a press to put the press out of operation. They'll pull it out before the foreman comes back to check. One broken machine closes the whole line down. This happens three or four times a week. The people want to loaf—they get paid just the same. If there's not another line for them to work on, they'll get sent home. Not at full pay, but maybe the guy who broke the press did it just because he wanted to go home. People never say anything, even if they saw it happen. Nobody would talk to you if you told on someone. One guy who works in the office told his son, who works on the line, what to do if he ever wanted to break the machines. The kid started on the line and knew all the tricks.

The evening shift—it starts at four—is the worst. Most of those guys come in after they've been drinking, and they want to go back and drink some more. They'll play all kinds of games. ✔

AUTO OPERATION

DRIVING SCHOOL OPERATOR

"What motivated me to open my own school was that I wanted all the money for myself," says Molly Z. who started out in the driving school business as an instructor for another firm. So with another former instructor, she formed a partnership, a small operation conducted at first out of one of their homes, then from a small office. They instructed teenagers who were applying for their first license, as well as adults whose lives had changed through marital or employment circumstances and who suddenly found themselves having to either dust off a disused skill or learn it, in middle age, from the very beginning. The school prospered; the partners hired several instructors, and they were able to skim hundreds of dollars a week off the top of the receipts for their personal use. After they moved to larger quarters, however, they got overextended and never made any money. But in the early stages, it was a good life.

It's very difficult to get good instructors. The burn-out rate is very high. People who take these kinds of jobs are not all that stable. They'll try this and try that, then come to us dead broke, all glassy-eyed thinking they're going to earn $500 or $700 a week. Well, that isn't the case, because by the time they finish paying the insurance, car rental, gas and oil, and working like crazy, they may come out with $200 a week.

Many companies don't charge for training, and we didn't at one time, but finally we got tired of training the new instructors and charged them $200. We had worked out a deal with a loan company that the instructors could go to and sign for the money if they didn't have the $200. Then the instructors would have to go through a series of tests to be licensed by the state. That would take about two weeks, but if you wanted them licensed faster, or if they had trouble with the tests, all it took was a payoff in the state capital. You can pay off and get anything you want these days.

So we got the instructors licensed, and we'd take the first $100 out of their checks, which was for an accident deductible. If they had an accident, there was no way they were going to avoid forfeiting that. Then they had to pay a bond. We're giving them a brand-new car, and we've got to know who they are, so we charged them $200 or $300 on that. Driving schools say that at the termination of instructors' employment, they'll get the bond money back, but very few of them do. The contracts were always written to the advantage of the company and the disadvantage of the employee. We had lawyers constantly rewriting them after something didn't hold up in court. We were called into the state department of labor many times, but we could get around paying the bond money back by saying, "Well, this instructor had an accident," or "He threw a rod," or "He was driving by himself and got drunk," or "A woman said he made a pass at her," etc. Those who made a really bad stink got some of their money back, but if we weren't forced to give it back, we didn't.

The schools ration out their students. They'll give each instructor five students, and they want the instructor to book each student every day, or at least every other day. So if instructors came in and said they needed more students, we'd say, "What happened to the five we gave you? It's up to you to have those people go out every other day. What are you doing wrong? Aren't you personable?" If there were four or five extra students, rather than giving them to an instructor who already had five, it was to our advantage to put another car out on the street. First, it gave us more advertising, because people would see the cars on the street. Also, we made money by renting the cars to the instructors. We made money off the insurance, we made money off the repairs. Believe me, there were ways the school never lost.

So when we advertised, "Earn $10 an hour as an instructor," naturally we got a lot of people looking for a fast buck. They'd come in thinking they were going to outsharp us. Well, instructors, in theory, could earn $600 or so a week, but they'd have to

28

work seventy hours a week and get money by dragging out students' lessons for as much as the market would bear. The more they book their students, the higher the percentage they keep. If they work twenty hours, they might earn $4 an hour. If they work over forty, they might be getting $10 an hour; so naturally, that's the incentive. That's why this is a job that will burn you out very fast.

Remember, the students getting into our cars are terrified to begin with. Many are women whose husbands have told them, "You'll never learn. I'm disgusted with you. You're ruining my car." So they want to hear someone who says nice things to them, and that's what the instructors are paid to do. Many students don't have a car available to them, and they can't rent a car, so the schools are really the only way some people have of getting a license. Now there are many different ways that you can talk to people. You can undermine their confidence and put the fear of God in them, and that was one of the things we did. Instructors will precipitate crises for the express purpose of saying, "See, I told you you couldn't do it." You could rile up people—get them very nervous—and throw them out into a traffic situation they're not ready for, like driving on expressways or in snow. They'll say, "Oh, I can't possibly do that," and you tell them they can't avoid driving on expressways or in the snow, and they'll keep pleading that they're not ready. So you tell them, "Well, you see now, we need more lessons."

Or you give them maneuvers that are so precise, they can't do them and lose control. Say they're parking, and you tell them, "Line your car up with the lead car, cut your wheel, and go back, back slowly," and they might hit the curb. So you tell them that if they do that they'll fail their road test, and if they fail it three times in one year, they've had it. And they've got to get their license, because they're taking a new job and have no transportation. So we tell them they need at least two, and possibly more, hours on parking. What's the person going to say?

You can always work a few hours in without very much problem, because you're the expert; you can get them to the point where they look upon you as God. You can say, "It's up to you if you don't want any more lessons, but if you have an accident, your insurance rates will go up, so in the long run isn't it better to pay $40 more in lessons than $100 more in insurance premiums?" Or tell them that if they make a mistake typing a letter, they can always start over, but if they make a mistake driving, they could lose their life. If you call any driving school and ask how long will it take you to drive, they'll say it depends—which is true, but they stretch the truth. When you see a lot of money coming in, you get greedy. You take advantage of people. So if you can keep a student out an additional three or four hours, you get more money, and you justify it in your own mind by saying that the person really needed the extra lessons.

Of course, there are some people who are very difficult to teach; they don't learn as fast as other people. But by and large, the instructors are taught to fend for themselves; they get five students, and it's up to them to get forty hours a week out of those five. There was one operator who was indicted for charging people several thousand dollars, and they never did get licensed. We had some students like that who had paid several hundred dollars, and a judge made us refund some of their money. But basically, we keep them coming back. We try to be diplomatic and tactful, and when they make a mistake in traffic, we tell them, "Don't get excited. I told you you weren't ready. We'll just have to go out a little bit more." Remember, the students have no self-confidence, and that's basically what you're taught to give them, that and the mechanical skills of driving. So you give them their self-confidence once you've got all the money you can get out of them—yes, that's about it.

I've known instructors who have become, shall we say, good friends of students and taken them for money. They were taught like instructors in the dancing schools. They were personable, and there are a lot of lonely women in their forties, fifties, or sixties, who, if a nice guy comes up and talks to them, are going to go. I knew an instructor who used to "borrow" money from his students. That sort of thing goes on constantly. If a woman gets ripped off, she's not going to tell anyone about it; she's too

30

embarrassed. The instructor would just say, "Oh, that's a figment of her imagination. She's a frustrated woman on the make for me."

We used to work together with body shops and garages. When we'd get to know them well and do enough business with them, they'd pad the repair bills. Sometimes the insurance adjuster wouldn't verify it at all, he'd just take the word of Harry at the garage, if the garage were reputable. Nobody is beyond stooping to make a few dollars—at least I didn't find that they were. ✔

SERVICE STATION NIGHT MANAGER

Wally G. has worked in various capacities for a large service station near a state toll road. Formerly a night manager, he is now a mechanic and tow-truck driver. Much of his station's towing business comes from a contract with the toll road commission and others with a new-car dealer. In the one case, he tows vehicles, many from out-of-state, that have broken down on the toll road; in the other, he tows the cars that have broken down in the hands of the new owners back to the dealership. In both cases, he can identify a double standard in pricing.

Sometimes, I will have to tow a car back in off the parkway because they have no spare tire, and I don't have the tools to change a tire on the road. The people we pull in off the parkway we will charge $10 more for a tire than what it usually sells for, just because they are broken down. We take advantage of the situation. Usually, we sell a radial tire to our regular customers at $10 over our cost, but we'll charge someone broken down on the parkway $20 over cost, which brings it up to the manufacturer's suggested list price. The regular customer gets one price, and the sucker off the parkway gets another.

We also have contracts with car dealers, where we tow one of their lemons that breaks down back to the dealership at a fixed price—$10. One dealer, I've noticed, always ups his towing bills to the customer. I brought one car in to him and billed him our usual $10, and I saw where he marked down $20 for towing on the customer's repair bill. He does this all the time, anywhere from $5 to $15 over what we charge him.

When I was night manager, I would rip off the owners once in a while, because I felt like I deserved it. Someone would come in and want a tire repaired, which ran anywhere from $3.50 to $5. Well, no one would be there but me, so I would pocket the money. I would sometimes change a valve, a hose, a belt—some small part like that—and just pocket the money. A couple of times this might have been worth maybe $10. When I put in my hard work, I felt like I just wasn't making enough.

Of course, customers sometimes ripped us off, too. One guy came in off the parkway in a van—we'd towed him in—and replaced his alternator. He said "Let me get in and see how it runs." He drove around a little bit, then split without paying the bill. That occasionally happens on a tire job. They say, "Let me test it," and they're gone.

SERVICE STATION ATTENDANT

Dean T. worked for a year-and-a-half at a cut-rate gas station that also had a policy of paying wages on a cut-rate basis.

This was one of those pay-and-go type stations. No credit cards, no checks, just cash. We bought our gasoline from a minor supplier, who bought it from a refinery. The gas was not really that good. A lot of people complained about it, like their engine would knock or something. I suppose it was a problem of low octane or water in the gas.

I would check the tanks for level and for water content. I'd put a stick into the tank—it was like a ruler in inches, but it was about ten-feet long. If the level measured five inches, that meant there were maybe 1,000 gallons in the tank, six inches 1,200 gallons, etc. You put this red stuff that's like a glue and comes in a can on the bottom of the stick, and if it comes in contact with water it turns green. God, I'd put that stick in, and sometimes it would come out eight, nine, even ten inches of green. Remember, gas floats on top of water, so when you get down to the bottom of the tank, you may have a lot of water. With ten inches of green, that could mean 2,000 gallons of water on the bottom of the tank. I'd tell the managers, but as far as I know, they didn't do anything. I went through three managers while I was there. You are supposed to have your tanks cleaned after every winter, but our managers never had it done while I worked there, and I was there for a year-and-a-half. We'd just get around that by not pumping too low, but it can get kind of bad when you're waiting for a load to come in.

We didn't have a cash register; all the attendants worked strictly with a roll of cash in the pocket. Any shortages on our shift would be deducted from our pay. I figure the managers ripped me off for almost $900 in pay. They would inventory at the beginning and end of a shift, count up all the oil, etc., and read the pumps for the total sales in gallons. If the cash we turned in didn't match the sales, they would split the shortages evenly among the employees and take it out of our checks. This, I'm sure, was against the law. It's like accusing you of stealing without proving it. There are shortages in stores, but they can't charge the clerks for what they lose from shoplifting. Then they deducted the shortages from our net earnings, which was really dirty because we were paying taxes on what they took from us. Maybe someone on the shift was taking it, but we all ended up paying for it. I had a friend at another cut-rate station, and they were taking his whole paycheck. He couldn't decide what to do; he didn't want to steal, but he was not getting paid, so he started walking off with $50 or $60, because everyone else was doing it.

A lot of guys who work at stations get into "hanging the pumps"—I think because the shortages are being taken out of their checks. Someone would come in and get $1 worth of gas, and the attendant wouldn't turn the pump off—he'd hang the nozzle, but keep the pump running. Then someone else comes in and says, "give me $5 worth," and they'd keep that $1 on when they started pumping, so he'd end up with $1 less gas than he'd paid for. A lot of customers are really spacey. They'll look at the price and say they want so much gas, and go on talking to the person with them. They don't notice the $1 already on the pump.

When you add oil, they're sitting inside their cars and can't see you when the hood is up. You tell them they need two quarts, so you bring two cans out and stick the nozzle in one can and add the oil, then take the nozzle out and put it back in the same can—and you never open the second can. Then you put the empty can on top of the full one and throw them both in the trash barrel at the same time. After the customer leaves, you pull the full one out of the trash and sell it to someone else. Drivers should really get out of their cars and watch attendants. Other things, like transmission and brake fluids, worked the same way. People know what they are going to pay for oil, but they don't know the price of brake fluid, so we'd up the price, say, fifty cents. Or they're not going to know how much fluid you put in. They may be down a half-pint of transmission fluid, so we'd grab a can left over from some other customer and pretend we were opening it, and charge them for a full quart. Or they might ask for a 10W40 in a high-grade oil, and we'd bring out the cheap stuff from our company and charge them for the high-priced stuff. They couldn't see what we were pouring in. I think a lot of times it is the consumer's own fault for getting ripped off. Sometimes they'd tell me to check their oil after they'd just had it changed. I'd pull out the stick, and it would be all black and they were down a quart. They wouldn't believe it and would have to come and look. There are a lot of drivers who pay for oil changes and don't get them.

Finally, I got fed up with paying for shortages and being shafted—God, I worked outside for eight hours straight in the dead of winter for $2.75 an hour—and I talked to the guys who were tanking the gas in about getting the attendants into their union. So they sent me down to their union office, and I talked to the guy there and everything. All the attendants at my station were gung-ho for the union, but the union guy said, get some more signatures—they wanted to organize several stations. I got the signatures of my own people, but I never got the chance to get anyone else's. I made the mistake of leaving a piece of paper at the union office with the names of the people I did sign up, and every one of us got canned. I don't know how the owners found out we were trying to get the union in unless they were paying off the union to feed them this information. ✔

As someone who raced cars, Terry H. knew the basic mechanical principles of an engine. When he worked one summer as an attendant in a service station, during free times he would help the regular mechanic. From this he learned that the work done wasn't always the same as the work promised.

This guy brought a station wagon in that was shaking left and right, so we said we'd check it out and find out what was wrong. After looking at it, the mechanic said "Oh, it needs rings, it needs a valve job, the crank has to be taken out, and everything else." The man approved the work, but it turned out all it needed was a valve job. We replaced five valves, a set of head gaskets, intake valve gaskets, and I think normally a job like that would run maybe about $200 or $250. He charged the man for the entire amount of work, somewhere in the area of $700. He did not replace the rings, he did not hone the cylinders, he did not take the crank out, like he said. He always did one portion of the work that he said he was going to do and got the engine running fine. The customer couldn't tell, because he couldn't see in the engine. I just wrote the customers' tickets up, but when I'd go in the back to help out, that's when I became aware of what was going on. I mentioned it to my boss, and he said that he would handle it, but the mechanic is still working there today. ✔

PARKING GARAGE HIKER

Parking garage hikers park and retrieve customers' automobiles, generally for pay of approximately the minimum wage level and whatever tips they collect. Nonetheless, some hikers, like Henry T., do remarkably well financially, and it's not the tips that make the difference. But even though he finds hiking cars lucrative, Henry is now looking for other work. "I don't particularly like ripping off people," he says, "but that's the only way you can make money in a garage."

As a hiker, I expect tips, but if you work strictly for tips, you wouldn't make any more than $10 or $15 a night, if you were lucky. From the very beginning, I was taught that tips aren't anything. I was shown where the money was at the first night I was there.

First of all, you would overcharge the customers—anywhere from 75 cents to $1.50. It's kind of hard to add up the time when we're charging by the half hour, and people don't pay any attention anyway. Sometimes they give you a twenty, and you give them change back for a ten, and if they don't say anything, you don't say anything. Or sometimes you mess with the tickets. You give them tickets that have already been paid for by other people and have longer parking times on them. If they argue, you just say, "It is stamped on your ticket, and that is all I go by. I just work here."

Overcharging them, though, is the main way you get it. I have made $190 in one night, mostly on my overcharges. One guy I know who works evenings at a garage told me that if he doesn't make $160 a night, something is wrong. That's $800 a week ($40,000 a year). If you work the day shift you should average, oh, $80; on the evening shift, say, $150; and the midnight shift, well, $60, except on weekends, when there's a lot more. And that's tax-free. We try to screw everybody, because you can't keep your average up if you don't get the money from everyone that comes through. You figure every ticket is worth so much money to you.

36

You would be surprised how few challenges we get—it's probably less than 2 percent of the time. People leave their cars, go into a restaurant, have a few drinks, eat, are feeling good, come out, get in their car, and go. The only thing they're concerned about is going on to other things or that they have a long way to get to where they're going. People set themselves up. They'll be drinking, or they leave their trunk keys in the car, or leave valuable stuff in their car, and when they come back, they expect it to be there. If they leave the garage and find something is missing, they want to scream, but they are gone. Once they leave the garage, we are no longer responsible, and we tell them that right there on their ticket—but they never read their tickets.

The owner knows all this goes on. This goes on everywhere in the garage business. As long as you don't mess with the owner's money, the owner won't mess with you. A good hiker's got to learn how to be aggressive with people and bluff them down. When people argue with me, I agree with them. "Hey, listen, this isn't my garage. I only make the minimum wage here. I don't get a dime of this. You're right, they charge folks too much money." You have high turnovers in parking garages, because some guys don't get very good at ripping off, and you have to be good; otherwise you just don't make it. You have to know your math pretty well and have to think figures quickly—faster than the customer. If they catch you, you just give them their money. Once they get that, they are satisfied, and you can always dummy up, "Oh, I'm sorry. I'm only human." ✒

PARKING LOT AUDITOR

After her husband of several weeks walked out on her, leaving hundreds of dollars of unpaid charges on her accounts, Betty W. took a job as an auditor in a downtown parking garage. She did office work and took the initial complaint calls that stemmed from customers later finding their fenders crumpled or articles missing from their glove compartments. Betty found the job quite unpleasant and left as soon as a better one came along. "I felt the owners were real rich people," she says, "and that they were out to rip off everybody. Their attitude was the hell with the workers, the hikers, and the parkers."

You know how a parking garage has a sign, like $1.75 in big characters, then in small print it has what the rate is for each additional hour. Our sign just said $1.75, and a lot of people assumed that was for the first hour, but when they would come back for their cars, the cashier would say it was $1.75 for the first *half-hour*. And that's where the arguments would start. There were a lot of fights, and the manager even carried a gun.

There were also a lot of arguments about the clock the cashier punched, which would time the customer to the minute. If you parked at 3:08 and were punched in at 4:09 when you came back, they would charge you for the second hour. If you were just one minute into the next time, they would charge you the whole amount. And people might be on time coming back to get their cars, but by the time they waited in line to get their tickets stamped to pay, the time could go over the limit.

The hikers, the guys who parked the cars, drove real fast, and a lot of times they'd bang up the car. Sometimes, the drivers wouldn't discover the damage until later, and they'd call for the manager. Even if the manager were there, we were told to say she was out and she'd call them back. If they called once, she would never call them back. Sometimes they would have to call back five or six times before they got to speak with her. Her standard procedure was always to deny it—it all depended on how persistent the driver was. If they were persistent, then she would say they'd have to make out a report and get an estimate. Then for the next two months she'd try to stall them and wear them down and also threaten the hikers with lie detector tests to find out who did it. Eventually, the person might get his car fixed but would have to take it where she wanted them to.

I saw the police officer come in for payoffs. He came in irregularly and was handed an envelope by a relative of the owner. They never spoke. The cop, who was in uniform, just said, "Hi," and he was handed an envelope—how much was in it, I don't know. They money was a payoff so he wouldn't write tickets when the hikers parked on the sidewalk in front of the garage when it was full.

People would call in saying such and such was in their car when it was parked, and now it was gone. I'd get a call of this nature on the average of once a day. The guys maybe would take something out of the glove compartment. There was a lot of turnover among the hikers. ✔

AUTO SALESMAN

Auto salesmen have long had a problem with their public image and Art D. found their reputation to be thoroughly deserved. After losing his sales job in another field, he tried selling cars and found he was very successful at it. Yet, despite the fact that only a few years ago, as an auto salesman, he was netting $1,800 a week, he got out with the feeling that it required just "a little too much chicanery and schlocking of my customers." He's never regretted leaving.

On day one in the automobile business, I sold my first car. It was a five- or six-, maybe seven-year-old car that had been well kept, but it was terribly overpriced. I sold it to a kid who was a cook at a restaurant and had no father or mother—he lived with an aunt. She had a fairly steady job and was going to cosign for him. I didn't know what I was doing, I simply sold, sold, sold. I just hung in there at the high-dollar price, never coming down, never making a concession until I thought I had the customer—and then I gave him $100. I laid the kid away for a gross profit to the house of $1,800 on that piece of junk, and I went home with something like $500. After I realized what I had done, and this is the honest-to-God's truth, I sat down in the corner and cried from shame.

The price for a used car is determined by what the market will bear at an auction, on a day-to-day basis. Dealers—and there are thousands of dealers in a big city—may have several cars that, for some reason, they can't move in their market. Let's say they sell a lot of Firebirds or TransAms, and they just took in several older four-door sedans on trade. They'll tell their used-car manager, "Take these three pieces of shit to the market and dump them." Basically, the cars go out there just as they come in. Sometimes when dealers have a bomb that's been sitting on the lot for three months, and they know it's a structurally un-sound car that's been in an accident, they'll tell the used-car manager to dump that at the auction, too. They hope it will pass right through; cars are not screened there, and the buyer is just another sales manager. It must be fun seeing all those sales managers trying to screw each other. What an animal crowd, but it all balances out. They go out and screw somebody, and some-body else ends up screwing them.

When these guys bring the cars back to the dealership, they usually mark them up $1,000 from raw—the price they paid—but the raw cost is also arbitrarily set. So, although a salesman knows there is a $1,000 markup on a car, he does not necessarily know if the markup is based on the true cost or a falsified one. If our sales manager has bought a contemporary, desirable car, like a Camaro, Grand Prix, or Monte Carlo—it doesn't necessarily have to be clean—he starts talking it up to his salesmen before the car is even driven back to the dealership. He says he paid $1,800 for it—when he actually paid $1,500—and that it looks like it is worth $3,000 easy. So he says, "Now, we can't really mark this one up only $1,000—this car is too damned good—let's mark it up $1,200. So now he wants a 50 percent profit on the sale in terms of the asking price. He wants to mark up a $1,500 car by $1,200, plus the $300 he has already cheated on. Well, if the salesman is smart, he won't ask three grand for the car; he will ask $3,500, so now you have the thing perpetuating itself. You can expect this, because the sales manager is going to bullshit the salesmen as much as possible. The salesmen can never tune into exactly what the sales manager has done in the pricing.

There is a trade bible, a tiny little book that fits in a shirt pocket, and only sales managers are allowed to carry it. Sales-men caught handling these books are usually admonished for it, because it gives them insights into profit possibilities for any given car. The book is put out by an auction-monitoring com-pany, sort of like a newsletter. It gives the prices on what cars are actually selling for at auctions. There are also red books the consumer can get copies of that publish used-car prices. So you may wonder how a used-car dealer can justify a price spread in, say, a Camaro from $1,500 to $3,500. I worked for a dealer who never bought anything that didn't look like it was in mint condition. He'd take the cars through an expensive process of face cleaning, and he'd mark them up in excess of $2,000. His whole success depended on presentability and image. There are that many customers who are simply not aware of what a used Camaro should sell for.

The greatest source of trade-in automobiles and automobile purchases is impulse buying. People will buy anything you try to sell them as long as it is hip. They may have a three-year-old car but want to keep current and updated with a new one. Or they may be seventeen-year-old kids with a first driver's license who see a four-year-old Firebird they want, because they want to be cool. How many people like that do you think there are in this country? Count them by the millions, because they are what allows Playboy Enterprises to make money and McDonald's to sell hamburgers. That is what America is all about. Some sales managers tell you not to show the car until you have sold it. In other words, just sit there and sell yourself. Be the best salesman there ever was, then go out and show them the car you have "personally selected" for them. So how much you can mark up a car depends on many factors; the most important are the buyer, his age, impulse capability, and the condition of the car. They can take an engine with 30,000 miles on it, steam clean it, and then spray it with a clear adhesive spray, and it looks like new. But it boils down to the fact that anything a seemingly knowledgeable salesman says is believable. Selling cars is not a matter of whether one merits a certain price—that's totally irrelevant to a salesman in the car business.

Baiting is done quite a bit in the daily classified advertising, because how else do you get people into your showrooms? All you have to do is put out an ad for a new full-size car for $4,995 and say no more, and they all come in looking for it. All they find is a one-tone, small engine, black-wall tires, no radio, no air, no power windows, stripped, new car that *has not arrived yet*—it is on order. Do you know anyone who would want to buy a totally stripped, brand new car? But what we advertise as bait, we have, even if it is on order. In the case of used cars, you either put a stock number on it and sell it to an auctioneer in time to prevent people from bothering you with it when they come crashing through your doors on Saturday morning, or else you keep the piece of junk in stock and take them straight to it. When they say, "This thing is no good," you simply usher them to another car, because that is salesmanship.

I used to have a friend whose ads made us all laugh. They'd say, "Reprocessed cars. Assume payments." Well, people who have a mooch instinct read that word "reprocessed" and think they're reading "repossessed." "They took it away from some turkey who couldn't pay," they tell themselves, "and now I can assume the loan and take over the car." Literally, according to this dealer, the car was reprocessed, from the west end of the lot to the east end. Okay, maybe he washed a window. When the customer asks about the repossessed cars, the guy would say, "Oh, yes, come this way," and that was the last he would hear about the ad. From then on, my friend was just selling cars. He'd show them a couple of cars, and already he'd get the guy into a multiple thought. Multiple thoughts lead to further confusion, additional ones lead further, and before you know it, that ad will be forgotten. After all, customers don't come in to deal in semantics—they were looking for a car, anyway, weren't they? In case they challenged him about lying in his ad, my friend would just say, "Oh, no. The *Daily Bugle* made that mistake."

When I was selling new cars in the mid-1970s, a full-size automobile was priced to allow a 22 to 24 percent gross profit to the dealer. The luxury cars sometimes had 30 percent or more. Midsizes were 16 to 20 percent, and compacts 10 to 15 percent. There is a cost figure against which a salesman works—it is not the true cost from the factory; that also is inflated for purposes of paying the salesman. If you think you have sold a brand new car close to list, and you think you have made a $700 gross profit, you can be assured that you've probably made a $1,000 gross profit. But you will be paid 15 to 25 percent of what you assume the gross profit to be—not the real one.

Depending on the dealers, they may give you a shot at more net profit if you sell rust-proofing or add-on equipment like stereo radios, etc. Say you sell an acrylic glaze finish that has a suggested retail price of $125. It costs dealers about $15 to apply, so they will gladly pay you 50 percent. All they want is $50 out of it, and the rest is yours. If you think you can sell it for $200, more power to you. I used to be asked to hustle rust-proofing and give a big spiel on how terribly reliable ours was compared to what another rust-proofing firm offered. Before you knew it, I didn't even want to sell ours for $125—I knew I was only going to get $25 or $30 of that—so I would go for $250, because ours was so much better. The customer didn't have access to our price list. That's a cardinal sin, showing your prices. You show as little pricing as you can.

Knowing the price structure, sharp customers who go in and start offering to buy a full-size car at 25 percent off the top know they will wind up with a deal at 21 percent. They'll have bought themselves a car and allowed the dealer to make $200. If customers are sharp, you bend with them if you are smart. You look customers right in the eye and let them name their terms. Have them say everything they want to say and gradually negotiate only when your profit condition is at stake. Always show maximum respect for their needs. Don't haggle, don't seem cheap, just let customers do their thing until you have carefully guided them into making you the offer. This is a technique used by all good salespeople—it reverses the challenge. It says, "What would you like? What would you pay?" It's the old, "Would you, if I could?" routine. If I go to my sales manager and get it to happen for you, would you, if I could? Boom! Now you have a commitment. When they say "Yes," you get them to write that down and put their signature on a piece of paper and give you a $20 deposit as earnest money. That's refundable on the spot, but you make them work to get it back in case you don't sell the car. So then you go to your sales manager, because you have to bounce every deal off him so that he can feed you strategy and you can go back and close the deal. Sometimes he will go back with you to the customer and supplant you.

"You know, Mr. Jones," he will tell the customer. "I am thinking of firing this guy. He keeps coming to me with these half-assed deals that show me how I can make $12 profit on a brand new car. This kind of salesman I don't need; I think I'm going to get rid of him. Can I get you up another $300 to make it a fair deal for you and a fair deal for me? I'm sure you have been around the business, and you know you have made us a tremendously fair offer—for yourself. But I would like you to have a little consideration. This guy has four kids, and if he makes a buck-fifty on this deal—and he won't even make that—he won't be able to feed his fat friends and his family. Now why don't you allow me to deliver this car to you tonight? I saw your trade, and it's not a bad car—I can make it like new and put it right back out on my lot and probably make 200 bucks profit. So with that and the extra $300 you give me now, I can make this a really fair deal. This guy gets to keep 25 bucks for himself, you have yourself a car, and we're a reliable neighborhood dealership. . . ." So there you are. It's called a T.O.—a turnover. The salesman turns over the customer.

The customer's response, if he is a fair person and knows the market and has already picked out that car, is, "Hey, I know you want $300 more, but I offered you what I did. Well, maybe I was a little too demanding. I'll give you $150." The sales manager says, "Oh, gee, that's awfully nice of you, but I don't think I . . . hold on a minute. Let me go talk to my boss, O.K.?" So now the second T.O. is in the making. It's probably not a T.O. at all. He'll just take the salesman to a back-room office, and the two of them will sit there and talk about booze and broads. Or, "Do you think we can get another $75 out of him?" or "Do you think we can sell him rust-proofing?" Finally, the sales manager will say, "You go back and let him know I have lost interest in selling him the car. I'll be on the phone for the next half-hour. Go in there and hit him for $250." So you hit him for $250, and the counteroffer is $200. Now you either go back to the manager or act as if you have the authority to deal conclusively. You rush him to the write-up man who draws up all the papers, and you have yourself a sale. Gross profit: $400.

If customers will not play the game and stick by their first offer, then you go into your routine: "Hey, wait a minute, I'm not going to fail to satisfy you, a neighbor of ours . . . a nice family man . . . (or some shit like that). Let me make one more effort on your behalf. Listen, if I only make 25 bucks on a deal, that's better than nothing." So you go back to the sales manager, and he looks at his nitty-gritty profit figure, and even for a $100 profit over his concocted cost, he will sell. They all do. They all have too many cars on their lots.

Consumers do have access to actual factory prices. There's a company that sells a computer composite of automobile prices, and they'll help anybody buy cars at $100 over dealer's cost. If these people come in and challenge our concocted cost price, it's, "Get the hell out of here, you asshole. We deal in our figures, not yours." Or you can also go on the offensive, where you switch into your take-it-or-leave-it attitude, with an indignity angle. "Sir, when did this car arrive on my premises? Have you access to my books to know how much my overhead is, from the day I received this car from the factory until today? Can you tell me how much I spent maintaining this car on my premises? Am I not a businessman, etc., etc." If the customer won't budge, it's just good-bye, and thank you, because for every intelligent penny-pincher you see, there are hundreds of impulsive liberals who just live life for the fun of it, and whether something is going to cost them $100, $200, or $300 more, they don't really give a shit.

Sometimes, when a guy schlocked and mooched us until we had no profit left in the deal, the sales manager would say, "I'll fix that son-of-a-bitch." They might drill holes in the side panels to make it appear as if they'd drilled them to insert the rust-proofing nozzles, but they were just holes. Or they might coat the underneath part of the car with some phony material that adheres, but which isn't even rustproof. Everything is placidly done. You're always screwing somebody, but they never know you screwed them. You only laugh after they leave.

The really obnoxious part of the whole affair is when they come back with something wrong. I worked for one dealer, and every colleague and every employee that had stayed with him over the years claimed that he took one major manufacturer for over $10 million in warranty work. Customers would come in for something routine, and a mechanic would take a little bubble of oil and burst it near some critical area and show them the oil "leak." (At this point, Art recounts the sort of phony repair described by the auto transmission repairman, on page twenty. The customer is shown the same defective part the shop keeps around as evidence for all such repairs.) When customers came in, they signed a piece of paper authorizing the service manager to look into their cars. What they were signing on copy 5, was an acceptance of service performed under warranty. Now this particular repair was supposedly not covered under warranty, so they charged the customer cash for the "repair." Then they'd take the serial number of that car, and by manipulating things, turn around and hit the manufacturer for payment for a repair that should be covered. They figured there was very little chance that there would be contact between the factory and the owner.

These are the sort of stories that flow among the salesmen when nothing is happening. The "Larry Doyles" (the *Lay Downs* who beg to be sold a car) aren't coming in, so what do people of low self-esteem, who know they are trapped in the rat race, do? They sit there, and out comes the profanity, the comedy, the horror stories. It's no wonder, because most dealers treat their salesmen, whether they're productive or not, like paper cups. The old guy got started by gypping and trading and going to the office every day for twelve years, until he built it up to a corner lot. Finally, he picked up an assistant just as capable of spotting the fast buck as he was, and the corner lot turns into a tremendously profitable business. Now the old man drives the top demo with all the horns and whistles, he has a big home, and he is a millionaire. Now you're a salesman, standing on the floor eight, ten, twelve hours a day, under constant pressure from the sales manager and the owner, who has no mercy—that's how he got to be a millionaire—and some asshole comes in and says, "I want to buy a car, and I'm going to make your life miserable for

48

the next hour-and-a-half." That's the automobile business.

But for all the larceny among car salesmen and dealers, you can triple that among the customers. They will come in with a 110,000-mile car on which they've had the odometer turned back to 58,000 because they know they'll get a few hundred more in trade-in. Customers know that appraisers will knock off $150 or $200 if they hear rear-axle noise, so they pack the differential with grease. Or, they'll tighten up the brakes or patch up muffler holes with adhesives. They'll misrepresent the fact that the car was in an accident. The opportunities to doctor up bad cars are unlimited. ✔

AUTO SALESWOMAN

Because her father had been an auto body repairman and she had been exposed to cars all her life, Genevieve M. thought that selling them might be an appealing way to earn a living. Like Art D., she had the title of salesperson, but because her employer kept her so much in the dark as to pricing, she came to regard herself as little more than a go-between. After a month-and-a-half, in which she sold about ten cars, she departed the showroom for a sales job in another field.

I answered an ad that said, "Salary plus commission." After a couple of weeks, I complained to the sales manager that I hadn't been paid any salary. Nothing happened, so I went to the owner and said, "This is insanity. I'm supporting a daughter, and I'm not going to work here for nothing. The ad in the paper said 'salary plus commission.' " He said, "Do you believe everything you read?" But he finally did come up with $50 a week salary.

They would never let me know the prices on the cars, so I had to take their word for what my commissions were. The lowest commission I got was $25, and I may have got $50 on a couple.

All I know is that I never made any money there.* Every time I asked them questions about anything, they'd just pat me on the shoulder and say, "Don't worry about it, Genevieve."

What made me the maddest was when I was dealing with a friend of my family's who was in the market for a new car. He came in and bought one of the big ones from me, and the manager's son, who was the assistant manager, said, "Boy, you've got yourself a nice little deal there." Apparently, there was a pretty decent commission involved, and they weren't going to lie about it too much. It was going to be the biggest thing I had sold yet. They had a rule that if a "closer," as they called a manager, comes in to your deal, he's entitled to half your commission. I didn't need any closer. This was between the man and me. He was happy with the car and said, "Get me this price, and I'll take it." So then this "petsie" of the place came in and asked the man, "What color would you like, sir?" He said "Green"—and the guy takes half my commission.

The people I worked with were either alcoholics, or they had no scruples at all. The newer ones were like me; they didn't know what was going on, and every two days there was a turnover. I asked a salesman whether this one car out front had a six- or an eight-cylinder engine. He said, "What does he want?" I said, "A six," and the salesman told me, "Then that's what it is." The sales meetings were the most degrading things you could possibly imagine. The sales manager was an ex-marine drill sergeant, and he'd talk to you like dirt and call you every name in the book. You would ask a simple question, and he would give you an obscene answer. That's supposed to motivate you. They would lust after every breathing female who walked in the front door, and after work, it was right over to the local bar to get wiped out. In all my life, I've never met such low life anywhere. ✔

The reason is self-evident, when one compare's Genevieve's commissions with those of up to $500 that salesman Art D. earned.

CONSTRUCTION

MANUFACTURERS' REPRESENTATIVE

Larry W., currently a manufacturers' representative, has also worked as a direct salesman for producers of hardware that go into the mechanical systems of new buildings. As a manufacturers' representative in business for himself, Larry buys the manufacturers' products and sells them himself, generating his own operating profit. As a salesman, he functioned as an independent subcontractor, supplying both the components and the labor for installation. Beyond that difference, his method of operation in the two roles is similar. Most of the experiences he relates below, however, stem from his time as a directly employed salesman.

We call on architects, mechanical engineers, and contractors to tout the good points of our products. When there's going to be a new commercial building, plans and specifications are prepared by the architects and engineers. Then the contractors place formal bids saying they will adhere to the plans and comply with the specifications and do the job for X number of dollars. We, of course, hope the architects and engineers call for our product when they write the specifications. Many times they specify generic names, or they may specify three different product names—those they think are reliable or for which the price is right to do a given project.

Cultivating architects and engineers is a long-term project, and it may take two or three years from a cold start before they even mention you in their specifications. Your product may not be well known. Why should they take a chance on you? There are new products coming out all the time, and designs for old products change. A lot of times personalities have a lot to do with it. If you or your company raped somebody in the last five years and that individual has got a long memory, he is not going to name your product.

51

Most bidding is advertised through a trade service that puts out a newsletter that tells what jobs are bidding when. We would bid for jobs through the mechanical contractors. If you have contractors you're friendly with, they'll call you for your pricing. So we have to cultivate the architects and engineers to get written into the specifications and the contractors to get the jobs.

Here we've got a project, and let's say you're a mechanical contractor, and the contractor down the street is a mechanical contractor. I'm bidding as a separate subcontractor, and you and I know each other pretty well. Say I'm bidding against twelve other subcontractors. It would be nice to know what my competition's price is, and I know that if I give you a $20,000 edge, you will tell me everybody else's pricing. There's a number that's put out called the "street number," which is what the job is expected to go for. Say that's $100,000, and I could really do the job for $60,000. So I bid you $80,000—in other words, I'm giving you $20,000 under the street number, and you tell me my competition is at $89,000. Okay, so I'm really only giving you $9,000 at this point, but you're still getting a better number from me than from anyone else. Meanwhile, to your competitors, I'm bidding the street number, $100,000.

You and I are in collusion, and historically this is the way it has always happened. This is how we are taught to bid. You have to learn this to get jobs. There is, however, a logical reason. Why shouldn't I say that as a subcontractor, I could do business with you cheaper than I could with someone else? If you are a much better contractor than your competitors and watch out for my interest instead of trying to screw me all the time, it's true that I can do business with you 10 percent cheaper. So that could justify the difference in the bidding—which is every bit a sham.

Sometimes, if you have a favorite-son relationship with a contractor, and you know you've got a better number than anyone else, you might just bid him and ride with him. If he gets it, you get it. But this doesn't happen very often, unless, over the years, you get an inside track. You are pushed by your corporation to get information and to get as much money for their products as you can, and establishing a favorite-son relationship is one way of doing that. Some contractors want your low number going in, and they'll play real straight with you. If you can do the job for $60,000 for somebody who is straight, above-board, and won't screw you, you'd give them $60,000 immediately and forget about it. But the other guys who don't play straight and who get all the funny numbers, you start bidding at $100,000, if you can get that, or $89,000 out of them, and that's fine, too.

Companies I have been involved with have given away free systems to contractors as payola. If we've got a project with a lot of our money in it, it's nothing to give contractors a $5,000 system to go into their office or to another of their jobs. If it takes giving something away to get future business, you give it away—no one will ever know about it. To get an $89,000 job that I could have done for $60,000, I have to give contractors a $5,000 system for their office. I just close the deal and call it two different jobs: A and B. I get $89,000 for the two of them, and I'm still making money for the corporation. The contractor is always willing to write two purchase orders to take care of the billing, and the charges for the components and labor are easy enough to fudge, so the only one who gets raped on these things is the owner of the building.

There may be a case where three products are specified, but mine isn't, and contractors have the option of submitting a voluntary alternate. They may say that if they furnish my equipment, or someone else's, the party they're contracting with can deduct $2,000 from their payment. But when they say $2,000, I've probably given them $6,000, so they take the other $4,000 and put it into their pocket.

Contractors perpetuate the system, because they want the good numbers (estimates). All our work is custom—there's labor involved, and that's why there is no such thing as a fixed price for our system. No two people estimating from the same price sheets could ever come up with the same dollar-and-cents figures. As a salesman and subcontractor, I may be submitting bids to twelve different contractors. Since you never know who's telling people things, you generally give all twelve a different estimate. If you're out at $85,000, and your competitor comes in with

$84,980, you know someone told your price—you can tell who's talking. I'm giving my low bids to the ones I think may get the job, and, of course, my competitors are doing the same thing.

Many times a mechanical engineer designs a job that won't work. As a subcontractor, my obligation is to make it work. Sometimes I'll try to change the specifications or make suggestions that are going to benefit me, just like any other thing. If I can find an easier way of doing things, why wouldn't I suggest it and try to help myself? If I can think of this ahead of time so I can give them a similar, but easier, job, then I can bid it cheaper. That's what the contracting business is all about, and that's why some get jobs and others don't.

Architects and mechanical engineers are hired by the owners of a building to protect their interest. When something they design doesn't work, they are liable, and at that point they will trade with the contractors. They will let a contractor put in something of less value to make their system work so they don't have to pay the money out. Sometimes they may compromise performance of the systems by doing this, but that's hard to determine. About 40 percent of the time, things don't work the way they're designed to work in a complicated building project, so there are always gives and takes. Many times, nothing is sacrificed. Designers may not know they can buy a piece of equipment cheaper than the one specified. There may be a product that is 99 percent as good as the one specified that costs two-thirds the price. If they're going to trade off, they'll let the contractor put in the cheaper one. That may make money available to clear up other problems. Many times there will be money designed into the building so they can take care of these boo-boos. Sometimes the owner knows this; many times he doesn't.

As a salesman, when I do architects a favor and save them from one of their mistakes, I may be allowed to write the specs on the next job with more in them than I'm going to give. So everybody else will bid on a Cadillac, and only I bid on a Chevy, and I give him a Chevy, which is what he wanted in the first place. It's payola, but there's no money changing hands, and no one will ever prove it. Contractors also make boo-boos. It may cost you money to save their asses, but you make it up next time by getting a job you might not have gotten otherwise.

There are a lot of schlock products put into a building if the architects and engineers don't watch the job very closely. If you're an owner of a rental building, you don't want schlock equipment that you'll always have to be servicing. It's just smart business to get longer-lasting stuff. Unless, of course, you're just planning to get something built, rent it, then bail out, selling it to somebody else as an investment. If you're building a condo, that is where you put in light switches that last only half the cycle. There, the guy getting ripped off is the one who buys the condo. If you're buying a condo, get one that has been converted from an apartment, and you'll find better doors, light switches, appliances, and everything.

Rarely does anyone go around and make sure all the specifications are adhered to unless there is a problem. So when there are contractors and subcontractors all the way down the line going for the low numbers, there is no fat left in the job at all, and they will do everything as cheaply as they can. This isn't necessarily the best way, because good contractors are selling their services, they have a reputation to maintain, so they're going to want to do as good a job as they can for the money. For that reason, I think it is better if everyone isn't going for the low number—and that there is a little collusion.   ✔

GENERAL CONTRACTOR

As a general contractor, Eugene C. builds commercial, industrial, and residential structures. He's been in the business forty years, and now with a payroll of about fifteen, he does $750,000 annual business. Not all jobs make him money, but when you have a loser, says Eugene, at least the next time you're smarter.

The cost of an acre of ground in the suburbs may be $15,000, but before you can put a stick on it it's $75,000. Sewers, hydrants, electricity, gas—these are costs to the developer. If you are building five houses to the acre, that's $15,000 a house before you even lay the foundations. So the contractor has got to skin, cheat, connive, and save in every way possible in order to bring home a house for $50,000, 60,000, or 70,000 at today's labor and material costs. Of course, we're in a ten-cent business. Ninety percent goes to labor and material. Then, literally, before we can get a permit to develop a hunk of land, we've got to donate some for the school, library, playgrounds, parks, or whatever, and put in the utility systems, curbs, streets, and sidewalks. The village requires all this stuff so they can tax a $60,000 home instead of a $30,000 one.

When a homeowner has to take out a permit to make an improvement, it's a ripoff if it's not coordinated with an inspection. In one suburb, I had to pay $100 just for the privilege of doing a little remodeling on one job. I've heard of permits costing in the thousands of dollars. It's just a shakedown for money that goes into the city fathers' pockets. Then unless you give the bastards money on the side, they'll draw lines for you. You accepted the job based on the plans, but when you go in to get them approved, they'll change this and that unless you pay them a thousand or two under the table.

You've got to cut corners, either on material or labor, if you bid too cheaply. You've got to look for edges. When you're writing the specifications, even though part of a wall is twelve-inch block, you might use eight-inch block, if it wouldn't make that much difference. Or, if the specifications call for wiring, you would use the lighter fourteen-gauge instead of the twelve and give the customer an electric system that's borderline by today's standards. Generally, building codes will ensure that the job is done properly. I wouldn't go below code, because if you've got a license, you're sticking your neck out if you do.

I just did a $30,000 job on a parking lot. The customer won't let the bank release the money, because they don't want to pay the $3,000 in extras required by defective engineering in the original plans. So we're at an impasse. To arbitrate you have to sue them and give a third to a lawyer. Should there be a lamppost in the middle of a sidewalk? We had to move the lamppost, and that increased my cost. But who pays for that, the contractor or the customer? Another job might have a six-inch difference in grade, where I have to bring in 150 yards of extra material, because the engineer specified the wrong bench mark (reference point). Doctors bury their mistakes. What is the contractor supposed to do if the plans aren't intelligently drawn?

I don't know how many millions of tax dollars have been spent on extra sewer capacity to take water that should be going back into the ground. The uneducated public is to a great extent responsible, but the politicians and engineers are directly responsible. Instead of building systems that dump the rain runoff from a parking lot into the sewer, they should build holding tanks with drains that diffuse the water into the ground, where it belongs. That way we save on taxes and we don't waste what God gave us. ✔

CAULKING INSTALLER

Because he frequently supplemented his income by burglarizing homes and fencing the stolen jewelry and appliances at a friendly neighborhood hot-dog stand, it was perhaps fitting that Milo V. took a job with a contractor who he says was "the biggest con artist I have ever met." As Milo would later personally learn, "He would steal anything that was not nailed down." As for normal workaday operation, he would simply substitute cheaper materials on the big industrial jobs—office buildings and garages—he contracted for.

Instead of caulking windows, etc., like you do at home, we were caulking mechanical joints, vents, and stuff like that to keep the rain and elements out. My boss would work on contract, and he had a crew of about fifteen or twenty guys. This one job specified a two-part material, which is a sort of rubberish material with an activator. Instead, we put in a water-base material that's a lot cheaper—less than half as much as the two-part—and which will wash out in a rain. To the layman's eye, it looked the same. This was a big garage, and we were caulking inch-and-a-half joints between fire walls. On a job like that, we would have used hundreds of cases of caulking.

This time he caught himself. The concrete was leaking, and the rain started washing out our stuff, so we had to go back and cut out a lot of the material we'd put in. Where this happened, we put in still cheaper material that would not retard fires. It would break down under heat, but the two-part material wouldn't. We were also supposed to put some kind of insulation in between the walls, which we didn't. If the work leaked after they had paid him, there was nothing they could do except make him come back and do it over. But if he wasn't in business, they couldn't. He's in another state now.

I did ninety days because of him. I was greedy—my wife was pregnant, and I needed some cash to make a down payment on a house. He offered me $3,000 to steal a machine from a construction site. It was easily worth $25,000. He gave me a dump truck and a low-boy trailer to put it on and sent me over there one weekend. It turns out the cops were watching him and me, so they chased him and pulled him over. He got out of it and went on his way, and then they came back for me. I got ninety days in jail and four years' probation. They didn't put him away—he had a little more money than I did. But he never did pay me the three grand. ✔

58

CROOKS

THIEF/ARSONIST

In the twelve years he has been a professional thief, Clayton B. has never once been busted. During that time, he has perfected the skills he needs with the help of occasional instruction from older professionals in the field. He has also picked up a drug habit and requires $200 a day to satisfy his heroin addiction. At times, Clayton has regretted being a thief and once tried to further his eighth-grade education, but he found school too difficult. What he really would like to be if he could, he says, is an archeologist.

I go into homes, but sometimes I'll go into a business if I'm being paid to do it. Somebody may want something out of a business, like a trailer load of stereos, or they may want some of the books destroyed, or they may want their own building burned for insurance reasons. I make contact through the people I work with, or someone will put them on to me. There would be a couple of different people to middle for me and the people who want their shop burned down. Whatever the reason for the job is no concern of mine. If people want a place burgled, I don't know, at first, whether it belongs to them or to one of their competitors, but I will find out. First, I will check the grapevine: Who turned them on to me; then I'm going to backtrack and find out who they went through and any other information I can. It may cost me a couple of hundred dollars paying around, but I don't walk into anything blind. I'm not going to get set up. If I get a funny feeling, if the people seem kinky to me, then I'll get someone to middle the deal. I won't meet them.

Maybe 10 or 20 percent of the time, they're having jobs done on their own property. The rest of the time it's against competitors or other people. These are small shops, bigger scale businesses, and some factories. I don't really want to know someone's reasons. The less I know, the safer I feel about it. I've been offered work that involves violence, but I don't get into that. Like I say, I'm a thief.

If people want their doughnut shop burned down, I try to find out how much insurance coverage there is on it. I don't want to make $500 and find out the owner made $50,000. On the average, I will make $1,000 or $2,000. First, I break in or crack a window. Then I use a half-gallon of gasoline, every-day driving gas. I never use much. For a timing device, I run a fuse—the kind you buy in an army surplus store—into the building and run the other end halfway down into a lighted cigarette. If the cigarette and fuse leave a trace afterward, I don't know about it; the follow-up really isn't my worry at that moment. Gas is detectable later, but most of the people don't seem to care how it gets done, just as long as it's total. I've had them blow out on me, because I used too much gas. The gas blows up, but the fire goes right out and doesn't demolish the building. About a half-gallon is just right.

Even though arson isn't a specialty of mine, I'll do it if there's a dollar in it. On the jobs I do for other people, I make about $25,000 a year. When I'm working for myself, it's about $400 or $500 a day, or two grand a week. A lot of my money goes right into drugs—about $200 a day. I don't work weekends, though. Even thieves have got to take a break once in awhile.

I've had old-timers who know their trades teach me a lot of things. They teach you everything you want to know at their house, or whatever, then you go out on your own and do it. They don't take rookies on, and they're not going to get caught for the sake of someone learning. I've gotten onto these guys through my environment, growing up, knowing people. They know ahead of time who you are and what you can do. Normally, they'll teach you as a favor, then someday they'll turn around and ask a favor of you. There's a lot of honor among good thieves, people who know what they are doing and who make their living that way. Right now, I've got a guy who's teaching me safecracking.

I can do safes, but I'm not that heavy into them yet. I just play with the tumblers. Usually when a burglary is set up, they put the books, or whatever, in a spot where they can be had very easily. If there's a safe I cannot get into, I'll go back to my contact and tell him he's got to put the stuff in a better spot or leave the safe open. The guy inside the company doesn't do the job himself, because of fear of getting put on a lie-detector machine and blowing the job. I guess the insurance companies, if they think it's an inside job, kind of give them the third degree. A lot of times, the insiders don't have the heart to do that kind of job, or else they don't know how.

A majority of buildings have alarm systems, but a good 20 to 40 percent of them don't even work. They're just up there, maybe to scare off an every-day street thief. Maybe someone had the building before them, and the new owners never even had it hooked up, or they didn't want to spend the money. How you crack those that work is somewhat a secret on different levels. If I told some of the secrets of cracking them, then the people who make them would come up with better systems. Some I can't get past myself, and then the job has to be arranged another way. Sometimes I will go in just to find out what kind of system they have—going in and applying for a job or pretending to be looking for someone in the company. This gives me a chance to identify the system, because in most cases the main box is in the front office. I can get by most of them, but I'm not an expert. An expert can get by them all.

They may have circuit breakers on windows, so when the window is opened, the circuit is broken, and the alarm goes off. Some may be silent alarms that are hooked up to a central office, and you never know the alarm is going off. That's why I never go in upon entering a building. I make my entry, and then I leave. That way, if there's a silent alarm, I'm not in there; I'm down the block or up on a roof watching. If everything is okay half-an-hour later, I'll come back and pull the job.

Electric eyes give me the most trouble. These are just beams of infrared light going from one box to another. They usually put them at the doors or the main aisles, knee-high or waist-high. Unless you have infrared glasses, you would go right through them and never know you had. But with the glasses, which you can pick up in any surplus store, you can see the beam of light and go over or under it.

If there's a watchman, I more or less follow him and watch him make his rounds so I can find out his movements. When he goes past one station, you make your entry, get your goods, then sit there and wait until he comes by again. When he punches in at that station again and leaves, then you make your exit. I would never take the chance of running out unless I knew exactly where the man was. Normally, watchmen don't give me any trouble. About half of them are armed. I never carry a gun, because I'm not out to hurt people. If a watchman caught me, I would temporarily give up until I had the opportunity to jump him. I would use physical violence to get away, if I had to, but not to injure someone purposely. I wouldn't carry a gun, because if I got busted, it would be for one thing, not a half-a-dozen more charges.

I got into this business doing home jobs. Mostly I'm after jewelry, because carrying a little briefcase doesn't create any suspicion. I stay mostly in the suburbs or the areas of the city where there's more money, unless I hear from an inside source that even though a house is in a slum area, the guy's got $40,000 there. Normally, I just wait for the people to go out, where I don't know, just out, day or night. If I'm not sure they're gone, I'll knock on the door as if I'm looking for someone and give them a phony name. I'll dress neat and clean in ordinary street clothes, or sometimes I will take a worker's approach—a TV repairman or something like that. To avoid leaving fingerprints, I wear surgical gloves. They're clear and tight-fitting, and you have to be at arm's length to notice them.

Usually, I make the entry by picking locks. All locks are pickable, even dead-bolts. It requires a set of picks and locksmith tools. In this field I would say I am an expert. It takes me about thirty seconds to pick an average lock, even a dead-bolt. They all have tumblers. Usually I go in the back or side doors, never much in the front. The neighbors are as big a bust as an alarm system. A homeowner's best defense is dogs. If I find a dog inside, I'll try to come back in a few days with a bitch in heat I'll pick off the street in the ghetto. I let the dog in first. Sometimes I've had it happen that the dogs start to fight, and I still couldn't get in. But if they don't fight, I'll leave the door open, and they'll run right out together. But even with all the increase in security, I'm still earning my living this way. I have the advantage, because they don't know where I'm going to hit.

I still go in scared, maybe not as much as someone else would be, but there's always that gut feeling. I guess you never really overcome that. My biggest fear is walking into the unexpected and getting shot. Luckily, I haven't but I know people who have and have gotten killed. More than getting caught, that's a burglar's biggest fear. ✔

CHECK BOUNCER

"Joe Blow" calls himself an "illegitimate businessman." For the last several years, except for one period of employment, his "main thing" has been passing bad checks. In the last year, he estimates his total bounce at $150,000. "Every place uses a different system for verifying your identify," says "Joe Blow," "and I alter my program accordingly."

To get a driver's license, you have to have three pieces of ID. I can't make a credit card, so I have to get a stolen one. It's in the name of say, "Joe Blow." Then I get some friend's birth certificate and discharge papers (DD-214), and I change the names by whiting out the old data and typing data in. I "preimpose" the name I want to use: "Joe Blow," change the address and the birth date, then Xerox them. Then I go to a driving examiner, take the test, they take my picture, and I'm gone. I've got my phony credentials.

The address I give depends on what I'm doing. If I'm opening a bank account, I want a good address. I always give a fancy address, because those residents get more respect at the places where I shop. I try to avoid shopping where blacks, poor white trash, or people of lower incomes shop. So when I go to a bank to open a checking account, I'll give a phony address on a good street. I know it will be two weeks before the checks are printed, so I'll tell the clerk, "You know, I'm moving next week, and I'm not sure I'm going to take this apartment or whether I'm going to such and such an address. Is there any way I could pick up the checks at the bank?" She'll say, "Oh sure, Mr. Blow. I'll call you at your office." And I say, "Oh, no, I'll call you, since I'll be out of town that week." She says fine, call me on such and such a date. So I do, and now I've got the checks, and my "address" has never even been tested.

If I leave my house at nine tomorrow morning, I'm like a woman in a grocery store on a shopping spree: She's got twenty minutes to get all the groceries she can. It takes about six days for a person accepting a personal check to find out that it's bad. So I've got five days.

You can deposit $1,500 in a checking account and shop from 9 a.m. to 9 p.m. writing an average of $400 in each store, spending twenty minutes in each store. Sometimes they may want to call your bank and check the balance in your account, so usually I don't go shopping until after five, when the banks are closed. All the stores I go into take checks. I look the part of a middle-class executive or attorney. I'll put on a whole show for them. In the last year, I'd say I've gotten over $150,000 in merchandise. Everybody buys their goods from me.

But even though I got $150,000 last year, I'm starving. Most of it was in merchandise, and there's all that overhead. It gets to where the outgo exceeds the income. And the upkeep is the downfall.

CON ARTIST

"I am versed in the art of everything you can think of," says Brett I., with his characteristic immodesty. Although he says he has had many

64

jobs, Brett prefers to operate solely as a con artist, living off the fat of the land and "getting revenge on all women." Because he is seemingly consumed by a hatred for women, I have limited his remarks to his exploitation of women as a warning for their benefit.

I'm fantastic with women. I take care of my body, and I have eyes like you've never seen. I picked up a girl on a bus— she liked my conversation—and I got her phone number. I didn't have a car, but after picking her up at her apartment, I put on a big act when we came out the door. I saw this tow-away sign, and I said, "Oh my God, Janie, my car's been towed away." So I called the "towing company," which was really my number, and I faked a conversation: "You mean it's $50? I don't have $50—I only have $20." Janie interrupted and said, "That's all right. I'll lend you the money." So I said, "Let's just go out and get something to eat. I'll worry about the car tomorrow." She not only gave me $30 to pick up my car, she also took me out to dinner. My specialty is ripping off young women.

When a woman has something to sell: an apartment to sublet, furniture, whatever, she is at your disposal. She is vulnerable to anything you say. Once I answered a car ad, "Moving to Boston in one week; must sacrifice." Gloria liked my voice. I went and looked at her car, and I liked it. "I'll call my bank tomorrow," I said. "Do you want cash or a cashier's check?" It didn't matter. She gave me a couple of beers. By then, she was telling herself, "I'm not going to resist anything this guy tries, otherwise I'll blow the chance to sell the car." So I started making out with her, kissing her, and one thing led to another, and I balled her. I crashed there that night, woke up the next morning, and fixed myself some eggs. She had about $50 lying around that I could have taken, but I'm not a thief. So later that day I called her back—I didn't have to, I just did it to hear her expression—and said, "Gloria, look, I don't think I'll be buying your car." "You son-of-a-bitch," she said. "What do you mean?" I asked. "A person can change his mind, can't he?" She said, "Oh, I see. You got what you wanted," and I said, "Well, you were ready to give it to me, baby."

I don't rely on classified ads more than a third of the time. The rest of the information I need I get off of billboards and bulletin boards in supermarkets, or I can trace people through their auto licenses, etc. I play them for suckers, just so I can call them up an hour later and laugh in their faces. 🡒

DOOR AND PHONE SELLING

ENCYCLOPEDIA SALESWOMAN

Doris G. was "suckered" into encyclopedia sales for a large publisher after she read an ad that said she would be doing marketing and promotional advertising by giving people sets of the books free. Though she had only a high school diploma, she did have the sort of chutzpah that brought her about $75,000 a year as a salesperson and finally $150,000 as a district manager. She was locked up in jail in numerous American cities and towns and deported from Australia. For every ten presentations she made, she says she sold seven sets of books. In her current home state, she estimates there are 5,000 families who bought her books "and never knew what hit them." Everywhere she went, the public was, to her, "ignorant and waiting to be fleeced." Doris never minded manipulating other people, but despite her great success in selling, she eventually got tired of being manipulated herself and became disenchanted with the attitude of her employer, who "just wanted me to keep working till I dropped. I got out because I couldn't stand getting my people out of jail or fighting with the Federal Trade Commission or working twenty hours a day, seven days a week. I got out because I couldn't deal with it anymore."

I would cold-canvass, knock on doors, and tell the people a lie . . . that I was taking a survey of all young married couples in the area. Would they mind if I stepped in?—at which point I was wiping my feet off and walking in. Then I gave them my canned spiel that we were selecting several families in the area and giving them a free set of books. The only thing we wanted from them was a letter saying how much they loved our books and their permission to use it as a testimonial. It was just a gimmick—we didn't want the letter anyway. If you could have seen some of the letters; those people were illiterate.

Then we would tell them, "Naturally, you want to keep your

set of books up-to-date," and we would offer them our two revisional services at our "production cost," which would "amount to no more than the cost of a daily newspaper." How could anybody turn that down? One of the services was a book that came out every year, and the other was a spectacular question-and-answer service that would allow them to ask one-hundred questions on any subject in the world. We would tell them they could get plans to build a home or dress patterns or whatever they wanted. We all knew it was a lie. If anyone ever tried to use the service, we would be gone by then.

We never went into affluent neighborhoods. We'd pick on real idiots, illiterate old ladies, a lot of military personnel. They used to drop us right on the base, and at night we had to climb over the fence to get out. The majority of people who bought the books didn't even have children. When they did, we'd play on their future guilt. There comes a point where a guy realizes he is undereducated. This poor slob is busting his back trying to make a living, and he wants his kid to be proud of him. He wants his kid to grow up and have a good education—but he doesn't want to have any part of it. He doesn't want to work with him; he just wants the kid to grow up to be educated. So, if he has a set of books in his house, no matter what anybody ever says about him, he can always say, "Listen, I paid $650 for that set of books, and this bum of a kid never even uses them."

Most people don't buy encyclopedias until someone like me comes along and shoves them down their throat. Sometimes I would get a little too nervy, and the guy would open the door and start throwing my crap out onto the street. I would rule out poor risks myself. I didn't care how poor people were. If I felt I could get paid for the books, I would sell them. The people had to have an income. I would never pitch an old couple on Social Security—Social Security is not an income—because they had to live three years to pay off the books. Once you're inside, you'd be surprised at what people will tell you. If you know how to ask questions correctly, they will tell you everything you could ever think of, especially if you mooch them up a lot. If you present yourself as a market researcher, they love to talk.

We never talked to the customer directly, it was always in the third person. Things like, "Parents don't care enough about their kids to give them a good education. Who is supposed to care—a stranger, like a teacher?" I once told a man, "If you don't buy your son this set of books, he is going to follow in the same failure pattern you have already established." I took him right by the knee and said, "Come on, Joe. Do you want this kid to grow up to be a bum?" Do you know he bit? I made the sale. I would stare eyeball to eyeball.

If you can't control them, you can't sell them. If a guy starts giving you a lot of smoke about not needing encyclopedias because he goes to the library to use them, you say, "Oh really. I'm so glad. It's terrific to meet an educated person. Where is your library?" He wouldn't know, and you'd know right away he's full of shit, and you can lean on him.

You can always take an objection and turn it around. I would always absolutely agree with people when they said they didn't use an encyclopedia more than ten times a year. I'd say, "You're absolutely right, sir. These books are not intended for you. But what are you going to do when it's snowing outside and your kid has to write a report on Norway? Are you going to drive him to the library? Do you want to worry about him being out on the streets alone at night?" You paint a picture of little children sitting around the fire reading their books and getting smart, and the customers lap it up.

We told them the set of encyclopedias we were putting into their houses was worth $600. But even though it was "free," we got our money out of it. We would tell them that the question-and-answer service cost us on the average of $5 for every usage, or $500 for the 100 questions. We said the yearbook was worth $25, so $500, plus $25 a year over a ten-year period, is a lot of money, and people are not going to sign up to spend $750 for two revisional services. So we told them we would sell them the two services at our production cost, no more than they would have paid at the time for their daily newspaper. We would close them then on a program where they would pay $5 or $6 a month, or about $65 a year for the next ten years, and we said someone would come around every month to pick up the money.

So after they had committed themselves to paying $650 over ten years, we hit them with something called a conversion. We said $65 a year wasn't much and the payments would be easy, but did they really want some jerky kid coming around every month for the next ten years? "Your neighbors are going to think you don't pay your bills," or "You'll have to buy him birthday and Christmas presents," etc. We would then make it easy for them to pay off their ten-year obligation in three years, with larger monthly payments. If they agreed, we would throw in what we called "goodie" books free—a set of children's books, medical encyclopedia, dictionary, etc.

After we had got them closed on that, we would remind them of the $7.95 charge for postage, royalties, and handling on the yearbooks. (Royalties were bullshit. How could you pay royalties on a yearbook, for God's sake?) So we'd say we felt bad about that charge, but there was nothing we could do about it, because the government didn't allow prepayment of those charges on books that hadn't been printed yet. However, we would give them at no additional cost a custom-made bookcase for the entire set. It was really bad news—a piece of garbage.

On the conversion, they paid the same amount of money in three years they would have paid in ten—we just gave them the free books as an extra. In fact, there wasn't any ten-year program, until we were forced by the government to start one. The whole set of books with every piece of garbage in it cost the manufacturer no more than $100 to produce, and they are selling them for over $650. As a salesperson, I'd get a commission of $280 on every set. The field manager, the one who drove the car of the crew, got $45. The people who trained the salespeople got $20. The district sales manager got $70. You could buy the books direct from the publisher or even the district manager, but if you get a salesman coming to your door and honking his horn at you, you'll have to pay a commission of between 48 and 60 percent of the total sale.

We really had people by the short hairs. They couldn't drop out, because they had signed a contract. If they tried, we turned their accounts over to a collection agency. I used to collect delinquent accounts. We pounded most people into the ground. I'd get on the phone and scream at them, threaten them, lie to them—you did everything you could to harass them. You called them on the job or called their neighbors and told them you were with the legal department and asked them to go get the guy to the phone. We humiliated them. Of course, it was illegal, but we still did it.

If they think they can collect, they will sue, and if they think they can't, they will harass the customer into the ground. But once it gets to the point that they know they are not going to collect, they just leave you alone. They won't take their books back—they don't want them. What are they going to do with them—a three-year-old set of books you can buy in the Goodwill for $5—they're garbage.

We started getting black men, who were very aggressive hustlers. They were very good salesmen, but they scared the crap out of people in the white neighborhoods. I never worked a black neighborhood—you'd get killed. These dudes would come in with gold shoes and nine-inch afros, and I'd take them out. They weren't on the street five minutes before the chief of police was on the horn. I had a phone in my car, and they'd call me up and tell me to come down and pick up my man. If I had five people arrested in one night for soliciting without a permit, that meant I had to have $1,000 bond money on me.

You can get away with a lot on taxes. You're an independent contractor, so it's entirely up to you what you work and what you report. They don't deduct for Social Security or taxes. Of course, there are a lot of business deductions because you're on the road all the time. I didn't underreport, however, because I was always afraid I would get caught.

My advice to a customer is if you want to buy a product, go to the source. If you want a set of encyclopedias, call up the company. You can call up (a leading encyclopedia publisher), and they'll sell you a set right out of the box at maybe $250—instead of $800 or so if you bought it from a salesman. You can get a lot of other sets out of the box for $30 or $40—maybe they've been repossessed. If you read the newspaper, every day you can see used sets for sale. I mean, I dealt with encyclopedia salesmen, and I can tell you that they were strong-armed from the moment they opened that door. ↙

MAGAZINE SALESMAN

Living in an apartment hotel and washing dishes for a living, nineteen-year-old Kevin R. was ready for a change. He read a newspaper ad that promised free travel all over the United States for "guys and girls" doing "publisher's contact" work. This was just a fancy name for magazine salesman, but the idea appealed to Kevin, who had been selling in his family's businesses since his early teens and who regarded himself as a "damned good salesman." So he took the job, and soon he was on the road with a sales crew knocking on doors almost twelve hours a day, six days a week. In the course of their travels, they discovered that they were not alone in their field. "We had contact with quite a few other sales teams," says Kevin. "The magazine business is all a ripoff."

These were national magazines we were selling. You'd go up to a door with a "Hi, my name is Kevin R., and I am working my way through college." What it really boils down to is you are supposedly working for a $1,000 cash award, but it's all a lot of bullshit. If we went back to the same town and the people said, "weren't you here last year?" I'd have to lie. I'd say, "No, Ma'am, I've never been in a contest in my life." They would say that they'd never gotten their magazines and weren't interested. Other people would get violent and take your receipt and tear it up.
A lot of people would never get their magazines. When we

72

sold a subscription and collected the money, we would turn it into our boss, Mr. L., every night. This guy would just spend the money. I'd say in 75 percent of the cases, he wouldn't order the magazines, and the customers were ripped off. We gave them a receipt, but the company rarely responded. If they did, they would promise to do something about it, but they never did.

I was one of their top salesmen. I was bringing in over $100 a day and I kept saying, "Mr. L., I would like to know where my money is going." And he'd say, "Don't worry about it. You are making money." He'd say he was keeping a record of how much money I was making, so I said fine. Meanwhile, he was giving us $5 a day to eat on, and we were almost starving. They never paid me at all. I was supposed to get half the sale as a commission, $50 a day or $300 a week, and I think that company still owes me close to $9,000, which I'll never see in my lifetime.

If you went up to him and told him you were quitting, he would beat the shit out of you. The kids they hire are like slaves. He had a girl who was mentally retarded, and he used to beat the shit out of her because she wasn't writing any business. He kept her, though, because in a sales organization you always have to have someone who doesn't do well to bring the others up. He kept bullshitting the rest of us, telling us that she would make it one of these days. She wanted to quit, but she was afraid of the guy.

He got away with this because he weighed about 400 pounds, and everyone was scared of him. He was a big brute. They go for heavies to run these sales teams, and they all work by force and intimidation. He had a couple girls on the crew he was using for his own purpose of prostitution. They used to go to bed with him. He was married, but I guess they loved him because he was rich.

He slept all during the day while we were out working, and he was up all night. So the only way to quit was to try to sneak out at night with your clothes, if you were lucky, or split during the day while he was sound asleep and leave your clothes behind. But you understand, we never had enough money to leave on. For example, if you called Mommy and Daddy and had them send

73

you money, there was no way you'd get it because he got your mail first and opened it to check it out. If you tried to split with your subscription money after a day's work, he would have a warrant sworn out for your arrest.

Finally, I went to a Christian organization, and they got me out of this whole deal. We were in California, and he tried this shit with me, so I called the police and told them he had this girl under him as a captive. I ended up testifying against him. I hear they put the man on probation for a year, but, you know, he doesn't give a shit. He left the state anyway, they said. I never got any word from the company as to my earnings. I have records of every sale I ever made. The company is still operating, and I'm sure they always will be. ✔

WHOLESALE REPRESENTATIVE

"Right off my business card," says Harvey R., "I would be a wholesale distributor. In reality, I was a door-to-door business salesman." Harvey was a bona fide salesman on his regular jobs, but when business got a little slow, he would spend a day here and there as a "wholesale distributor" for another firm, hawking wares in which quality was conspicuously lacking. Nonetheless, many buyers were, indeed, ready customers, totally oblivious to the flaws that were built into his product line. It was, as Harvey puts it, "a monkey hustle."

This was a national company that goes under different names in different areas. We sold housewares to businesses or to organizations that were trying to raise money, or even to individuals who thought they were getting a good deal. We simply loaded our car up with merchandise, and they would give us a route, say an area of about a two-mile radius. We went out and called on every business—everyone from a mortician to a pet shop owner—and tried to sell them the goods. We would go to churches or high schools that were having fund-raising programs, or places that had bingo games or festivals and sell them our products for their prizes.

The fact is, this company was in the business of acquiring seconds or discards and selling them as bargain merchandise. Most of the merchandise was defective, and our tactics were to get in and get out as fast as we could. We sold sets of glasses that were misshaped, miscut, or had machine markings all over them; knife sets that were bent or had scratched handles, or the blades, which were real crummy steel, were not fastened properly to the handles. The lips of the carafes were flawed. The backgammon boards were chipped. We were selling our customers nothing but faulty garbage.

Yet, a customer could go anywhere and buy the same products, in good condition, cheaper than we were selling them for, or at least for the same price. The company was probably buying this stuff, say, a set of glassware, from the manufacturer for $2—on closeout because it was defective. We, the salesmen, were paying $13 for it, and we were telling our customers that this was a $60 retail set that they could have for $20. Let's say you ran a small coin shop, and you were on my route. I'd walk in and introduce myself, saying, "I'm Harvey R. and I work for——so-and-so Distribution Company. We just completed a sale out here (or 'we closed a show in the area') for some of our buyers, and I have a few pieces of my merchandise left. So rather than sending them back to the home company, I call on some of the small businesses in the area and wholesale them out at my cost. Let me show you what I have." Then I show them the fliers and say, "Let me run out and get one and bring it in." I show it to the man, go through the demonstration, and remind him that he is getting a $60 value for $20 and ask him how many can he use. Boom—that's it. They are taking your say-so—and we do have a pretty nifty demonstration that goes with it—and you make them think they are getting a steal. The clientele I am selling to is very sophisticated, but they are your common, everyday businessmen. Basically, we give charity organizations the same pitch. The only thing that will vary there is that you want to clear out your car so you give them a little better price on volume. The schools, especially, don't know what they are getting into, because they don't have the time to open up fifty sets and inspect each individually.

I have walked into shops and watched a guy spend an entire week's paycheck buying my merchandise—twelve or fourteen sets; it's incredible. This is a profit of $7 a set for me, and this guy is going to turn around and try to stick those on his friends for x number of dollars profit for him. People are not looking at the worth of a thing. They are just looking at the supposed savings they are making. They are always looking for that big deal that lets them go home and say, "Look what I got for a steal."

I got into this through an ad in the paper. When my own business got a little bit stale, I'd look for a way to pick up some money on the side. For the salesman, it was a dynamite business, and you could make a lot of money in a hurry. You got paid in cash, so you reported whatever you wanted to report as income. The average salesman pulled in at least $100 a day. You have to report something, but, Jesus, you can claim you sold twenty pieces at $2 a set, so you can claim you made $40 rather than $100 or $135 or whatever.

When I started out, I did not know the nature of the merchandise I was selling. They said the knives had rosewood handles, which was the best they used, and stainless steel blades, which was true, but no mention was made of what was wrong with them. Gradually, I found out, just by selling them, and God, on some days you'd have a whole carload of flawed merchandise. There was no mention of guarantees at all, but if a guy called up with a complaint, I would replace the merchandise, and hope he wouldn't see the flaws in the set I replaced it with. Of course, what we were telling them wasn't exactly true, either. This stuff wasn't left over from a show or anything. If the customer wanted 5,000 sets, I could get them for him.

This was a very aggressive outfit; they showed me a lot of good sales concepts and how to get into a lot of places. They totally beat the hell out of security systems and taught us how to gain entrance where it was technically illegal. They had it down to a fine art as to how to avoid being taken in by the police for soliciting. You'd say, "Wow, I'm not actually soliciting," and go into it like that, and the police would get so frustrated, they'd let you go on doing what you were doing. If another company moved in as our competition, the president of my company would go to any length to blow them out of there. He told us, quite up front, that he would spend any amount of money to destroy an outfit that challenged him.

We had to pay a security deposit, in the event that we damaged some of the merchandise in a car accident or whatever. Now, they tell you that the deposit will be refunded twenty working days after you quit. Two months later, after calling them lots of times and being told a bunch of stories, I have yet to see my deposit. ✓

TELEPHONE SOLICITOR

Responding to an ad that promised "tremendous salaries," Barry S. took a job soliciting sales by telephone. "I knew it was a lie right away," says Barry, "but it took me several hours to find out the extent of the lie." He left the same day.

This firm was in the business of selling light bulbs, and we'd get on long-distance telephone lines and call companies all over the country. We'd get the names of their purchasing agents, then ask to talk with them. "Hi, Jack," you'd say, "I was in your office the other day to deliver our annual gift to you, but you weren't in." You'd tell him it was a broiler, radio, or whatever, and you'd ask for his address. "By the way," you'd say, "our company pays for the gift, but I have to pay for the shipping charges. Do you think you could give me an order to cover the —?" Yeah, sure, he's happy to get the gift.

So you ask Jack, "How about if you bought 500 light bulbs?" He agrees and gives you a purchase order number, and you've made a sale. But those bulbs are going to cost him an arm and a leg, much more than he'd pay in a store, the salesman who was training me told me. This salesman thought it was very funny; he was cracking jokes about how they were rejects, and how the purchasing agent would get in trouble if his boss found out what a crummy purchase he'd made.

Some of the purchasing agents will curse you out on the phone right away—they've probably been stung before. Even though some of them may know it's a gyp, they'll go through with it anyway to get their free gift. If they ask you for a price, you try to avoid it, but half the time they don't realize what you're charging them.

What was really funny, the salesman told me, was that we never even sent them their gift. If they called back after several months asking about it, we were supposed to say, "Oh, gosh, there must have been a mix-up in the mailing room. We'll get it out right away, and by the way, maybe we could get another order from you?" If they ordered the second time, we'd send them their gift, because we realized the purchasing agent wanted to play the game with us.

Nora G. also lasted one day on her job as a phone solicitor. Outwardly, her pitch was promising free cemetery lots, but she suspected that her employer was actually trying to sell unlisted telephone numbers. (A telephone company official confirmed to me that these numbers are indeed collected and sold. Sometimes tradesmen or deliverymen will be paid to make note of numbers on their house calls.)

We worked from special directories that have telephone numbers listed numerically by exchanges. We'd go down the list until we found one missing, then call that. When the person answered, we'd ask if they had received the ads we had mailed out to the people in their area, and when they said no, we'd say, "Well, give me your name and address, and I'll send you the ad so you can see how to get a free cemetery plot." Some would be dumb enough to give their name and address, but a lot of them got mad and asked where I'd gotten their telephone number from. I would just say:"Oh, we're just calling at random." You had to be very aggressive, and I found it nerve-wracking. They never did pay me for the day I worked. ✔

PHOTO SALESWOMAN

The freebie is a common bait in the marketing of personal services, and the photo studio that Melinda B. sold for found it very effective in getting people into the establishment and into the clutches of the firm's seven high-pressure salespersons. High prices and easy credit rounded out the package.

This studio would use a phone room to make calls and get people to come in for a free picture and a string of phony pearls. The whole family would come in all dressed up. After the photographer took the pictures, I'd take the people into another room and pitch them on an $89.95 package: so many 8x10s, 5x7s, wallets, and all that. They'd usually buy that. Most people will go for that much. Of course, they'd still get the free photograph even if they didn't buy anything, but if they bought the package, they were allowed to choose their proofs.

"Proof-passers" were then supposed to sell the customers a photographic oil, a photo that's tinted in different colors and then framed. The oils could run up to $300. They tried to train me as a proof-passer, but I wasn't any good at it, because I couldn't keep a straight face; it was so ludicrous. Nobody was charging the kind of prices we were. The oils were nice, but they weren't worth $300.

Their credit practices were vicious. They wanted me to work in the credit department, but I said you couldn't pay me to go in there. They'd be verbally abusive to people on public aid, people who should never have signed the contract in the first place. Often, they'd miss a payment—they just couldn't afford the pictures. The people they preyed on were ignorant. Anyone with any intelligence didn't buy.

They just kept pushing people into signing. Finally, the police sent in an undercover agent who pretended to be a blind man. They actually took his hand and guided it to sign a contract—without (they thought) his knowing what was in it. After they did that, he put them under arrest for deceptive practices.

Nancy A. worked as a receptionist for a studio that offered passport photo service and had a tendency to charge what the traffic would bear.

We would sell passport photo prints for $5 each. If the owner saw someone come in dressed in a well-tailored outfit, or if they didn't understand English very well, he'd up the price to $7. If someone called on the telephone, we would tell them the price was $5. Then when a customer came in, I would ask if he had called. If he said no, then I knew I could charge him $7.   ✔

DWELLING

APARTMENT FINDER

They gave her a title of rent counselor, and Patricia K.'s job was to find apartments for prospective renters in a large city. The clients expected her firm's service to offer them exclusive listings. The firm was advertised in newspapers and on TV. In fact, most of the listings were taken right out of the daily newspapers, not all of which were current. The firm was eventually closed down by the authorities. Patricia said that when she started in the business, she did have a conscience, but she lost it when she saw that most of the customers were too careless to even read the contract.

We went through the newspapers pretending we were people looking for an apartment to rent. We'd call the listings in the classified ads and get all the information we wanted—like whether there was a yard, dryer, washer, etc., whether they allowed pets, etc.—then we'd leave a phony name and number and say we'd call back. Then we would prepare our own listing of the property from the information we'd just gotten.

Once in a while, landlords would call and give us their property to list once they found out we didn't have to list their apartment by the right address and that we would dissuade blacks and latinos from renting—in, say, an old Polish neighborhood. I would tell the landlady we wouldn't refuse to show the listing to blacks or latinos, but that I would attempt to persuade them to try something else if I could. Renters generally wanted a neighborhood that would be good for them to live in, anyway. But even with landlords calling us, only a third of our listings were exclusive—the rest were right out of the newspapers.

We provided nothing the people couldn't have found out for themselves, and we gave them no guarantee we'd find them a place. When I started out, the customer paid a fee of $30, then it went to $40, $50, and finally $100.

A customer would look at our ad in the paper, which might have listed six or eight properties, and would see maybe two listings that sounded too good to be true—a six-room house for $150 a month. There are some people stupid enough to think you can get that. So the customer would call our office, and we'd say, yes, it's still available. Then he'd come in and pay his $100 fee—cash only; we wouldn't take checks. He'd ask if I could guarantee that he could have the apartment, and I'd say, no, I can only guarantee it's still available, that all my listings were still available, for that matter.

That's when we gave them the "magics," special phone numbers that either the boss or a person hired by him to portray a landlord would answer. Each day of the week, we'd use names from a different letter of the alphabet. If you called Monday, Mr. Anderson would be the name; Tuesday, Mr. Brown; Wednesday, Mr. Carlson, and so on. The magic number was supposedly the landlord's number, so on Tuesday, we'd give the client Mr. Brown's number, and he'd call Mr. Brown, and the guy would say, "My father isn't home—can you call back later?" So the client would call again, and Mr. Brown still wasn't home, and finally, after getting the runaround for two or three days, he'd call again, and the guy would say, "Oh, my father just rented that property. Didn't he tell you?" This was just a stall we'd use until we could find something for them. Sometimes we could stall them for weeks. Other people, though, were smart. They'd check and find there was no such landlord, and that's how we got caught. My boss was stupid in a lot of ways, but he was a genius in making money. He had a lot of people paid off.

We got 100 new clients in every day at $100 a crack. He took more money from those people. Most of them were black and poor. I've had more than one customer pull a gun on me because they were mad they couldn't get their $100 back. I'd say, "The money isn't here. I can't do anything about it. It's in the safe." They wanted their money back, because they weren't getting any service. When I felt sorry for the customer, I would pull one

82

over on the company and give them the legit listings without charging them.

Landlords would complain when our clients would call them weeks after their apartments were rented, because our listings weren't kept up-to-date. The newspapers would call and say we couldn't use their listings, and I'd say, "Wait a minute. We're just making use of public information." We had six or seven lawyers working all the time.

We were competing with another company that told us they would run us out of town. They would tie up all our phone lines, just hang on them all day long. They poisoned one of the dogs that I took into the ghetto with me. They broke our windows every other week, until finally we just left them boarded up. They squirted Crazy Glue into our locks so we had to break into our own office. They threatened the girl friend of one of our guys with a gun, then sabotaged his car. We knew it was the other company, because the guy who ran it was present when these things happened. He had bodyguards everywhere he went. We were told he was with the Syndicate. ✔

ASSISTANT PROPERTY MANAGER

Property managers are commonly, though mistakenly, thought of as landlords. As such, tenants hold them in contempt when their air conditioning or the hot water ceases, but they hold them in awe when they suddenly recall their powers of eviction. In fact, property managers are administrators hired by owners to protect their property and maximize their earnings. They dispense, according to the terms of the lease, those services to which a tenant is entitled. Some act as true intermediaries in reconciling the sometimes conflicting interests of owners and tenants; others are clearly in the owners' camps. A woman just starting in property management once told me that one of the first things her boss said to her was: Give the tenants everything the lease promises, but remember, once they've moved in, "They're just so much horsemeat."

After a couple of years in a real estate firm, Trudy D. worked her way up to the job of assistant property manager. She handled both commercial property and residential units and dealt with owners ranging from individual landlords, to incorporated professionals and real estate investment trusts. She and her staff kept the owners' books, paid their bills, hired operating and maintenance crews, and collected the rents. Generally, Trudy says, upkeep on the medical buildings and business offices was well provided for, "But the apartment buildings were a different matter."

Apartment building owners are notorious for being nonchalant about upkeep. The competence of property managers is sometimes diminished by the demands of owners. If they don't want you to exceed the budget, or they won't raise the rents, then you're going to have to cut down on basic services, and you'll get an undesirable level of tenants.

When the heat would go off in two of our buildings in a fairly low-rent district, the landlords were never terribly concerned. They wouldn't put in a new furnace, even when we told them they had to. They'd say, "We'll just let it go for another year," when they planned to dump the building anyway.

Managers short-change tenants by not cleaning hallways. If they get behind in their payments to the garbage collection service, maybe it won't be picked up for a couple of weeks. Most of our buildings had no pest control. If you have a piggy neighbor, a whole building can become infested. Many owners have inadequate liability insurance coverage.

Once we got our tenants moved in and paid up, we'd write down every request they had, and depending on our budget, sometimes it would get done, sometimes it wouldn't. We'd only deal with emergencies. Some tenants even had toilets out of order for three or four days, and you'd just say, well, the plumber can't make it. There's no way they can prove he can. All they can do is complain; few of them want to go to the expense of hiring a lawyer.

84

It distressed me to have people call with complaints that were really justified—like leaks in the ceiling—and I'd have to lie to them, because I knew we weren't going to fix the roof for a good six months because of the budget constraint. That's the company line; be nice to them, but tell them lies. You can't tell them the owners won't undertake such an expensive project at the time—I mean, that would give them justifiable grounds for moving out under constructive eviction. Property managers usually get a percentage of gross receipts. Whether the maintenance gets done or not doesn't affect them at all.

A property manager is essentially a fence for the owner. We offer bookkeeping services, but that's about the beginning and end of any real responsibility. Landlords use property managers, because they don't want to be bothered. A renter often doesn't even know who his landlord is; it's not on the lease. As agents, the property managers are responsible for protecting the privacy of the owners. Unless you live in a place, your standards for that place are going to be low. When we're in danger of exceeding our budget, we just cut off services. If we didn't the owner would get another firm to manage for him.

Government bodies are very slow to act on complaints. They're just a bunch of bureaucrats, and unless it's a problem of rats or gas leaking, they don't want to get involved. Everybody is hesitant to bring in the government, because then there are usually problems for everyone.

We had a lot of tenant damage in our older buildings. One foreign couple skipped town after paying one month's rent. She didn't know about electric stoves and had been cooking eggs, refried beans, etc., directly on the burners. They had pulled down every lighting fixture in the place and pulled the lavatory fixture off the wall in the bathroom. Judging from the walls, it looked like they'd had a big fight with raw eggs. That cost us about $600. Things like that happen a lot. People have wild parties and just rip the place apart. They feel that if the landlord doesn't take care of the building, why should they?

From the tenants' standpoint, a resident manager can be more responsive than one in a central office. One problem we've had with them, however, is that if tenants pay their rent directly to them, there are instances where they have siphoned off a bit. It has to be a lax management situation for this to be possible, but maybe the guy will collect a couple of grand, and then he splits.

The way most leases are written—they are definitely in the landlords' favor—the tenant cannot withhold rent until problems are corrected. Even though it's 40° below and you have no heat, you have to pay your rent. The best thing is to get to a small claims court in a hurry. But you have to keep a record of everything, the day, time, to whom you spoke, and their response. I'd keep a separate journal just on the dealings I had with my landlord.

Let's face it: If you get evicted, where are you going to go? That's the root of it. ✔

REAL ESTATE SALESWOMAN

Right after she got her license as a real estate saleswoman, Myra L. went to work for a broker—someone who must also be licensed by the state. Salespersons cannot deal in real estate except under the auspices of a broker. Divorced and supporting her two children, Myra began her long-postponed career in real estate. She worked for four firms in as many years, and the experience gave her and, as she says, many of her colleagues, a profound dislike for brokers and the way they operate. She now plans to get her own broker's license and operate on her own. Though arrangements vary, as a saleswoman Myra received half the commission her firm collected on the sale of a house. Her income derived basically from listings she acquired and serviced (listings are agreements between people selling their homes and the real estate company), and the listings brought her a commission when the properties were sold. However, since the commissions were everybody's source of income, therein lay the seeds of many disputes.

When I started in real estate, I worked for a woman who gave me a contract that stated that if I wanted to buy a home to live in, I could do so without paying a commission to her. But, if I bought a house to sell and make a profit, I'd have to pay her a commission. Well, I came across a listing that looked good, and I told her I was thinking about buying it. She said, "Okay, but don't tell me about it; I'm not interested. By rights you should pay me a commission." And I said, "For what? I intend to live in it." Well, shortly afterward, as the sale was going through, I left her over a dispute. She changed her mind; she definitely wanted that commission. I finally had to go to court, after she tried to block the sale. She caused nothing but chaos, and I don't know what claim, under our contract, she had to the commission, since I'd bought the house to live in.

By law, you can't take your listings with you when you leave a firm, but you're entitled to your commission when the deal closes. But just try to collect it without a big hassle. When I left this woman, there were several closings for my listings that had not taken place. One transaction was with another broker, who represented the buyer. Brokers who represent the buyer do most of the work; they handle the financing and everything. The seller doesn't have to do anything except get an attorney to assure a good and marketable deed. I made all the arrangements I was supposed to make before I left, but after the closing, the broker deducted several hundred dollars from my commission. She said a lot of work had to be done to follow up after I'd left, but she didn't say exactly what the work was, because there really wasn't any. I had no recourse—the state will not adjudicate claims between salespersons and brokers—but to take it to small claims court, and I just didn't have the time to do it.

We were all entitled to service our own listings for thirty days exclusively, which was fair, because we work hard getting those listings. Well, one day they rerouted a call on one of my listings to another salesperson, and I brought it up. My broker said: "You're the most money-grabbing person I've ever seen." I said, "I'm working for money to support my children. If you want to work for nothing go ahead." She fired me. At Christmas, the salespeople were supposed to get a bonus as a percentage of their sales, but her partner later told me that nobody had ever lasted till Christmas, because she didn't want to pay the bonus.

The brokers want the best of both worlds. They tell you that you're independent contractors and thereby avoid paying unemployment tax and handling a lot of employee paperwork. Yet, many of them force you to come in for sales meetings—or else get fired—and what they call floor time. This means you have to be in the office, usually one day a week, answering the phones and doing secretarial duties. Some will tell you about this beforehand, and if you don't agree they won't hire you. This is their way of getting a day's work out of you at no pay.

I sold a home for an older couple, and the buyers, even though both of them worked, didn't have enough money to swing the deal. In a case like this, the seller will take back part of the financing. They'll say, "We'll pledge $5,000 to enable the people to get a mortgage at a bank." That's what happened in this case; the buyers bought it on contract. Well, the buyers' broker told them not to say anything about their bills, and when he set up their mortgage at a savings and loan, he misrepresented their financial position. He did not declare to the savings and loan that there was, in effect, something like a second mortgage on the house. I brought this to the attention of the state, and they did nothing about it. I also informed the savings and loan, but it turned out their broker and the loan officer were friends. This sort of misrepresentation goes on all the time with brokers, I'd say 50 percent of the time. They are going to stretch the truth as far as they can to get the mortgage money, because they want to make the sale. I was often in a position to present misinformation to a bank, but I never did, because the broker would take care of it. Brokers justify this by saying, "Well, they can make the payments, and the bank will make its own credit check." But the banks can't verify everything, like whether you own property out of town. Not everything shows up on a credit report. Maybe it does if you have bad credit, but if your credit is good, you're pretty well in.

There was a house listed by another broker, and one of our

saleswomen came in with her customer's offer, which was over the listing price. She called up the salesman in the other office, and she said she'd like to present the offer. He said he couldn't present it until day-after-tomorrow, because he was going to be out. He should have presented it, and our saleswoman was very angry that our broker didn't protest. Well, the salesman had prospective buyers of his own on the line, and so when they made an offer, which was lower than our customer's offer, he presented both of them on the third day, and his buyers' offer was accepted. The reason he gave was that his buyers were coming in with more money down.

Well, with the salesman's firm representing both the seller of the house and the buyer, they would collect 100 percent of the commission instead of splitting it with us, if our buyer's offer had been accepted. This stalling happens all the time, even though an offer is supposed to be presented within a reasonable time. Sometimes, the broker may be trying to favor a friend or someone, but usually it's a question of money. When salespeople represent both parties, they collect the commission as both buyer and seller.

Commissions are generally what the market will bear, and brokers are always reluctant to cut commissions. In fact, in the suburbs, a lot of commissions are going up from 6 to 7 percent. I don't know how they can justify that with the price of homes going up the way they are. There was a broker in the city who was charging 4 percent, when everyone else was at 6. He said that when he got started they refused to accept him in the multiple listings, which is a sort of trade organization among brokers. He said the brokers got together and chewed him out for cutting his commission and generally ostracized him. He had a terrible time.

There's a salesman in my office who earned $38,000 last year. He's worked for several brokers in the last few years and says they're all crooks. I had $3,300 coming to me from a closing I had arranged, and my lawyer told me he wouldn't trust any broker to hold money, except for a couple of the big prominent firms. He always put his clients' money into escrow. Salespeople go from office to office, because they are not being treated right by the brokers. I feel from my experience, and talking with others, that brokers have set themselves up as a privileged class, and salespeople are at their mercy.   ✍

FLOORING SHOP FOREMAN

Daryl C. is a shop foreman in a rather large operation that sells and installs both soft flooring (carpeting) and hard-surface flooring (tile, parquet, vinyl, etc.). He started out in the business more than twenty years ago as a wholesale salesman, then shifted to retail, and then contract. Before he became a foreman, he worked as a measure man and installer. Daryl is now with what he considers a reputable firm, although he has worked for what the trade calls the "borax houses," the high-pressure operations that advertise on late-night television. Reputable or not, however, his firm is not averse to perpetrating "a consistent ripoff that is almost a trade practice at this point." Their flooring materials are top quality, their installation is professional, and their service is good, says Daryl, "But somewhere along the line, I can guarantee you the odds are that you did not get everything that was written on the order."

How many yards of carpet are there in a 9 x 12-foot rug? If you answer twelve, that's not bad, and it is a hell of a lot better than 90 percent of the public could do. But if I asked you how many yards of carpet would there be in your living room, covered wall to wall, your answer would be, "I haven't the foggiest notion." I could put a tape measure on your floor and tell you "40 yards," and you would shrug and say, "Gee, that sounds right." Or, if I told you 44 or 39 or 43⅔, you still wouldn't know. Well, let's say it took exactly 40 to do the job, and I told you 44—that's a 10 percent ripoff. That's trade practice.

The dealer or the seller is the one who benefits from this. If the guy who handles the tape is getting commission based on total yardage, then he benefits, but the guys who measure are not always salesmen. They will just draw up a scale diagram, which they give to the salesman. From that, the salesman makes his estimate. He figures the floor area, the extra yardage required for a pattern match, and everything, and let's say he figures the job would require 42⅓ yards. At that point, he goes to his customer and tells him it takes 46 to do the job. He's already taken into account the pattern match and regular waste. He is just padding it 10 percent for his own and his boss's account. Or he may be doing it to cover the job he sold two weeks ago, where he was 4 yards short, because he made an error, and his boss won't let him off the hook. This sort of practice happens nine times out of ten, and all establishments do it most of the time.

Maybe one customer every six months will go around with a tape measure after we installed a carpet and say, "Hey, you billed me for 44 yards, and I only needed 40." We will ask them, "Are you taking into account all the factors? I have to allow three-inch trims at each end of the room, because your walls may not be perfectly straight and square. Now you add up that three inches at each end into the length and width all the way around the room, and that's another foot of carpeting, right? Now, you have a door to get into the room, and the carpet goes halfway into the door, doesn't it? There is another four or five inches. At the seam on the far side of your room, I have to trim an inch or two on each end of the roll, because the edges are never perfectly straight and square. . . ." When I get through with customers, I can convince them that 46 yards of carpet was a bargain.

Of course, I can tell customers it takes three inches of trim, because I've been in the business for a long time. In reality, I only take an inch-and-a-half, and on some carpets I will go nothing because I know they stretch quite a bit—like a rubber band. We could actually go in shorter than the physical measurements, because the particular carpet will stretch to cover it. In the large majority of houses, the rule of thumb is to add 3 to 5 percent waste factor, and that should cover all the carpet you need.

Now, if your room in fact takes 40 yards of carpeting to cover, it only takes 38 yards of padding to go underneath. The more complicated the room is, the bigger the difference—there is always less padding than carpeting. But you bill them for 40 yards of carpet and padding and labor. That's a built-in ripoff. That's the beauty of the whole thing right there. It allows for one inch of tacking strip, for the trim and turn-under of the extra carpeting, and the three inches on each side you allow for irregularities in the room. You need that much less padding on every job.

The only protection the consumer can get, is to go to three, four, five different stores and get estimates. Then take a look at the numbers. Most people won't do that. They will go to three or four stores but look only at the fabrics. Only one or two will go out and measure the room and give a confirmed figure. The customer will throw away the higher one and go with the other. Well, both of them could be high for that matter. Or there are people who will go to a store because their mother and grandmother bought their carpeting there. And they don't have the foggiest notion whether their grandmother got ripped off, or whether they will or won't—they just know that that's the store they always go to for their carpeting.

A typical job will average out pretty close to 40 yards. Let's say the carpet costs $20 a yard and the padding $2, the overcharge on four extra yards, plus the two yards of padding you don't use, plus the $3 or so per yard installation is worth a considerable amount. That's merchandise and labor the owner didn't have to buy and deliver. If a store does a million-dollars-worth of business in a year and rips off on overcharging, say, 5 percent of each job, that's $50,000 in income that the customer didn't get merchandise for.

Most reputable dealers stand behind their installations, but if you get these hole-in-the-wall operations, where the operator may buy a carload of samples and operate out of a spare bedroom, you run the risk of a poor installation. If your room is fourteen-feet wide, and the carpet comes from the manufacturer in the standard twelve-foot width, a seam should be made joining the two pieces of carpet together. A disreputable installer will cut the two pieces necessary—one twelve feet and the other two feet—and will lay them side-by-side and nail them to the floor or staple them together. There is no seam made. If the carpet is a plush or shag, you may not notice it—until such time as you have the carpet cleaned and there is a little bit of shrinkage and that seam gaps open. Customers may not be aware of what it should be, or if they challenge the installer, the installer will say, "That's standard practice. You have a seam in your pants and you don't complain about that."

Now if this same small dealer tries to do the installation himself or sends someone out who is only getting a buck a yard to do the work, he can't afford to waste the time on it, and he's going to use a knee-kicker instead of a power stretcher. If you kick it in by knee, you can only apply a limited amount of tension on the carpeting, and the installation won't be firm and snug—tight like a drumhead, as it should be. A power stretcher has a series of extension tubes and a crank handle, and it's adjustable so that you can put the proper amount of tension in and put the carpet in snug, tight, and secure to the floor in all directions. If it isn't secure, as it won't be when you use a knee-kicker, you are going to get wrinkles and buckles all over the carpeting every time the humidity changes. Consumers pay for an installation, and if it's not properly done, they are getting ripped off. I would cut the balls off any of my installers who tried to kick in a job without using a power stretcher.

In rental units, it's common practice to throw down carpet over a crappy, rough-poured concrete floor—just to keep the cost down. It is cheaper to carpet in most cases than it is to smooth the floor and put down tile. They hope the carpet will cover the irregularities, but after awhile, you begin to see them. Owners usually couldn't care less, because they don't have to walk on it. The renters are the ones who suffer; they pay for it indirectly through their rent, and they have to live with an improper installation.

You, of course, as a homeowner, have the opportunity to buy carpet wholesale, if you know someone in the trade. You go to them and pick out the fabric, and it may be an excellent buy at purely wholesale prices. But that carpet exists at the mill—in Georgia, California, Oklahoma, etc., and it has to be shipped. You have to pay the freight. When it gets to your house, and you have 100 yards on one roll, which may weigh 500 pounds, then the truck driver is responsible for getting it off the tailgate. He ties a rope around it and fastens the other end to a telephone pole, and drives away, and drops it onto the street. How do you get it into your house? Who is going to cut it and make the installation. You have to buy padding, tackless stripping, metal trim, and all the rest. When you get through, you could have gone to a reputable carpet dealer and come out with exactly the same finished price. Yes, your contact is doing you a favor—no, he's not. It's six-of-one, and half-a-dozen of the other.

"Borax houses" are a world all their own—high-pressure, high-volume, fast-track operations advertised over television. With them, the salesmen have a "percentage of profit" arrangement. After the direct costs for merchandise, delivery, and installation are subtracted, there is a split between the contractor and the salesman. For every additional yard they sell, they get a bigger percentage—the more the volume, the more they profit. These are former used-car, siding, storm window, and awning salesmen who haven't the foggiest notion of how to spell "carpet," but they do know how to sell. They know how to get a signed order back to the office.

High yardage is their most common gimmick, but it's so high that reputable dealers who only steal 10 percent would blush if they saw the figures. They have no qualms whatsoever about walking into a room that is 12 x 15 feet and telling customers they need 30 yards of carpeting. That's a 50 percent ripoff. They have no qualms whatsoever about not mentioning the yardage at all—just delivering a package figure at the end. "We will be glad to do this room for you for $300," when, in fact, it could be done for $200 at a fair retail price.

They will sell that $300 job on contract, and once a contract is

94

signed, customers have no recourse. They didn't buy the yard-age, they bought the package. Generally, a reputable shop will not work on a contract. The reputable approach is to specify the yardage. One factor with the "borax houses" is that they are dealing with a poorer, less-educated clientele. That poor son-of-a-bitch who buys from them doesn't know any better. He may have no more than fourth-grade arithmetic, and there is no way he can check their figures. If he gets his next-door neighbor and his three friends in, between the four of them, none of their answers will be right. High yardage is primary.

Misrepresentation of the fabric is another. They don't tell you what it really is—it is a propaganda of omission. They will tell you it is 100 percent virgin nylon carpeting, but there are fifteen different grades of nylon. Customers don't know that—they don't know the difference between first-generation, second-generation, and third-generation fibers. Third-generation nylon is like third-generation computers. What IBM can do now, they couldn't even dream of thirty years ago.

When synthetics first came out, they were not suitable for floor coverings, which take a fantastic amount of abuse. Since then, they have developed yarns specifically for floor covering that have substantially more body, hold dyes better, and have what the trade calls "memory." When a 100-pound woman puts all her weight on a spiked heel, the impact can be as high as 100,000 pounds per square inch. The yarn is compressed to nothing. But if it has memory, when she steps off it, it will come back—after an hour it will stand back up again.

The schlock outfits, however, will sell the cheapest stuff they can find, made out of the cheapest yarns available. Most of their fabrics won't even get on a wear-test machine, much less come up with a wear-test result. Yes, they sell 100 percent virgin nylon but both the nylon and the customer are about to become something other than virgins. At least, it's going to get you something on your floor.

Of course, they want your financing business, too. Federal law now requires truth in advertising, which must show the figures. You can read them on late-night TV, while the joker is talking.

95

Don't listen to him, but read the printed figures on the bottom of the screen: 28 percent per annum. You sit there thinking: How can anyone in his right mind pay that—but, of course, you and I go out and finance a car, and we really don't look at that paper either when we sign it, do we?

All the same rules of soft-floor surfaces apply in hard-floor sales. They will sell you sixty square feet when only fifty are required. I will point out that I have to balance the pattern in the center, and the end pieces all have to be trimmed, and I need extra pieces to get into the doors, and then I will automatically throw 10 percent more at you, if you tell me you want them laid diagonally—and I can keep adding it up to where I can actually sell you double what you need. Incidentally it does take an extra 10 percent for diagonals, but sometimes it only takes 5 percent. If you lay out the pattern right, you can use half of one side down the other.

If you do not have the expertise, you can assume that you're getting ripped off. In all the years I've been in this business, it has fascinated me that these things happen—and nobody knows what the hell is going on.

SEWER REPAIRMAN

At age fourteen, Joe P. ran away from home and slept on park benches. His first means of support came through a lucky encounter with an "illiterate hillbilly" who befriended him, took him home, and gave him a job on his roving crew of sewer repairmen. For twenty years, Joe cruised city and suburban neighborhoods with other crew members, mostly southern, conning homeowners into sewer, roofing, and masonry repairs and landscaping. Early on, he learned that the hustlers in the crew earned much more money than the repairmen, and so he got his "hillbilly" friend to teach him how to hustle by reading people's faces. "I can watch a person's face intently and tell what they are going to spend," says Joe. "Sometimes they do not have to say a word." In the course of his career, he traveled from the midwest to California, sometimes with groups of crews in several trucks, looking for "fish" (easy marks) and selling his services with approaches ranging from sad stories to postures of expertise. He prided himself in never ripping off "a working stiff" and instead sought people with money—lawyers, doctors, celebrities. "When you took $500 or $5,000, it didn't hurt them at all." He retired from door-to-door work, which he calls the biggest ripoff in America, after he was boasting one night in his living room with some of his associates, and his teenage son came in and asked, "Isn't there another way you could make a living, Dad?" Says Joe, "My conscience got to me after awhile. I have six kids I'm raising, and I would rather see a fourteen-year-old boy go to school and be raised the right way than having him fall in with a bunch of thieves like me."

I know almost every sewer company in the area, and I never found an honest one in my life. I used to have a crew, and we'd drive down alleys. We might have eight guys on the truck; six would be hustlers and two laborers. Every sewer company sends out trucks like these. Then you'd start going door-to-door with cards, saying, "Hi. I'm a sewer man in the area, and I've been doing a lot of the people's work around here for years." Maybe you have, and maybe you haven't, but what you say the average public believes.

Just to win their confidence on a job, you'd suggest they get three good estimates. You'd know you had them in the palm of your hand, when they would say, "Yeah, I agree, but I trust you." So you tell them you are there to check their sewer trap and see about cleaning it. Some of the guys would open the lid and say, "Damn, it sure is filthy," and there would hardly be anything in it. When the customers looked in and said they didn't see anything, we'd say we could tell it was filthy (even though it wasn't) just by looking at the water level. So we would offer to go down and clean it out for a very low price, and the customers would go for it.

Then we'd say, "Oh, well, as long as we're down here, turn on your water so we can see if it is coming out of the pipe all right. We'll check it out for you free of charge." So when the customers went into the house, one of the guys would take a crowbar and break the clay that leads from the house into the sewer, or loosen some of the bricks on the side of the sewer. Now, instead of a cut-rate cleaning job, they've got a repair job. Or we could say, "The water's coming out of your line real slow. It needs to be rodded." The guy down in the sewer would take a brick and lodge it in the pipe, so it really would look like the line was bad.

Sometimes we would drop things into the water and tell the homeowner: "Do you see that? You're not supposed to see anything from your bathroom in that water. If you see toilet paper or prophylactics, that means you have a main line blockage, and it is backing up." One of the greatest con guys in our business once dropped some prophylactics into a sewer, and the customer went in and beat his wife half to death because he never used them. It was all really a comedy to us but a heartache to someone else.

All we wanted to do was get the rod (a cleaning device) inside the line, so when we started pushing it to the street, we could say: "Oh, oh. I hear something!" We would start feeling the rod and holding it like we were banging on something and say, "You have a broken tile." All of a sudden, a $10 job comes out to be a $2,000 job. So we'd get hired to dig up the street to replace the one broken tile, and half the time we would not replace anything. We'd just cover it right back up as if some work had been done.

Some of the jobs we did were legitimate—there was a real blockage or they had roots growing in the line—but compared to the phony stuff, these were nothing at all. When I was looking into sewers, I might run across one blocked line in a month's time. People will get their lines rodded because they're running a little slow, but in most of these cases it's due to the pitch.

When sewer repair got a little slow or risky, or good leads materialized in other endeavors, Joe and his crew would switch businesses, though still using the same well-honed sales pitches. As it turned out, they were all well versed in the art and science of landscaping.

We'd pick out the most important tree on somebody's property—everybody has one: a blue spruce, a red maple, etc., and we'd tell them, "It's dying, it has red spiders/mites/aphids/ etc." Sometimes, we would put our own little bugs on the trees. One guy used to carry a jar of spiders in his pocket, and he would spread them all over an evergreen while he was waiting for the people to answer the doorbell.

You can take any evergreen, any tree, any bush, and you will find infection on it of one type or another. You will find a living bug or a fungus, or something, but nine times out of ten it is not harmful. The big thing is to win the confidence of customers— persuade them that you know what you're talking about. Once you convince them they are about to lose all this, you tell them it will cost $500, you spray everything, and then you beat it.

Sometimes we used a proper spray, and other times we just sprayed them with water. We used to joke about how the bugs were washing. If the guy was suspicious, we might put coloring in the water. I remember once I didn't have a truck to go get some dusting sulpher, so I dusted a guy's evergreens with kitchen cleanser for $145. Usually, we just went for a one-shot application, but if the guy was a fish all the way, we'd come back several times and get him for more money. Sometimes I had the right equipment—$3,000 power sprayers—and sometimes I started the year off taking the bus with nothing more than a pair of trimmers in my bag.

I might get a job, like spraying some evergreens, for only $45, so I'd try to put a "build on" to raise the price. "As long as I'm here," I'd say, "I'll have the men clean out your gutters." The guys would go up the ladders and rip open a couple sections of the roof and say, "Hey, look at this. It's a big mess up here." I'd climb up there real fast and say, "Holy Christ. The whole roof is split. You must have had a lightning storm out here in the last month." Well, just playing the odds, you know they had one.

You make them believe you are doing work up there—you'll be carrying things up and down; they won't know what you're doing—and most of the time you are just putting little patches on. You know the old man or his wife are not going to come up the ladder, so you know where to put your shots.

If I were a consumer, I would get estimates from three or four people on the kinds of jobs I did. I would check the repairmen through the city, the police, and the Better Business Bureau. One thing people should know if they don't want to get ripped off is: Don't go outside with repairmen. If they can get you outside to look at the sewer trap, the roof, or the landscaping—they've got the job sold.　　　　　　　　　　　　　　　✔

WINDOW INSTALLER

Gus J. worked for a small, family-owned business that ordered cheaply made windows from a manufacturer and installed them in customers' homes. Though they did offer to replace defective windows, as Gus says, "Once the window was put in, our people couldn't care less."

The business advertised in magazines and had salesmen following up on the calls they'd get, giving prospective customers a lot of baloney. Most of our customers were very gullible people. The salesman would play the wife against the husband, or vice versa. You know, they'd kid the guy, "Hey, who's wearing the pants in this family, you or her?" Then they'd end up selling the guy $2,000 worth of windows just by getting him flustered over not being the boss in his own house.

The double-pane windows we installed were not a good product for this northern climate. They had metal frames, and the metal sweats in the winter, just like a water pipe sweats in the summer—it drips. The guy who broke me in told me that when I installed a window in the winter, I had to make absolutely sure I got the job done in two days. The first day the customer will notice that the window is starting to drip, and so you tell them

100

you don't have the outside finished yet. The next day you finish the outside, get their check, and get the hell out of there, because that window ain't going to stop dripping until spring.

When we received the windows at the plant, half of them would be defective because of bouncing around on a truck for a thousand miles. They were double-pane glass with a vacuum between the panes. The glass was so cheap and flexible, the panes would touch, and you'd get a rainbow effect. The customers would say, "My God, what's that?" and we'd say, "Don't worry; we'll replace it," even though it might be three or four months before we'd get around to it.

One of the boss's relatives, who didn't know much about the business, would measure the customers' old windows, and he'd always get the measurements wrong. On about 30 percent of our jobs we'd have trouble getting the new window to fit properly, so we'd have to fake it and build up the sides of the window with strips of plywood. A lot of people wouldn't say anything, but people who knew something about home repairs would ask why we were putting all that stuff in there. Then, I'd have to think of something cute off the top of my head, which was embarrassing for an honest person. Even if they fit right, there was usually something defective.

Some installers use foam rubber strips on the sides of replacement windows when they don't quite fit into the old track, so they have a foam cushion that makes the window seem tight. I've seen stuff like that crumble to nothing in three years. That's all that's holding the window, and in three years that's going to rot out, and you'll have drafty windows.   ✍

REFRIGERATION SERVICEMAN

As a refrigeration and air-conditioning serviceman, Harold E. is happily self-employed with all the business he cares to handle. He works a three-day week and figures on earning $45,000 a year. Although he does sell and install units (and "There are no bad units manufactured"), most of his work consists of servicing existing units in homes and small businesses. A good deal of his business stems from correcting repair work done by those among the 70 percent of his colleagues he regards as crooks.

Any high school sophomore could be a good refrigeration man. It's not a complicated technology. You have to know a little physics and chemistry, and some pipe-fitting and basic electricity. Still, an air-conditioning unit looks to the average layman like an IBM computer. And when a rip-off artist does the work, the customer can't check it.

I go in where the rip-off artists stop. They're butchers and don't know what they're doing. Their wiring is bad; yet the controls are incredibly simple. I've seen them cross-fit everything so the customer has a completely sealed unit that doesn't blow cold air—it doesn't blow anything; it just runs around in circles. Every few weeks there's a whole new shipment of so-called "air-conditioning" men from the technical schools, and they're bad. They come and go every season and fortunately go out of business very quickly.

These newcomers have a standard markup on the book price of parts of about 1000 percent. They'll charge $35 an hour, plus a charge for the service call itself. Whether they do anything or not, the customer will get screwed for the service call. There will be people who'll call me and say they've had four servicemen in who've charged them a fortune, and the unit still doesn't work. They tell me they'll pay me if I fix it, and if I don't, they won't. I say, sure. I fix it, and they're happy. I'll back up my parts, and I'll back up my work.

I charge $25 an hour, and I charge for fixing, not looking or thinking. If I'm there for fifteen minutes or one hour, it's $25. I don't have a set markup on parts. I do what sounds good. For a motor that cost me $50, I'll charge the customer $125, but I'm still 25 percent cheaper than my competition, so I'm not screwing anybody. There is a question of when enough is enough. You do what the market will bear, granted. If it sounds too high, drop it a little bit. But as long as you're less than your competition, the customer is delighted. I don't screw anyone intentionally, unless I don't like them. If I don't want their business again, I'll give them quality work, but I'll just charge them a lot of money for it.

I would say that 80 percent of the time on calls, I'm paid in cash. This year I expect to make $45,000, and I'm going to pay taxes on $8,000 of it—that's what I'll get in checks. I file for whatever is legitimate. The federal government can't get me on anything, and that's beautiful. This is common in my business. I would say 80 or 90 percent of air-conditioning and refrigeration business is cash money. Of all the trades, this is the very best. I've been audited five times. Let them audit me—my records aren't altered.

I have no regrets shorting the government. I'm a very honest man. All of my bills are paid on time, and I try not to screw anyone. I'm proud of this. I may be a dying breed, but I am a very honest man. ✔

ALUMINUM SIDING SALESWOMAN

In the popular mind, ripoffs abound in the field of home improvements. Unscrupulous salesmen, shoddy products, and ill-trained workers all have helped contribute to the tarnished image that the business frequently deserves. Carol W. started in the aluminum siding trade working the phone room soliciting prospective customers for a small, highly mobile, "rinky-dink outfit." When she realized that the salesmen were passing up a lot of good leads, she went out in the field herself and pushed siding until one sale nearly backfired. Thereupon she was brought back to the phone room, and it was only then, one hot, summer day when she was trying to swat horseflies coming into her office from the warehouse, that she learned the nature of the product she had been selling.

If you could sell, they'd let you. I'd been in sales before, so I got a sample case with Alcoa stuff in it and went out selling. They were advertising Alcoa siding, and when the salesmen pitched it, they pitched Alcoa, so that's what I told the customers they'd be getting: aluminum-backed vinyl siding. It turned out what they were putting on the houses wasn't Alcoa siding at all.

I sold the chief of police in a little town, and the guys in the office almost had a fit. They had to specially order Alcoa to put on his house, otherwise they figured they'd have problems with him. If one of the brothers who owned the company had gotten the lead he would have dropped it.

This switching wasn't general knowledge in the office. I found out when I was running around trying to kill horseflies. I ran into the warehouse—I had a can of spray in one hand and flyswatter in the other—and saw some guys carrying some siding out. It was so crappy it took three guys to carry it—one on each end, and one in the middle, so it wouldn't buckle. It would just fold right up it was so flimsy. It wasn't anything at all like Alcoa's—it was real shitty stuff, a complete ripoff.

They didn't dare sell in a larger city because of the Better Business Bureau, so they sold in all the surrounding towns and to farmers and rural people. The first thing they would do in a new area was open a phone room, then we'd just go through the directories calling prospective customers. They'd go to one area and rape it and move on. That was the only way they could do business.

Our salesmen used to take a piece of steel wool and rub it over the Alcoa samples to show people that it wouldn't scratch. Our installers were siding a farmhouse one day, and the farmer came out to show his neighbor what the salesman had shown him. So he rubbed steel wool over his new siding—and the paint came off! Paint coming off was a frequent complaint.

I think they got a lot of complaints on the installations. They had a regular team that followed the salesmen around the country. Those guys used to do installations in record time. It was unbelievable how fast they could put that crap on.   🖊

104

EDUCATION AND TRAINING

COLLEGE ADMINISTRATIVE ASSISTANT

Alvina D. worked in the administrative offices of a small college. The school caters to minority students, many well into adulthood, and their enrollment is made possible through federal funding. Although the college had the usual "laudable aims" and generally got uncritical press coverage, Alvina concludes that most students got little out of their experience. "Basically," she says, "all they were getting was a piece of paper."

When people read about the school, it sounded good, and they believed all the stuff they were reading. They believed it catered to minorities, that its main purpose was to accommodate black parents who couldn't achieve education in the daytime because of their work schedules, and that it was for people who had already acquired necessary skills but were lacking a degree to back them up. It was especially for those people who were not considered college material by schools. Our philosophy was, nobody was turned down. Although we were not accredited, we awarded both bachelor's and associate's degrees.

We would go into underprivileged areas, like the housing projects, and find students and suggest they apply for a grant. It was so easy when students out of the projects applied for grants—they always got the full amount. It was as if whoever were approving them was afraid someone was going to accuse them of being prejudiced, so they always awarded the full grants—they always got the full amount. It was as if those who were approving them were afraid someone was going to accuse them of being prejudiced, so they always awarded the full grants. We would have the students fill out a form for a basic educational opportunity grant (BEOG), then check to see if they

105

had written everything down honestly. Their father made X thousands of dollars a year, their mother made Y thousands, whether they lived at home, etc. Well, we would change all that, because there was no way they were going to get the money if they put down the truth. If someone put down an income of zero, we would put down at least $7,000, so it looked like he was making enough to live on. These were applications for grants of up to $1,500 a year, from both BEOG and the state scholarship commission. I counted 500 applications myself one day, and all of them were for the full $1,500. If student applicants hadn't signed the forms, rather than taking the time to get them to do it, we'd just sign them ourselves. We would change everything on the applications, and everyone would get awards. The money would just keep rolling in.

What happened was that none of the students were really showing up for classes. Out of 400 or 500 students, maybe only twenty-five or thirty showed up, and they didn't come on a regular basis. Because federal money was going to the school, we had to account for the students' attendance. So we had to make up false attendance sheets. All the people in our office signed these attendance sheets in the names of our students, and we'd submit it to HEW for audit. The auditors would see the students' names and dates on the sheets and not question it further. It didn't seem to enter their minds that these were forged, nor did they ever think of going to a student and asking, "Listen, were you here on Feb. 24?" We'd just say, "This student was here, and there's the name and date," and that was just one more check for $1,500 for the school. We claimed an enrollment of hundreds, but that was a lie. Actually, there may have been only fifty students there at the time. In the first few years, we never had HEW inspectors coming in—that's only been recently.

When someone is going to school on a $1,500 scholarship, there's no way we're going to fail them. They're always going to pass, whether they do the work or not. We had a program—if students were twenty-five or older and had worked in, say, an accounting office for the last two years, we'd tell them, "You don't

106

have to go to school to be an accountant, because you already know that—the only thing you're lacking is a degree." So the students would list everything they knew how to do and put it into a portfolio. They'd write, "Know the basic techniques of accounting, from experience on job." Okay, there's some credit. Then, "Can apply basic techniques of tennis" because they'd played in high school, and that's some more credit. And on and on. So they give you maybe sixty-five credits for all the things you know and they tell you, "Okay, now all you need are fifty-five more credits for a degree." So you take a couple of classes, maybe do a research paper, and within a year you've got your degree. I knew someone who got fifteen credits in horticulture for growing houseplants. You could come in with a high school diploma, and if you had a lot of outside experience, you could get a degree within a year.

We also had another program, where they'd give you a book to read, but you don't have to read it. Then when you're ready for the test, they give it to you and tell you to bring it back next week. So you take it home, and if there's anything you don't know, you just consult your book, right? You go back with your test, and you've got an A, and you've got your credit. One student was three credits short of his bachelor's degree. Well, at other schools he would have had to enroll in a course. Not at our school. He just talked to one of the administrators, and the next thing I knew he had a grade card to prove he'd earned the credits. All he said was, "Money can do anything."

They made us all apply for grants. We were supposed to go to school, but we never had time for it. Still, we applied—some of us were making really good salaries—and we all got grants for $1,500. They'd say "Apply for a grant. It's so easy to rip off BEOG." So we just took our applications and lied. When graduation was small, they would give the administrative staff and faculty degrees to make the class look larger. Like, typists, whom they'd given titles of "director of word processing," would get bachelor's degrees. Of course, they were doing the school a favor; they'd got the school a $1,500 grant, and the school rewarded them with a degree.

VOCATIONAL SCHOOL SECRETARY

Margaret F. works as a secretary in the administration of a private vocational school that specializes in training nurses' aides. Their revenue comes from student tuition, and the school keeps the money flowing in by using high-pressure recruiting techniques. The school operates in a predominantly black neighborhood and draws many poor and often illiterate older applicants who migrated to the area from the rural South. Most students, Margaret says, are not aware that a government-funded CETA program exists that would give them the same kind of training free, nor are they aware that most of them won't get the job they hope to get upon graduation. There are also other, competing schools, says Margaret, "but they are worse than ours."

The school trains women in basic nursing-aide skills. But although we have registered nurses teaching the course, it's really a hard-sell business campaign, not a school. We advertise in a brochure. When the women call in and we get their phone numbers, we never let them alone after that. We keep calling them and sending them letters. "When do you plan to start class?" It really is harassment.

Sometimes they sign up. The tuition is over $400, which a lot of these people can't afford. They can pay a minimum of $13 a week, but even if they can't afford that, we're supposed to encourage them anyway. A lot don't finish—a goodly number, after they've spent $200, figure they can't afford to continue, so they drop out. They are entitled to a refund, a percentage based on how long they've attended, but the school doesn't explain that, and most haven't read the contract. If they don't demand a refund, they don't get it.

There's no screening of students, and a high school degree is not required. A lot of applicants have only gone through third grade and can't even read or write. If they sign, they're in. As long as they can make scratches on the application, they're accepted.

The curriculum is bona fide, but the teachers (there's a large turnover) say our equipment is out-of-date or it doesn't work. We also don't have a lot of things we should have to teach people how to work in a modern nursing home environment.

They still try to push people through to get their full tuition. The midterm test is very short, and they're helped through it. If they fail and have to take it again, they're coached so they pass. They're also coached on the final. Even so, you'll have a woman winding up the course who's paid all her money, and she'll get a rotten evaluation from the teacher—and that's what you go by in the placement business. Her evaluation will say, "This person needs maximum supervision, not recommended for private duty; recommended for nursing home duty only." One of our students has a barbiturate problem, but we're still trying to shove her through the course anyway. But she's not going to function well as a nurse's aide.

Although we give the students a certificate, state law does not require a nurse's aide to have one. Some places won't hire you without one, but others don't require it. It's possible to come in off the street and get a job as a nurse's aide.

The school doesn't say anything it doesn't have to. A lot of students want to work in hospitals, but we don't tell them that hospitals are not hiring many nurses' aides anymore. And if hospitals hired them at all, they would put them through their own training program. Hospitals are phasing out nurses' aides and replacing them with licensed practical nurses. Our director, however, soft-soaps this and says, "Yes, we qualify you for working in a hospital," which is true, even though the hospitals probably won't hire them.

A lot of our students don't realize that the only jobs available to them are in nursing homes, where they get terrible wages, $2.50 or so an hour. They could earn the same doing almost anything else. Private duty jobs are better, but the only ones that come in are a long way away, and they generally need people with cars. If students don't grill the interviewer, she's not going to give them that kind of information. We have a lot of angry graduates not working in the nursing field or where they expected to work.   ✔

TEACHER

Our school passes children on to a higher grade whether they're making it or not, which isn't fair to the child. If children haven't made the grade level, then they'll always be behind. As a teacher, you try to gear yourself to those children who are having trouble, but if you've got twenty-nine other kids on a level a year above them, even with extra help they won't catch up. They go along and usually become disruptive in the classroom to compensate for what they can't do—they may become the class clown. By the time they are sixteen, they're ready to drop out.

Our administrator will say retain them, but then, come the beginning of the next year, he'll change his mind, because he's unwilling to have an unpleasant confrontation with both the teacher and the parents. He makes a show of exercising his responsibility, but ultimately he's not.

Teachers today have no responsibility for giving counseling or afterschool help. There is a need, but we're not required to do it. If teachers do give extra help, in the evening or over the summer, they charge a stiff fee. If students need special help, they are taken out of class and dealt with by people provided by the government under various titles. Staying after school is out the window because of busing. With the unions, we get paid for X number of hours, and that's it—good-bye. Sometimes, teachers work with youngsters during recess or before school, but a lot of them don't like giving up that cup of coffee or cigarette—that's their free time.

A good number take work home, though we're not expected to. Grading papers is more or less voluntary, though we do have to keep adequate grade-book records. Some teachers spend a lot of time grading, and others don't. Teachers can find ways of grading that don't require a lot of paper reading, and they can also fix up their grade books so that they look fine if someone is coming to check them. Principals may come around to check them every week, or every month, and some never look at them at all.

110

Sometimes I think school boards work in ignorance. They believe what the administration tells them, even though it isn't true. We tell them everything is fine, everyone is learning well, everyone is doing his job—and that's not always true. Our principal lies to everybody about things there is no reason to lie about. When he lies to us, we just close our eyes and make believe we don't know what's going on. Undoubtedly, he's protecting his job.

When board members visit a school, they are steered away from what they shouldn't see. I used to feel I could approach the board with a problem. Now I probably still could, but not without risking my job. Although some board members invite us to speak up, you're never quite sure if they mean it. Lots of times they are green, too. So much is done today with public relations—especially by those in charge. If you don't think something is going well, it's almost better to keep your mouth shut. If it came to a showdown between me and the administration, the cards would be stacked against me. There are so few jobs in teaching, you're not likely to get another.

Administrators can mislead the board through their reporting. There are different ways of classifying student achievement scores. There are different norms for country schools, urban, inner-city, etc., and you could match your scores against the scale that makes them look best. When you're afraid your teaching might be judged on the basis of the students' test scores, you could help in some ways with the answers. When you're giving directions, you can almost give the answers by just changing the inflection of the voice. (You read a question, putting emphasis on the correct answer.) I haven't known this to happen, but it could.

Tenure is good for the teachers, but it doesn't make better teachers. Some, who shouldn't have received tenure in the first place, hide behind it. Until you get tenure, you kind of keep your opinions to yourself. Most districts require two or three years' satisfactory service before they grant tenure. It's usually the principals who rate teachers, and most of them are not qualified to do so. It's very expensive to get rid of a teacher. Some-

111

one said it costs $30,000 or $40,000—it has to go through the courts, and they have to prove you unfit.

Sometimes, I feel teachers are given jobs they are not fit for, especially those with tenure. When enrollment shifts come about, you either take the job they offer, or you're out. But that doesn't mean you're prepared for the job, and that's not the best thing for the youngsters.

Some parents in a community demand and are given more respect than others. Some are given special privileges, like getting a specific teacher for their child, while others could make a similar request and not even be considered because of their lack of status. You kind of know the ones who get what they want; they usually are on the various school committees.

There are a lot of people in education today because it is a well-paying job, especially for women. I think we're getting people who don't know their subject matter, who are learning it—sometimes not even fast enough—as they teach it. They're in teaching for the money, the good hours, and long vacations. What really kills me is when teachers say they hate kids. I don't think they belong.   ✔

SCHOOL SOCIAL WORKER

As a school social worker, Harriet D. counsels children having social and emotional difficulties in school, and in the process she works with their parents and teachers. She has seen the concept of ripoff well implanted in some young minds.

Kids can rip you off easier than adults. There are some children who start with a delinquent ego, and they never enter the counseling relationship with the same purpose you do. If you know the personality of the child, you can tell if he's conning you and has no intention of making good use of the relationship. There are children who are masters at manipulation and control, and they are going to control the counseling relationship as best they can, just as they do in the classroom. You have to be aware of their attitude, verbalize it, and help the children see exactly where they're at—then they can't pull it. There's a lot more manipulation by kids at the high school level, when all of them are going through an identity crisis. They're all putting on to a certain extent—they don't want to show you how they feel about things. ✔

RESEARCH SECRETARY

Taxpayers are both amused and angered when government spending of a dubious nature comes to light as one of Senator William Proxmire's Golden Fleece Awards. Many of these awards are given for research projects. Greta S., an employee of a large university, was assigned to a research team as a secretary, and though her duties consisted of basic filing, dictation, and typing, she found that the game of getting a grant involved much more than a stenographer would imagine.

The researcher, a medical doctor, was responsible for the content of what came out of his office. He was responsible for the research proposal and, once he got a grant, for the research itself. He had a team of research assistants, mostly graduate students from the psychology department and the medical school, who were supposed to perform extensions of the doctor's work. Their work was tied to their academic programs, and they got lower wages than I did.

The doctor was starting a research center in conjunction with a hospital and the university itself. But when he came in, he had no idea of what his first research project was going to be. Then he was told the government was funding projects in a particular area, so he decided to develop a proposal in that area.

To make a proposal to the Department of Health, Education,

113

and Welfare, you have to have read all the previous literature on the subject and know where you're coming from so you sound halfway intelligent. So, the doctor sent me and his other assistants to read all the available literature on the subject. Then we made outlines.

He didn't read any of the literature himself, and he didn't even look at our outlines. He just took a kind of passive attitude. "I'm just going to sit here and let everybody else figure it out—I'm not going to do anything about it myself." So, he didn't do anything, and all his research assistants agreed that he had no conversance with the subject matter at all. He didn't even have any experience in that area. He was good at taking suggestions and delegating duties, but he made no suggestions himself and didn't even read the final proposal as it was written by his researchers. His work was mostly confined to political maneuvering.

There was a tremendous turnover of staff. People kept quitting on him. Yet, it was a big deal for a grad student to get his name on a research project like this. There were two guys mainly involved in the research. The doctor took them separately into his office and told one he would get his name on the publication and would, in fact, get sole credit for it. Then he called in the other guy and told him the same thing. When he heard I had told them about this, he was furious and told me to confine my work to secretarial duties. He eventually got the grant. ✔

GRADUATE STUDENT

After her divorce, Mary J. worked in several low-paying jobs until an advertisement for a private university in a large city caught her eye. The school offered a program leading to a master's degree in *vocational* counseling, a field that deals with clients over the age of eighteen, as opposed to *educational* counseling, which deals with students under

114

eighteen. With a B.A. in sociology, she was eligible for the vocational program, but lacking education credentials, she was not eligible for admission to the educational counseling program. This didn't matter; she was interested in the vocational program so she enrolled in it. In a very short time, she learned that even in the halls of academe, there is not always truth in advertising.

Although the university advertised a program for an M.A. in vocational counseling and accepted students for it—they never offered it. In my case, I didn't get to take the courses my transcript and my degree say I took. At the start, I signed up for a course in vocational counseling and went to the class. On the third or fourth meeting, I began to think that I was in the wrong room, so I asked the teacher, "Isn't this Education 408, Techniques of Vocational Counseling?" The teacher said, "Yes," and I said, "Well, aren't we going to talk about that?" And she said, "No," and I said, "Why not?" "Well," she said, "because educational and vocational counseling had been combined into a general course." I figured that course was a fluke, so I went ahead and got my grades and credits. But the next semester, it was the same thing. I signed up for a vocational counseling course that turned out to be educational counseling.

The faculty members didn't know anything about vocational counseling and just went along with this misrepresentation by the school. They were getting money from the state for vocational education—the state employment service was sending their own people through the program. The program was withdrawn later, but it's incredible that it was listed in their catalog for a while, and they charged you tuition for it, yet they didn't even offer it. I got my degree in educational counseling—even though my degree says vocational. On the other hand, how many people are going to complain? Who's going to say, "Hey, my M.A. is no good."

I had to do everything on my own and make it my business to know what I needed for vocational counseling. One professor who taught human development would not change the requirements: He demanded that I test two twelve-year-old children.

115

He said I should go to a local school and get them, and I said I had no credentials to do that. In lieu of a thesis, I had to do a two-term practicum where you practice on clients under a teacher's supervision. The teacher was unable to spend time supervising us—she said she had too many people—so I had no direct supervision. The first time she was supposed to supervise me, she was interrupted and had to leave. The other time she said she forgot to plug in the audio equipment and couldn't hear me.

At the university, they charge you a student union fee, but they don't even have a student union, just a lounge with a Coke machine. Someone said the money really goes to the building fund. They did open a ping-pong room, but it was closed at night, and I was a night student.

After I got my degree, I tried to get a job with the state employment service, but I waited a year on the list, and nothing ever happened. I was told I had to pay off someone, but I wasn't told whom. I had very high grades, and I know there were openings, but I could never get interviewed. Every time I'd go down, they'd say, "No, your name hasn't come up." ✔

ELECTRONICS

AUDIO ENGINEER

Jerry P. is an engineer for an audio equipment manufacturer. Although his product line is nominally high-quality electronic components, Jerry admits that his firm and others in the audio field "are mostly selling hype."

What's unique about our industry is that we're selling a myth. We're trying to perpetuate the notion that we're producing equipment that rivals a live performance. This is impossible, because any five-year-old can tell the difference between live and recorded sound. The equipment we manufacture is very expensive pre-amp and power-amp "separates." It's worth it in terms of labor and our costs, but whether the customer needs it or not is secondary. In my opinion, it's over-designed. There's no way to evaluate the accuracy of sound reproduction because of its inherent subjectivity. In our advertising we'll state our design superiority and its benefit to the customer, but whether or not these design differences truly make an important contribution to improved sound quality is questionable.

Consider what, for instance, customers are spending in terms of what they are receiving. All the quality parts and specifications are in the equipment that we say are there, but are they important? Are the thousands of dollars people spend on this equipment going to make a substantial difference over another product? The law of diminishing returns definitely works here. I've done a lot of evaluative testing, and if people have already spent the money on a product, they absolutely hear the difference between that one and one of supposedly lesser quality. When you test the same people blindfolded, using the same equipment, rarely can they tell the difference between electronic units. But, generally, if they know what unit is being

117

listened to, they will pick their favorite brand or the most expensive equipment being evaluated. We have a bias that controls what we hear.

Just as there are minimal differences among electronic components, there are gross differences among speakers. Among electronic components, the factors of difference are 1/100th of a percent, compared with a 100 percent difference among speakers. There's a lot of profit in speaker manufacturing, and, as a result, there are a lot of people in the industry—and a lot of flim-flam. For every one of us in quality electronic components, there are one-hundred manufacturers of speakers. Speakers are more of an art than a technology, and any guy can cut holes in cabinets out in his garage and stick speakers in them and go hawk them anywhere he wants. Speakers are the easiest things to get into and the most open to ripoffs. Dealers will have their own house-brand speakers built with the cheapest cabinets and cheapest drivers that they'll sell as loss-leaders. The speakers they list at $129 retail, say, 12 x 14 x 24 inches, cost them anywhere from $14 to $32. That gives them a lot of leeway in pricing when they're selling an entire system.

When you hear speakers in a showroom, there is no guarantee whatever you'll like them in your living room. The only way you can evaluate a speaker is to listen to it in your own environment. A speaker with a lot of "presence" is a speaker that will sell itself. It has certain things that fool your ear, like a lot of kick at the bottom end, yet this is just a resonance. It sounds like there is more bass, but, after a while, it becomes tiresome. It also has an overabundance of highs to make it sound more vibrant. In a showroom, the environment is not under the customer's control at all—it is under the salesman's control. At lower volume levels, the human ear doesn't pick up lows and highs as well as it picks up mid-range sounds, so all a salesman has to do is slightly raise the volume of a speaker and it sounds better.

Basically, a salesman can sell anything he wants. That's why manufacturers are quite willing to give a discount of 50 percent off-list to employees of audio shops. That's standard practice in the industry so they get their products into the salesman's home.

118

"I own these," he'll say, and his justification for owning them is to sell them. Sometimes manufacturers will give a salesman more than a 50 percent discount because it is self-serving for them. Dealers, on the other hand, usually get 40 percent off-list on the merchandise they are selling—that's virtually standard in the industry. Another incentive are "spiffs"—kickbacks—from the manufacturer to the salesman. If he sells your product, which you have a warehouse full of, you give him $15 apiece, or whatever.

Despite the improved warranty situation, due to trade commission pressure, litigation on anything takes so long that the customer's new protection is really null and void because of the realities of bureaucracy—and manufacturers recognize this. Even though a warranty says that you can return something, there are always a lot of delays and red tape, and any aid it gives is little more than a psychological factor.

In terms of what you spend, if a $1,000 system gives you 100 percent satisfaction, you could spend $400 and get, perhaps, 80 percent satisfaction. However, this is difficult to say absolutely because our industry, by its nature, is without many objective standards. On the other hand, if you spent $1,500, you might get satisfaction of 150 percent, and if you spent $2,000, you could get 130 percent. The results you get are a matter of knowing how one component affects another.

Basically, though, if manufacturers are able to build up a mystique around something, they'll sell a million of them whether they are any good or not. ✔

MIDDLE MANAGER

Steven F. is a middle manager in the engineering end of an electronics manufacturing firm. His company is long established and reputable and has consistently used quality components and work procedures that make its trade name worth $20 or $30 more than its competitors' on similar products. Foreign competition, however, is forcing the company to change that policy, and the company feels unjustly treated by the American government, which, it says, does not enforce existing laws that keep off-shore manufacturers from selling their products here at below fair cost.

One of the largest retailers in this country has a private-label electronics product made for it that has a metal cabinet—what we call a "hot chassis"—which, if a child were to spill a soft drink or drop a safety pin or some other conductive object into it, it would be absolutely lethal. Yet, it meets the minimum Underwriters Laboratory requirements. Though we would not put out a product like that, that is the kind of competition we're facing. It's made by an off-shore manufacturer. Their only requirement is to meet UL standards. The Consumer Products Safety Commission has been looking at the matter for the last four or five years but has not come up with anything yet.

I'm in a battle with our manufacturing segment over certain parts of their process; they say the processes are necessary, and we say they are an attitude. They impose a cost, part of which is simply the manufacturing people trying to cover their asses. Any new product is different; it poses threats because things could go wrong. These people are measured against the budget, and if they run into problems, their budgets will be exceeded, and their compensation will be judged on that basis. So they will always try to pad as much for contingencies into their estimates as they can. I'd do the same thing. If there's a possibility something could go wrong, I'd like to help myself, simply as a matter of preservation.

My company is owned by thousands of shareholders, and the reason it exists is to provide a return to the stockholder and presumably some kind of service to the consumer so that profit can be generated. Our stockholders play a minimal role in determining the destiny of the company. At the annual meetings, they are docile. Most of their reactions come from social rather than financial issues. Our corporate structure controls a com-

120

pany they don't own. It is self-sustaining and is probably more likely to take action that would guarantee its own existence and continuance than to maximize a return to stockholders. ✔

AUDIO EQUIPMENT DEALER

As a store manager for an audio chain, Marvin K. is responsible for both a retail and service operation. He cautions customers to be wary of "bargains" in the field of Hi-Fi as well as house brands. And, despite certain ripoffs in the field, Marvin believes customers sometimes cheat themselves by coming into stores with preconceived notions and not listening to his professional advice.

On rare occasions we pirate (sell without a dealership) certain equipment, which may give customers a repair problem if they move out of state. Some companies will not perform repairs under warranty unless the equipment was purchased from a franchised dealer. If someone bought a certain brand tape deck from us, obviously we'd repair it. But if people move out of the area, we're putting them in a bit of a bind when it comes to getting warranty repairs. We don't give them any warning of that problem—at least I don't. On the other hand, I will do almost anything not to sell that brand, because, though it's a well-known brand, its products are ripoffs. They purport in their specifications to be excellent to superb equipment. But I have yet to find one machine as quiet as they claim in terms of background noise. I point this out, but if the customer still must have the model, I accommodate him.

With few exceptions, there is no such thing as a bargain in Hi-Fi's. If something is at a low price, there is a very good reason, and it behooves the customer to find out why. A lot of cases you can't—that knowledge is beyond the customer—and the dealer isn't going to tell you.

In essence, fair trade still exists. Yet one company's line is seldom if ever discounted. They carefully monitor their sales. If

I were to discount them, they won't say, "Well, this is fair trade," but they will cut us off. Our only recourse would be to spend several thousand on a lawyer, take it to court, and be without the product for two or three years. Then we only *might* win. As a result, you still have fair trade among manufacturers for better and superb equipment. They get away with it, because they're good.

Flashy front panels, something like an extra midrange tone control—these are manufacturing ripoffs. Maybe this tone control will add $1 to the manufacturing cost of the unit. Practically, it does nothing. A couple of manufacturers with very high sales certainly overengineer their equipment.

Much of what has been written about TV repair fraud is applicable to stereos. In repair shops there is more chance of fraud occurring than in a situation like ours, where we run a repair shop as a nonprofit service. One such ripoff could be high labor charges for realigning an FM tuner—or the possibility of it never having been done. This is a fairly fine adjustment, and a receiver may be used in a system not transparent enough for it to make any difference whether it's done or not. There are no parts left over to show a customer; you just can't prove it.

Almost without question, padding of repair bills is encouraged by manufacturers, who grossly underprice their allowance for warranty repairs, thus ripping off the retailers. We get a fixed amount, just $7 for every receiver no matter what's wrong, and we have to swallow that if we want to remain a dealer—or else make up for it with nonwarranty repairs. In 80 percent of the cases, we lose money on warranty repairs.

One must be extremely careful of house brands, where maybe three different manufacturers build a component for a retailer. These are noticeably lower priced, yet a retailer may still see a 40 percent profit on them. There is almost no quality control, and variation from unit to unit will be great. In that respect, the specifications are a lie. There's a good chance there's something in the unit the manufacturer bought cheaply at surplus and designed the circuits to accommodate it. They may have capacitors in unusual combinations that can't be substituted because of

122

space problems. The units are then either beyond repair, or else repairs would be astronomical. The customer gets incensed, but the dealers say, what the hell? Most of their business is one-time only, so they come out ahead. One way to maintain our reputation is not to sell house brands, and have to try to fix them later.

🖝

ELECTRONICS INSTALLER

Before working in a regular TV repair shop, Mike T. did installation work for an electronics dealer who would "milk everyone for whatever he could get." His boss had various shops under different names, and when things got too hot for him, he would file bankruptcy and go into business under another name. When Mike was challenged by an irate customer in the field, he would simply say, "Look, I just pick up and deliver. If you think you are paying too much, you will have to talk to the boss."

I started out doing antenna servicing, where the customer would have called saying the reception on the TV was bad. Well, I'd turn on the set, and sure enough, the reception was bad. I'd check out the antenna system and find that it was okay, it was all hooked up. So I'd say, "I'll take the set back to our shop and check it out. Maybe there's a bad tuner, or it's not sensitive enough to signals, or maybe it just needs cleaning."

Back at the shop, I'd hook it up—just out of curiosity, because I wasn't hired as a technician, even though I could handle the work—and I'd find that it worked perfectly. Most likely, the customer's house was in a "dead spot," where the signal just can't reach the antenna properly. Maybe buildings deflected the signal, or the customer was in a valley or not in what we call a line-of-sight of the signal. So the set will sit there for a couple weeks, and the customer will call up and ask, "What happened to my TV set?" I'd get hold of the boss, and he'd get on the phone and say, "Oh, well, we had to rebuild the tuner, you needed this tube and that, etc." We hadn't done anything to the set, and the customer would end up with a $150 repair bill. This was his policy. I went out and did my job, and he would get on the phone and give them a lot of phony charges.

It's not hard to take a TV or radio, clean it, and make it look like new, especially the parts inside. There are sprays that will blow the dirt out of the chassis. It's not hard to take parts out of a TV and redo them totally, recoloring them, putting new numbers on them, or just cleaning them with a degreasing compound. This will take the ink off a particular part, like a capacitor, and if you wipe it off well enough, it will look like a brand new part. You can tell the people who peek inside that you have replaced the parts. We, of course, never showed the customer the "old parts" we had "replaced."

It is not an uncommon practice to take used parts and charge new parts' prices for them. For instance, you might take a tube or resistor out of a new unit that doesn't work right, even though it is technically a used part, because the unit was previously sold. Parts, however, do have a life expectancy, and when you use used parts, they should be working at their full capacity. Yet, it is hard to say how soon a part will go out, and there is really no method of testing.

Once my boss and I were checking a sound system in a pizza place, and I found the problem involved some bad connectors on the cable. He said, "Naw, we'll replace the cable in the entire place." He told the guy, who said, "Fine, go ahead." While the guy was out on deliveries, I replaced the connectors, because I knew they were all that was bad, but my boss told him when he got back that we had replaced all the cable. Well we didn't know it, but the guy had marked all his cable with a yellow crayon and said there was no way he was going to pay for cable when we didn't replace it. But even though he caught us, my boss persisted in saying we had replaced the cable. He was a nice guy—a real darling.

He would try to wiggle out of all kinds of situations by insisting that he did the work, even though he hadn't. It was really a matter of his word against the customer's, and let's face it, the average customer doesn't know from beans.

ELECTRONICS REPAIR APPRENTICE

While still in high school, Calvin F. started out as an apprentice in a repair facility of a television and radio store. He started out sweeping floors, then, as he learned the technical ropes from the technician, he was given simple repair jobs to handle. Like Mike T., he did a lot of antenna installations, but most of his work is now inside as an assistant, at the workbench. Though he expects the boss to allow for overhead in his bills, Calvin is sometimes amazed at the spread between what he is paid and what the customer is charged for the work.

It varied how many people worked in the shop. There was one skilled technician and maybe five high school or college kids who'd kind of hang around and pick up what they could. The technician and I really had a good system going. He would go to each set and figure out what was wrong, then tell me what to do. He would do the brain work, and I would do, say, the soldering. I'm getting $3 an hour, and the technician makes about $8. The sort of formula they use is that Pete, the technician, will triple his labor—the labor charges would be three times his hourly pay rate. But no one ever keeps track of the actual time. Pete just says "It was kind of hard for me to fix," or "It took me awhile," and the boss will put an arbitrary, higher labor charge on that one. But the customer is charged the same rate, whether I do the work or the technician does it. And I would say that at least half the work done in that shop is done by guys like me who are getting $3 an hour.

I started out doing antenna work, which involved getting up on a nice high roof. He wouldn't pay me the minimum wage, because I wasn't eighteen yet. I'd get paid about $6 for a normal

125

antenna job, which he would charge $120 for, and I know all his parts cost him less than $50. He would charge $200 to replace a picture tube in a TV set, and the tube would cost him $60 or $70— the rest was labor, supposedly. I'd been working there six months when they started me replacing tubes. It's not a complicated job, and someone relatively inexperienced can do it. It took me about a half-hour to do, and then at the end, the technician had to spend five or ten minutes adjusting it, and that was it. Together we could easily do ten or fifteen color sets a day.

I got to the point where I could probably fix turntables faster than the technician could, because I was working on them all the time. I did the entire repair without anyone's help. There are only a certain number of things that can go wrong with them, and usually it's one thing that involves replacing maybe one rubber part. I would spend a half-hour, or an hour at the most, repairing a turntable, and I could put out ten in a day. He would charge about $30 labor on each, which is about normal in the industry, so that would be $300 he'd pull in for work he was paying me $30 to do. That was a pretty good markup.

It's common in the electronics repair business to hire someone at, like, two-bits an hour to do whatever they can, even though they're billing the customer ten times that amont. Of course, he'd say, "Hey, I've got all this overhead—insurance, light, heat, rent, etc." and he is right up to a point, but how right is he? Sure, it took me a little while to learn each job, but he couldn't say he paid a lot to train me. He did all right. He'd have a new car every six months or so, and usually it was a Cadillac.

I know he was selling demonstration TVs out of the showroom as new ones to people who wouldn't know. Some still even had tubes, where everything now is solid state. Some of them were eight years old—I knew because I saw the dates and the letter codes on the chassis. If he knew the person knew it was an old set, he would say it was two or three years old and maybe give them $50 or $100 off. But all these sets had been used. They were running in the showroom, and so their part-life was somewhat less. He just tries to get away with more than he should. ✔

ENTERTAINMENT AND RECREATION

CARNIVAL WORKER

Carnivals are the glittery, bittersweet world of honky-tonk, hustle, and broken dreams. As a teenager, Sara M. ran away from home to work the carnival circuit from the Great Lakes to Texas as a jointee—a person who runs the game concessions. She soon proved her skill in bringing in the marks (customers) off the midway into the various emporiums she operated: the hanky-panks, the alibis, and the flat stores. In short order, she worked her way into an arrangement whereby she took $250 a week off the top of her receipts and never paid taxes. Although she enjoyed being a carnie for about three years, she finally left the business and enrolled in college.

Sara found when seeking a job that carnival people don't ask much about a person's past. Good female jointees, she learned, generally earned more than males, and poor neighborhoods were better draws than wealthier ones. She found her marks to be quite ignorant. "They're so slow at a mental process that it's easy to take them for what they've got," though children are not so gullible as they used to be. Incidentally, she says, the first rule of a carnival is, "Never rip off a kid. When you burn kids they never forget." Unless, of course, they're "absolute assholes, smart-mouthed kids who'll stop at nothing to keep other people from playing. Then you burn them for every penny they've got."

Hanky-panks are the skill games where people have to do something, like bust a balloon with a dart. If they don't do it, they don't win anything. The more baskets you make or toilet-paper rolls you get through the donicker (toilet) seats, the bigger the prizes—and the more you pay for the privilege of doing it.

We've got to get a certain amount of money in before we can

127

let a prize go. The odds are in our favor that people are going to miss five or six times before they win. The idea is to keep them there.

A good bushel-basket agent will top anybody on the midway. The jointee tells you to toss two softballs into a bushel basket. It's almost impossible, because they usually bounce right out. If you get one ball in, the jointee takes it out, which makes it doubly hard to get the second one in, and you have to get two in to win. If you do get them in, this is where the alibi comes in. "You went over the foul line," the jointee will say, or, "It hit the rim when it went in."

In a lot of cases, the agents' alibis are legitimate. They will explain the rules beforehand, but people break them. We have signs up, but people tend not to read them. But in alibi games, even if a mark doesn't break the rules, you have to use an excuse or you'd never make it—you almost have to cheat in order to survive. Even if the player insists he was right, you wiggle out by alibiing. That's how the game got its name—you alibi and alibi. You keep telling him he went over the foul line. He can't prove he didn't. Even if a player's wife is standing right next to him, most of the time she's looking at the basket and the prizes.

A good agent just works customers into believing they have a chance to win. You always give them a faint glimmer of hope, and they'll keep trying all night. You keep saying, "Come on . . . win it for the little lady," and she's punching him in the arm. We're all miniature psychiatrists out there. If the mark has spent up to $500 to win—then by all means give the mark the dog, because you've already paid for it. It's a standing rule that if they lose $100 or more, you give them the dog. But don't give it to the others, like the lucky guy who wins on his first throw. That's the whole idea behind the alibi.

A flat store is another kind of alibi, but with more money and tougher odds. It's where the guy is out-and-out lying to you. A flat store may have four agents; it's a square tent, and it's got one man on each side. They play a little game called football. You have to roll a bunch of marbles into numbered squares, and your squares have to total a certain number in order to win. Some

128

holes they deduct for, so you go up and down, up and down. If you go over the total you have to reach, then you have to start over. The agent is sitting there adding the marbles up and dumping them so fast you don't even have a chance to count the numbers or add them up. You just take his word for it. Very seldom do you reach the required total until you've spent $500 to win a TV they've paid $75 for.

The "tip-'em pop bottle" is an alibi joint. You get what looks like a big meat fork, only it has smaller prongs, and you have to push a pop bottle up from its side onto its flat bottom. Unfortunately the bottoms of the bottles are not straight across—they're on a slight angle, or they're uneven—and they play on a heavily waxed board. It's almost impossible to get them up.

I had a dice game in Texas, where gambling was legal. In a dice game, the odds are automatically in the house's favor. The customers would bet that the dice would come up under 7, over 7, or on 7. Under and over was 1-to-1 odds; on 7 was 2-to-1 odds—you could triple your money. Some people will bet under 7, some on 7, and some above 7, so there's going to be one winner and two losers in every game. The only way the house could lose would be if everyone bet the winning place, and that just doesn't happen. Even though the 7 winner gets 2-to-1, the money from the under- and over-bettors pays for the winner, and the house breaks even.

Only a few carnivals—the crooked ones—have rigged dice or wheels. I know of one down in Alabama that the sheriff is in on, and he gets a take of what everybody makes. One customer went to the sheriff and accused a jointee of gambling with him and taking all his money. The sheriff said, "Oh, you were gambling. Well, I'll have to take you both in." Very few carnivals are crooked now; the business is getting a little better reputation. They want to come back to the same spot next year. They know if they have too many alibis and flat-store games, they'll burn the spot.

We have a patch agent, a guy the joint owner pays $50 or so a week to take care of policy protection. They hire local cops. Most of the time the cops look the other way. It's not that we're doing anything illegal—it's just that we can talk faster than and out-think the person who's playing the game. If a customer raises a fuss, the cops will come by and tell the customer to cool down—they will generally take our side because of the payment. In most cases, customers figure they didn't do anything wrong—well, they probably didn't—but if we gave prizes away freely, we wouldn't be in business after five hours.

Sara M. learned tricks of money handling, both as a carnival jointee and as a cashier. She discusses them.

In a joint you never hand back change. You say, "Yeah, I've got your money right in my pocket," and you keep them playing and playing until finally, "You ran out of money; you only have one throw to go." You don't even have to be dishonest—you just keep handing them balls and reminding them how many throws they have left. There's generally a little disbelief when you tell them they've used up their $10, but you say "Here's your prize," and they'll say, "You mean I paid $10 for *this?*" You keep them playing until you can afford to give them a decent prize, so other people will say, "Wow!" and want to play themselves.

Double-counting is where you count a single dollar twice. A guy buys a fifty-cent ticket and gives you a $10 bill. You give him back $8.50 instead of $9.50. You double-count a $1 bill. Most people count their change when all the bills are $1, but if you show them a $5 or $10 bill first, they could care less about the singles. In some shows, double-counting is the ticket seller's livelihood, especially among the older carnies. I knew a one-armed guy who was the best double-counter in the business. He could convince a mark that he had $9 there when he really only had $7. "How many times do I have to count it out for you?" he'd ask. If an agent can double-count without getting too many complaints, the owner will overlook it. I've done it—we all do it. You do it in a situation where you know you can get away with it. In many cases, marks will walk away and leave change behind. They'll buy a fifty-cent ticket and leave the fifty-cents change. When they walk, you always set that money aside. If they don't come back in ten minutes, it's yours. You can always tell them that someone else behind them picked it up. If they catch you double-counting, you just say, "Oops, I'm sorry."

Watch young and old people giving you change. A lot of times they will give you an extra dollar. You buy something for $1.50 and give them a $10 bill, and they'll give you $9.50 in change. Very few people count their coins nowadays—men are the worst; all they worry about are the bills. Clerks will just hand you the coins without counting them out, and rarely do customers count them. It's harder for carnival people to short-change that way because we deal mostly with quarters.

Short-change artists will confuse the clerk at the register. Generally, this is done in small groceries late at night where there's a good crowd and only one clerk. The customer will buy, say, a pack of cigarettes and say, "All I have is a twenty." So the clerk gives him his change, and then he'll say, "Oh, here, I've got a dollar. Give me back my twenty. A lot of clerks, assuming the customer is honest, will just take back the change without counting it and give the guy his twenty back. Except that the dollar he suddenly came up with he had pulled out of the change the clerk had given him in the first place. So he's shorted the clerk $1 just by confusing her. Then he may ask her to change a five, and this just keeps going back and forth until she's totally confused. I've seen this happen to very experienced cashiers— they just don't count the money. This happened to me once, except I had already short-changed the guy the first time around, and when it was over I had $3 of his, and he only had $2 of the store's.

If you take $5 or $10 out of your apron every night and put it in your pocket, the owners will overlook that, but if it's more, they'll fire you and blackball you. There are absolutely no taxes paid on most of the money in a carnival. The only time you pay taxes is when you own something. Owners will withhold taxes from the ride guys, but a lot of the time they won't be paid to the government. A lot of shows avoid paying unemployment taxes for their employees by saying the employees work on a daily basis.

131

The "Coney Island" is where you force the marks to play, actually pulling them in and physically forcing them by poking them in the back with a handful of darts. You tell them to play and play, and they do.

Pickled-punk sideshows are still around in some southern states. These are fetuses anywhere from three weeks to ten months old. They get deformed ones from hospitals, put them in formaldehyde, and display them as human oddities of what happens when a mother takes drugs or catches German measles. The kid is supposed to be buried, but the carnival guys approach someone in the hospital and say, "Well, if you get anything interesting, I'll pay a couple hundred" and they get them.

When you first get a job with a carnival, they'll ask you what shows you've been with, but they never ask if you've been in prison or anything like that. There's no stigma to it. Carnies are normal human beings like everyone else. ✔

USHER

As an employee of a large ushering service, Eric R. works various jobs ranging from airport security to large private wedding parties. He enjoys the work, which he has done for two years, more than any other job he's ever had. Of course, it is perhaps not the regular duties of ushering that Eric enjoys as much as the fringe benefits the job provides.

At the airport, the work involves security. Passengers cannot get to the gates leading to the airplanes unless they go through us first. We run the X-ray machines and check purses and briefcases for guns, knives, pointed sticks—anything that could be used as a weapon by a potential hijacker. In a day's time we collect maybe twelve or fifteen guns and fifteen to twenty-five knives. If the point of a knife blade extends over the pas-

132

senger's palm, we take the knife away. If they have a permit for their gun, we can put it in the baggage and ship it, but if they don't have a permit, it's good-bye gun. We turn it over to the police, who work right in the airport with us.

Once I saw a police officer take payoffs for letting a gun through. I didn't say anything, because I knew they would get me for it good if I did. The guy had a .45 automatic, loaded. He didn't give any excuse. He just said he had personal reasons why he was carrying the gun. He told the officer, "How about if I slip you a few in a very secretive way?" And the officer said, "How much are you going to give me?" I heard the figure $500. I guess they went through with the bribe, because there was nothing said.

When I work as an usher at a ball park, I would take a few bribes myself. Say I'm seating people, and they want a better seat. They will slip me $35 or $40 to get them front-row seats. I have worked rock concerts at the door when there are sellouts, and somebody will offer me $100 to let them in. That goes on quite a bit—a lot of the ushers get away with it. I usually charge $75. I tell the customer, "Give me $75, and you've got yourself a deal." If they want to see the concert bad enough, they'll pay.

I make more selling tickets than I do from my pay as an usher. Last night I worked a rock concert and sold two tickets for $150. They were stolen, and I'd paid $20 for them. That was a $130 profit. People who are working ticket sales for the concert are pretty loose—they make their bucks on the side, too. They keep a certain number of tickets aside because they know ushers are going to be working that night, and we'll buy—we want to make some money, too. All the ushers—at least those who have been around enough to know what is going on—operate like that. I probably pull in $400 or $500 a week on the side in bribes, illegal sales, and what have you. Everyone has to make a buck today.

I'll also work private parking jobs for something like a big wedding reception in a private home. They'll invite me in to eat. Some of the women will end up getting drunk, making plays for you, and enjoying life. While everyone is partying, you'll end up in somebody's bedroom with one of the woman stragglers. Usu-

133

ally, she is a young chick, one of the daughters or something. I never take anything from a house, but the women will go around and get their hands on some cash for me. The uniform gets them, probably. It's a pretty good racket.

I'm a damned good-looking stud. I was out in California a couple years ago, and I worked for an escort service, where the women call up for men to escort them. Most of the clients were older women and really wealthy. The company billed my night at $100, of which I got $70. The women would take me out to the theater, restaurants, or whatever, then give me a tip for going to bed with them. I worked three nights a week and had enough cash to live the rest of the week. I worked out there about two years before I got tired of it. You know, there are more women in California than you can shake a stick at. ✔

BLACKJACK DEALER

After attending an independent gambling school in Las Vegas, Daniel L. went to work as a blackjack dealer in a small casino off the strip. Starting on the swing shift (6 p.m. to 2 a.m.), he soon saw that there was no such thing as "after hours" in the round-the-clock Las Vegas operation. And though his school trained him to pick out people trying to cheat the house, he soon learned that casinos watched their dealers much more carefully than their players.

There are seven spots to a table, so you can be dealing to from one to seven people, depending on how many are playing. The object of blackjack is to come as near to the number twenty-one as possible. If you go over twenty-one, you bust— you're out. Players have the option of taking a card at any point, but dealers have to follow house rules that say they have to take a card anytime they have sixteen or less, and every time they have seventeen or more, they have to stay.

134

It is a tremendous advantage for players to identify the tens and aces, because if a deck is ten-heavy, it will favor the player. If they have sixteen, they don't have to take a card. But if a dealer has sixteen, he does, and if there are a lot of tens in the deck it is likely that he will bust. I was dealing a single deck, though we didn't deal down to the bottom to prevent people from counting. Some players, however, will try to mark the tens. We used to deal two down-cards to each player, and when they picked them up in their hands, they could put a slight lengthwise bend in a card, which will raise it up about a 1/32-of-an-inch off the felt when it's face down. So if that card later becomes the dealer's down-card, the player can see the top card is not sitting on it evenly. I never caught anyone doing this, but I was taught to guard against it in school. I did, however, encounter another kind of marking that I was supposed to catch but didn't.

If you take one card out of a deck, and you put a fingernail mark on the edge, you can hold the card away from you, and you won't be able to see it. But if you put the card in the deck, with all the other cards around it, the notch is very conspicuous. Some guy did this against me. He started with $25 and ran it up to about $400 in twenty minutes. I was taken off the table, and after they examined the deck, they found the guy had notched it. A mistake I guess I was making . . . when you deal a single deck, the index finger of the hand that you hold the deck with should be across the front of the cards so the player can't see them. I wasn't doing that.

Another way players cheat the casino is capping the bet. Let's say you've bet $10, and you push another $10 into the circle while the dealer is not looking. I've caught people doing that, but I didn't turn them in, because often when people are capping bets, they will often tip the dealer. This is called toking. Players will put money on the perimeter of the circle in addition to a regular bet in the circle. They are betting two separate sums of money. Let's say they put $5 in the circle, and $2 on the perimeter, and they win. They will get $7—$5 that will be matched for the bet they made for themselves in the circle, and

$2 for the bet on the perimeter. The dealer gets that $4 as a tip, so obviously he hopes that the player wins and the house loses.

Toking or placing a second bet is perfectly legal, even though it puts the dealer into a conflict of interest. Mathematically, however, it's not a real problem, because ultimately the house is going to win anyway, so the casino doesn't care. In fact, tips enable the house to pay dealers a low salary. When I was working, 75 percent of my income was from tips, and we'd only report 15 percent to the IRS. A dealer walks a very tight line when he's being tipped. You can be friendly, but you can't tell people how to play their hands. If you're too helpful, you can lose your job.

Probably the largest type of cheating I saw is when the dealer works with the players. Usually, these collaborations are with an old friend or someone who is new to town—it's not going to be someone who lives in Vegas; that would be much too risky. In most casinos, when a dealer has a ten or an ace showing, he looks at his underneath card and sees what his points are. If it is not blackjack, he knows whether he is pat or not. If he is pat, he doesn't take anymore cards; if he is not pat, he will have to hit. Now, there are numerous ways that he can signal this to the player he is working with. If he has his weight on his left foot, it may mean that he is pat. They can work out a variety of signals ahead of time: which foot you shift your weight on, where you hold your index fingers, which way you are looking, etc. A player who knows what he is doing can use this information to win consistently. Mostly, if there is collusion, it will be a pit boss who will pick up the signals. A dealer I knew had his casino card revoked and was kicked out of town for doing this.

Players can be booted out of the casinos if they're caught cheating in minor ways. If it's no more than a few hundred dollars, they just ask them to leave and write it off as a business loss. In Vegas nowadays, if someone steals a lot of money, they don't get their arms broken, they get sued, civilly and criminally.

Another form of cheating is made possible by the way the tables are set up around the pit. The dealers work back-to-back, and a player at one table can see players at another table as well as the back of their dealer. If their dealer has a ten up, he has to look at his bottom card, and if he is sloppy in doing this, a player at the first table can see what he has from behind his back and signal a partner at the other table whether the dealer is pat or not. We were instructed to add another move when we were dealing, which is when we look at our underneath card, and to slide one hand under, on an angle, so no one behind us could see the card—but it still goes on. I've heard that one casino in Atlantic City determined that this method of cheating was so effective that they've instructed their dealers—regardless of whether they have a ten or an ace up—to play out the hands without looking. They were willing to take a percentage loss on this, trading one risk for another. The best part of it, from the casino's standpoint, is that it prevents the dealers from collaborating with players, while it also stops collaboration among the players themselves.

Players who count the cards can change the odds, which normally favor the house. There are all sorts of methods for counting cards intelligently. The simplest is just plussing and minusing the deck. This means you give twos through sixes a value of plus one, sevens through nines a value of zero, and tens through aces a value of minus one—it's just a binary system that tells you where the weight of the unplayed tens are. As you get down toward the bottom of the deck, it can be very useful in telling you how to play your cards. I've been told not to deal to certain players because they were beating me by counting. The pit boss would just say, "Skip that player." There is really nothing wrong in counting. I'd say that if there is a ripoff, it would be the house not dealing to counters, for the simple reason that counters can beat them—which they are entitled to do. The house also has "mechanics," dealers who are tricky with cards, they can send in to burn the counters, although I never saw this happen.

In Vegas, everyone is looking for an angle, and the matter of cheating is a question of whether something pays or not, and whether or not you're going to get caught doing it. One of the reasons the IRS is struggling to get into the cages where the money is counted is that it is generally known that the managers

137

are constantly skimming off the top. A lot of things in Vegas shocked me, but I was probably pretty naive. The only woman I met in the beginning was very attractive, and I'd talk to her on my free time. It turned out she was a hooker. My pit boss carried a gun around in the back of his pants. It's grotesque in Vegas. It's an ugly place where the buck is god, and all the people worship it and get myopic in the process. The whole town is keyed up for one thing: fleecing the tourists who are passing through. And they are very successful at it, too.   ✔

MUSICIAN

Paul N. is a professional musician in his early twenties who is trained in both classical and popular piano. His gigs range from the usual assortment of wedding, club, and school dances to nightclub and cabaret jobs, both locally and on the road. Like all professionals, he likes to be recognized as such, even though he has not reached the big time and must be content to play his keyboard at $35 to $50 an engagement. Paul can play anything from swing to classical to cocktail. He plays Bach for drill and whatever the customer wants for hire. He sees himself and others like him very much the servants of commercial tastemakers. "Look what's on the radio now," he says. "A bunch of white guys trying to sound like black guys. What's distributed—from the first note to the stocking of the record shelves—is all controlled by corporate executives."

If I followed every union rule, I'd never work. They say: Don't play for under scale, don't play with nonunion musicians, don't play for free, etc. When I play for free, I risk being found out, but I'm trying to further myself, and any exposure I get is good experience. I don't think I'm ripping anyone off—the union doesn't own me. And being a union musician doesn't guarantee me an income. I'm an honest dues-paying

138

member—I expect to get jobs from them, but I never have gotten one through the union. Most of the work I get is from referrals.

Even getting scale wages ($35-$50) is extremely difficult. You may get a percentage of the gate, which, after everyone takes a cut—the booking agent, the talent agent, the club owner, bartenders, waitresses, and bellboys—it isn't that great. And you don't even know when you're getting the amount you're supposed to get either. The union is filled with claims every week from musicians complaining about not getting paid.

Quite often, musicians rip each other off. Whoever gets the gig gets paid, and often the musician will keep the money and tell the others he'll send them a check—and he never does. When you go on the road with top names, you won't see your checks for months after the tours. Most musicians are paid by personal checks until they get to the big time. So as long as you're just jobbing locally, most of the pay is tax-free.

Usually we play forty-five minutes, with a fifteen-minute break—that's standard, though it's violated quite a lot. If you practice five to eight hours a day, you can have a lot of contempt for an audience if they're belching, eating, or telling loud jokes while you're playing. That's why a musician will take a thirty- or forty-five-minute break—because why should he play his brains out when nobody is listening anyway? The guys who hire you complain about that all the time, but if you don't like the audience, that's the way it is.

Sheet music isn't used by professionals—that's just for people at home with pianos. Professionals rely exclusively on tape recorders or lead sheets. The lead sheets have the lyrics, melody, and chord names. Most working musicians have fake books, which are just collections of lead sheets. Fake books violate every copyright law on the books, and so, naturally, they're illegal. The original composers or artists are getting screwed because they're not collecting the royalties they're entitled to. Fake books are usually printed on the sly, and you can get them through the grapevine if you have the right referral. They're about $20 for 500 to 1,000 songs. Theoretically, whoever pays the musicians is responsible for getting a license to play a song—even something like "Stardust" in a little roadhouse—and then the writer is supposed to get a royalty check. Nobody ever enforces it, though. There wouldn't be any musicians playing weddings or anything if they did.

Once, I walked into what I thought was a new recording company, thinking, wow, this is great, having it so handy. I'd made an appointment and brought in a cassette of songs I had written. Later, I got a letter saying how great my material was, and just sign on the dotted line, and you can begin recording in Memphis. And you owe us $5,000.

This was just a company of "sharks"—composers and musicians who have no real connection in the music business. They just have a couple of studios and get all their money from hopefuls who want to compose or record. If you're a lyricist, they'll say, we'll put your song to music for a fee. They have a standard tape that fits virtually anything, and they'll just twist it around to make it fit your lyrics and charge you an outrageous sum of money. Then, they'll get you to come into a studio and record it.

These sharks told me they'd double whatever I agreed to invest and promised promotions on radio, national recording contracts, and all that. They might drop off a demo tape at some little radio station, and it won't get played, and then they'll say that was their promotion. It's mostly naive people who know nothing about the music business who get ripped off by sharks. Nobody I've ever heard of succeeded by going to them. You should never pay to record. Go through standard commercial recording companies—they'll pay you and cover your expenses as well. ✔

HEALTH CLUB INSTRUCTOR

Doug N. got a job as an instructor in a health club that specialized in body-building. His audition consisted of posing in a swimming suit to

140

show how well built he was and a strength test to see how much weight he could lift on various kinds of exercise machines. Doug says that despite his lack of formal training, he is a good instructor, though he wishes he could give more individual attention to his students. Many of them are brought in through what he regards as high-pressure tactics. As a result, Doug learned that his job involved more than building muscle in his students—it also required using his muscle to make some of them students in the first place.

These health clubs will advertise that you can get a first workout free, or you get thirty visits at a real low price, but they don't tell you directly that you have to use those visits in thirty days. So, you sign up for that initial thirty-day trial and pay an introductory fee. One place in the form it tells you you get your thirty visits for the trial price, then somewhere else it says you have thirty-day free trial. But you don't put the two together, and in the process, you're also signing a commitment that if you decide after the trial period (they don't say after thirty days, they say, after "the trial period") to come to the club, you're agreeing to a membership contract for a year. So you may have used the place five times, and you'll go in there a couple months after you first signed up, and they'll say: "Hey, you haven't paid your year's dues," or something like that.

It just blows my mind that they can pull something like this, but they do it. One of the guys who got into one of these contracts told me about it, and, man, I could not believe it. After their trial period is up, they are committed. If they want the full program—swimming, track, body-building—they might be paying $400 a year, maybe a little more, for that. The cheapest they can get out for is, I think, about $275. People are hooked because they sign a contract.

The people who go into it are kind of duped. They do not know what they are getting into, and they try to get out. A lot of the guys there are businessmen in their thirties; they are pissed off at their companies, or they want to lose some weight or build themselves up or something like that—they don't know what they're doing. So one of these guys may be in the office talking to the manager, and he would call in a couple of us instructors to stand around in our swimming trunks. We're the muscle men in there to look tough. The dude will be sitting there, and he will be looking at me and the other instructor trying to figure what's going to happen to him.

First, the manager tells the guy he ought to stay in the program. He says, "Hey, wouldn't you like to look like Doug over there?" At that point, I might spread my legs a little and flex my muscles so I look even better to the guy. Then they ask him, "Aren't you ashamed of your body?" and stuff like that. They try to shame him into it by having us in there just to show off what we've got.

Then, if that doesn't work, they'll tell him something like, "If you are not in shape, how are you going to protect yourself? What would you do if you were walking down the street, and you have to come in contact with Doug, and you bump into him, and he doesn't like it and just hauls off and wipes you out?" Now he thinks he is going to bump into me or one of the other guys from the club sometime, and we're going to work him over a little. That really pisses me off—using our muscles for that. They don't come out and tell the guy we are going to rack him up if he doesn't pay. It's just a "Well, you know that we'll take care of you." We are just showing our muscles.

At this point, some of the guys will sign up. The manager will say, just try it for a year. Give it a chance to work. We are going to put you under the personal supervision of Doug, and he is going to see that you lose that stomach, or whatever else the guy needs. Well, I can't give them individual attention; we have too many people. We give them full instruction on how to work our equipment, but after that, they're pretty much on their own. But they think it sounds good, so they will sign up.

Some guys don't want to pay a damned thing; they just want to get out of the place, and they tell the man to go screw himself. With these guys we just try to scare them a little more. The manager would say to one of us, "Come here," and he'd have one of us stand right in the path of the dude, and the other stands in front of the door. Then he says, "Wouldn't you care to sit down and talk about this a little more?" The average guy going to a health club is nothing. I'm a pretty big guy, in good shape, and he just looks at me and feels like, "Hey, man, he could cream me right here."

I've only had physicial contact with a guy once. There was this big dude, and I knew there was going to be trouble. He got up and just told the manager, "Your muscle doesn't scare me any," and started off to try to slug me. I caught his wrist just before he made contact and gave him one sock in the gut, and he doubled up. I just picked him up by the collar and told him if he wanted to get rough, I would get rough right back. He just didn't want to have anymore, but he said he would sue me, and the man said, "Hey, you started it." I just took the dude and told him to sit down. He did, and the man told us two instructors to leave. It is up to the manager what is going to happen next. Hey, if a guy really wants to leave, I'm not going to lay a hand on him.   ✔

FOOD AND BEVERAGE

DAIRY MERCHANDISER

For several years, Ernie W. was responsible for the retail product line of one of the nation's largest dairies. In this capacity, he was given the title of merchandiser. His primary role, however, can be more bluntly expressed. "Actually," says Ernie, "I was price-fixing."

Pricing of milk is set up through the federal milk-marketing program. The federal government says how much the farmer gets. Of course, the government is full of lobbyists who say, "Oh, we have to have a price increase." Well, the dairies are glad to see the farmer get a price increase, because then they can kick their prices up. The problem is, the farmer gets nowhere near a fair proportion of the ultimate price raise the consumer pays. As the government allows bulk milk prices to increase, dairies bump their prices, too, but they kick them up ridiculously. Usually, if, say, the farmer got a three- or four-cent per hundred-weight increase, we would raise our prices that much on a gallon, and 100 pounds of milk will make about twelve gallons. So that was a much greater percentage increase for the dairy than it was for the farmer. I'll bet that for every nickel the price of milk goes up in the store, farmers are lucky if they get a penny of that. The middleman—the dairy—is getting the money. Of course, dairies can say their labor costs go up, and they do, but nothing like the way their prices do.

My higher-ups decided they wanted certain products priced at certain levels, depending on what areas we were in. They wanted to get their profit up when they saw dairies elsewhere improving their earnings, so they sent me out to meet with several other people from dairies in our market area to fix prices. We would usually go to a motel and hire a meeting room or just have a lunch over in a corner. We met whenever there was a

145

need, especially whenever the farmers got a raise. I definitely went to those meetings with the authority to negotiate, and whatever we had all decided at the meeting, the dairies would live with. Of course, you could get your butt chewed out for not getting prices up enough. They would tell you, "Hey, come on, we have to live with this for another month, and so-and-so in Memphis is getting a lot more than that."

What we were doing was clearly illegal. We took some security precautions—I didn't want to go to jail. My higher-ups always told me before I went to these secret meetings, "If you get caught, we don't know who you are." I told my boss, "Just like it later happened in the Watergate thing, I am not going to swing alone, pal. If I get caught, you'd better stick behind me, because if you don't, you'll go, too."

It was also my job to see that prices were fixed in all retail stores. If small, independent grocers were selling milk for twenty or twenty-five cents under the price we'd fixed, I'd go in and talk to them, explaining that this was silly; we could all make more money than this, so why don't they bring their price up to where everyone else is? I did the same thing with gas stations, cleaners—anybody who was using milk as a loss-leader to attract business. If they didn't agree, then you'd go to their supplier and say, "Jeez, XYZ Market is selling milk for eighty cents. Why don't you explain to them that we have them surrounded by stores, and if they don't raise the price up to what we want, we'll lower our price in those stores to sixty-nine cents and kill them." We didn't use any rough stuff—no more than breaking up a sign or something—just friendly persuasion. Most of the time the suppliers would tell the grocers they were not going to get any more deliveries if they did not increase their prices. That was illegal, but the grocers would have to go to court or try to get another supplier, and the other suppliers, of course, were in this group, too. The supermarkets got to the point where they would call me if they were putting milk on sale. They would say, "Look, we're going to have milk on sale, but don't panic. Next week it is going back to the regular price." Okay, no problem.

My dairy's net profits were so high they were able to pay for one plant in less than two years. And we were not the ones making the most money. There were five dairies in the area, and two of them consistently made more profit than we did. That's what we did—we tried to beat the other dairies.

Of course, the by-products—cottage cheese, coffee cream, chocolate milk—that's where the big profit is. We could put cottage cheese into the stores for nineteen cents, we'd charge them thirty-two cents, and they'd sell it for maybe thirty-seven. Any of the by-products were at least 60 or 70 percent profit for the dairy.

The butterfat situation is more or less a pricing ripoff. Butterfat is the most expensive element in the product, and the federal government regulates how much butterfat there has to be in milk, cream, ice cream, etc. Of course, the milk lobbies keep pushing to lower the regulations so they can make cream products for a lot less money. There was a big celebration one fall, when they lowered the butterfat content required by law on whipping cream, which you usually sell a bunch of over the holidays. Whipping cream used to be 36 percent butterfat, but they keep dropping it. I don't think they can drop it much further, otherwise the whipping cream won't whip.

They can charge almost the same price for skim or low-fat milk as they do for whole milk, because they can get away with it. There's been so much raving recently about cholesterol that a lot of people are buying low-fat milk. Back then, the cream floated to the top of those goose-neck bottles, and when the milkman left it on the porch in the winter it would freeze, and you would have a cream puff sticking out. The trend now is to lower and lower the butterfat, but leave the price the same so you make more money. It's just like the liquor industry when they switched to the metric bottles; the bottles are smaller, but the price is the same.

In one metropolitan area, we were distributing our products there, but we couldn't get a permit to go into the city itself. That was all politics. So we had to get somebody with a city permit to package them, and someone else with a city permit to distribute them to stores within the city. We had to pay both of them off.

147

How much, I don't know. But I know they got sealed envelopes. Of course, we had to pay off the union tremendously. I know at one time I gave our man $1,500 to pass on. Otherwise the union guy could simply say, "You are not going to deliver your products," and he could damned well back his words up. They'd just shut you down.

I think the dairy business is going to get more and more consolidated. The big ones are just going to keep buying up the small people. The small guys can't compete in prices with a national supplier, and the product is all the same. Everybody goes strictly by the minimum and makes all the money possible. With this situation, the small guys are going to go by the wayside.   ✔

GROCERY CASHIER

Lynne F. works as a regular cashier in a supermarket of a national chain. As a person working the cash register, she acknowledges that customers may not always be charged the correct price for any given item—sometimes because of their doing, sometimes because of the store's. In any case, she says, customers should know that the burden of determining the correct price for any given item is often on them.

Our chain runs ads with sale prices in the newspapers. The items in the store, however, are not marked with the sale prices—they just have the regular price on them. A lot of the cashiers are part-timers, and we don't always have time to read the papers to learn the sale prices, so often we don't know them. Even if you do know the sale price, you usually don't look at the item you're checking out—you're so busy you just look at the price. So unless the customer knows the sale price and brings it to our attention, we charge them the regular price. If I know an

148

item is on sale, I will ring up the sale price, but my responsibility as a checker is to charge the price marked on the item.

The same thing happens at other stores in the chain. I bought margarine at one last week, and it was marked the regular price, even though it was on sale. The pricers don't go back to the items on the shelves. Say bread, which is usually three loaves for $1 is on sale four for $1. They may put the sale price on the ones they're just putting up on the shelves, but sometimes they don't even mark them. They may put one big sign over the display saying four for $1, but the loaves themselves will say three for $1.

The other clerks know about this, and we complain about it all the time. The manager just keeps brushing it off and ignoring me and everyone else. He even brushes off the customers, unless they question it. In that case, he'll make an adjustment, but that's all he does. It's not up to the customer to correct this—it's up to the manager. If we advertise a sale, everybody should benefit from it, not just those who read it in the paper. A lot of people come into the store to take advantage of sale items. The company is profitting off of this, and the customer is suffering.

I'd say a customer could get gypped on at least ten different items on sale that are still marked with the regular price. The sale prices can make a real difference. If a customer came through with a basketful of all items on sale—let's say the regular price would be $20—the sale price would be about $3 or $4 less. That could be $3 or $4 times hundreds of customers.

Some customers will abuse the discount coupon system by waiting until you've rung up everything—and meanwhile the bagger is putting everything in sacks—before they hand you the coupons. Of course, you're not going to hold up the line and go through four or five bags to see if the customer had Peter Pan instead of Skippy peanut butter. And with $40 worth of groceries, how are you going to remember? In such a case, we'll just assume the customer had the right item, and we'll give her the discount. Sometimes, the customer will not have the right item, and to save a hassle I'll accept the coupon anyway, but sometimes I won't. If I take the groceries out of the bag and show them they don't have the item, they'll say, "Oh, I *thought* I had it."

Under the food stamp program, you can't tear any stamp worth more than $1 out of your book. Sometimes customers will bring a book that has a loose stamp from another book. They'll pretend to tear it out and hand it to you. But we can tell if it's from their book, because if it isn't, it will have a different serial number on it. Sometimes when you challenge them, they'll get mad and walk out. That rule is supposed to stop people from selling their stamps to other people.

The registers we have now automatically separate the items eligible for food stamp purchase from the ineligible ones. With the old machines we had to ring up each category separately. A lot of customers would let you ring up the whole order, then they'd say, "Oh, I have food stamps." Well, you either had to go back and void the whole order and do them over again separately, or you had to pick out the eligible items and deduct them from the total, and that was a big hassle. Sometimes, if they had only three or four ineligible items, we'd say, "Well, go ahead and give me food stamps for all of them." It was less trouble.

Customers often switch price tags, especially on things like frozen shrimp, because the price is sky-high. But we know the prices and usually catch it. On frozen foods the package is some-times so frosty it's hard to get the price tag to stick, but we have maybe fifty customers who try to do it all the time.

Some customers will keep something for a long time and bring it back all covered with dust. They'll say they just bought it and want to return it because it's the wrong thing. Sometimes they'll bring back meat that looks like they've had it a long time or they didn't refrigerate it correctly—and they'll say it's spoiled.

Customers are good at eating fruit. They'll walk past the grape stand and eat them right and left. They'll eat nuts while they walk through the store, and by the time they get to the register, there's nothing to ring up. Or they'll let their kids take candy, and they'll say, "Oh, that's right; he has candy." Otherwise, they'd forget. Or sometimes a kid will pick up candy or a toy and walk right past. When you ask if he got it in the store, the parent will say, "Oh, I didn't know you were going to take that—here, put it back." If you didn't say anything, the kid would walk out of the store with it.

If I see shoplifting, I report it. Usually, when it's late at night, a couple of men will come in and walk around a lot. When they're there for fifteen minutes and still haven't picked up anything, then you know they're up to no good. They usually stuff what they want—a bottle of wine or a steak—into their jackets. We keep the hard liquor behind the counter because it's more expensive. So they usually opt for a bottle of wine.

Our security guards are not very good. Their philosophy is, "Why should I get killed over the store's money?" Shoplifters are usually caught because one of the managers has seen them take something. But security guards won't challenge anybody on their own unless it gets outrageous, like if they take a whole shopping bag of stuff.   ✔

MEAT WRAPPER

Loraine O. worked in the meat department of two supermarkets of the same chain until she and several other women in her job classification were let go. As a meat wrapper, she was a member of the same union as the butchers, although her job consisted mostly of packaging the meats for counter display. Nonetheless, she did have to learn the various cuts of meat as she went along. Loraine wasn't sorry to leave that particular occupation. She found the work hard and a certain amount of antifeminism prevalent among her co-workers.

We put out three different kinds of ground beef: regular ground beef, ground chuck, and ground round. But basically there wouldn't be any difference among them; they were all the same. I didn't grind the meat myself, but the butchers told me

151

this, and I could see myself it was all the same color. The butchers didn't grind our own meat—what they ground came in boxes from Australia. It was just a box of lean beef in chunks, and they would take the fat they had trimmed from our regular cuts of meat and mix it with the Australian beef in the grinder. They have leaner meat in Australia, so to cater to American tastes, we had to add our own fat to it.

When I shopped in other stores, I'd watch carefully to see the difference in color in the different grades of ground meat. Ground beef has the most fat in it, ground chuck has less, and ground round has even less than chuck. But in my stores, they didn't even change the content of the fat. They put the same meat in all the packages, and people never knew the difference—there was the same amount of fat in all three grades.

I bought some of our chopped sirloin once and commented on how good it was, and one butcher said it was no different from the other ground beef—it was just my imagination. I said, "Oh, no. It tasted like steak to me," and he told me that it was the same boxed beef from Australia. I guess it was psychological.

You know how customers will pick out, say, a round steak and give it to the butcher and tell him to grind it up? Our butchers would take the piece of meat to the back, cut the bone out of it, package some plain ground beef, stick the bone on top of it, and wrap it for the customer. They'd save the piece of round steak and sell it later. No one ever knew the difference.

When I have meat specially ground, I always try to watch it very carefully, although in many cases it is impossible, because they do their cutting and grinding behind doors. But a lot of times when you have your own meat ground, unless they grind it twice, you will see some parts of it will be darker and some lighter when they hit the fat. Their own beef is all pretty evenly ground.

Sometimes when meat is on sale and none is out on the counter, they will say, "We will have it ready for you in five minutes." They may not be out of it at all, but they say they are and will make you wait for it. They want you to stand at the counter so you will buy more meat.

152

One time—I never really knew exactly what had happened—but one of the helpers hinted around that they had gotten in some bad meat. He sent me out into the store to get a bottle of peroxide and told me to be sure no one saw me taking it. Meanwhile, they closed up the whole meat section—not the counter, but they brought something down around the work area so that no one could see back there. They locked the doors to the stockroom behind the butchers' area; they made sure no one saw what they were doing. Apparently, there was some way they could doctor the bad meat with the peroxide. It was all very secret.

We had a deli where you could buy chicken and other cooked food in little tinfoil packages. I knew a girl who was working in that department and she told me how the butchers gave her chickens on the verge of spoiling to cook with a little barbecue sauce on them and sell them like that. She said she had smelled the chicken, and it was really bad. A lot of old people came in to buy the cooked food, and she said: "I can't do that to them." She refused to cook it and got into a big fight with the manager about it.

I remember hearing maybe a couple years after I worked at the store that they closed it down—I think because of short-weighing. Although I was never told to short-weigh anything, a man who worked in the Deli hinted around that he did. He told me, "Yeah, well, you gotta make money somehow."

It was kind of sneaky the way I lost my job. The first manager I worked for told me he didn't like women working the meat department. So he gave me a hard time; he even had me unloading a truck. I wasn't in the union yet, so he did everything he could to make me quit. I never refused to do anything—mop floors, whatever. But eventually I got upset about something and got a transfer to another store.

They were a little nicer over there, but one day they came along and said that we had to time ourselves on everything we did: working the electric meat wrappers, cleaning them, and all our other duties. Make sure, they said, to leave yourself enough time, because after that we would have to work at that pace.

153

Well, we did, and not too long after that, most of the women meat wrappers in all the stores were laid off . . . just the women meat wrappers. I guess they decided that the women meat wrappers couldn't put out as much as the men could. The union didn't do a thing about it. The union leadership was all male. ✔

DELI COUNTERMAN

The supermarket in which Jay O. works has a delicatessen that sells cold cuts, salads, and puddings, and he tends that counter until evening closing. When his products begin to lose their freshness, Jay is generally the first to know.

Ours is a smaller store, and things get relatively slow sometimes. Some items, like coleslaw, macaroni salad, and potato salad move well, but other things like some of the cold cuts just sit there. The food is displayed behind glass, but everything has a code on it that tells you when it's supposed to be discarded. When something gets out of code, however, my boss will just take the old one off and put a new one on, and we'll sell it anyway. It just about has to reek before you pull it out.

There is stuff in there that if people ask for it, I will tell them not to buy it. I tell them right out, "It will make you sick." These are things like beef loaves, head cheese, etc. —things that don't go quickly. Just about anybody can smell a piece of meat that's bad. He tells us that if we pull something out, and it just has a little mold on the top, we should wash it, that's all. Of course, we don't do that in front of the customers. Often times the ends of things are really stale. He will make sandwiches out of them, stick them in the case, and people will buy them. On the average, about three people come back every night with stale stuff. He doesn't work nights, so he doesn't know.

The company health inspectors okayed our delicatessen

kitchen, but the city has threatened to close us down because of unsanitary surroundings—loose garbage-can lids, etc. The problem is the manager: He's very old and just isn't aware of what's going on. I don't know why the store doesn't just close that whole operation: ✔

GOVERNMENT/PUBLIC SERVICE

STATE SOCIAL WORKER

One of the programs Maurice L. worked on as a state social worker involved withholding rents from slum landlords in an effort to force them to make their properties more habitable. He would go to court in case the landlord tried to evict the tenants, and he saw to it that rotten back porches, broken plaster, etc., were repaired before the rent was paid. His job gave him an interesting look into the world of slum landlords.

There's a whole class of slum real estate companies. In Eviction Court you'll see the same set of lawyers representing them. Usually a lawyer owns a piece of the company, and he writes their leases, handles the evictions, etc. — it's a whole field of law. They have nice offices and everything. They'll sell you a building, manage it for you, and send you nice statements and beautiful receipts for everything. Sometimes they end up owning buildings after selling them three or four times on contract. After that comes the firebug.

I knew a woman whose husband had bought a building, a nine- or ten-flat building, years ago. This was going to be their retirement. After he died, she continued living there and managing it. Then the neighborhood went black, and she was stuck there. Her own son wouldn't even come by and help her, so finally she turned it over to a slum broker to manage it. The first thing they do is scare you. "Don't come around your building without me," the broker will say. Then he sends statements every month. They would say: Collected X amount of rent, so many evictions, and paid expenses, like Joe the carpenter, for minor repairs. The broker actually paid $15, but sent her a bill for $25. Black carpenters couldn't find work at union wage scales

157

and were happy for these jobs, so the managers would give inflated receipts to the owners.

When she saw the statements, they didn't look that bad. Her broker had included receipts and everything, listing expenditures for fuel oil from XYZ, and insurance on the building, etc. She didn't learn till later that he was getting a salesman's commission from XYZ, and that he was also selling her the insurance. Finally, he talked her into selling the building, and he sold it to a guy who walked away with it. He sold it on contract with no money down to a guy who would make payments through him, so he would get a percentage. It ended up in court, and after we proved all these inflated things, he settled with her for $12,000 so she wouldn't sign a criminal complaint against him. Of course, she could fire her broker, but whom could she turn to? Another one just like him? ✔

PRISON MEDICAL TECHNICIAN

For nine months, Leo P. worked as a medical technician in a state prison. He undertook the job thinking he was in decent shape. "I'm 196 pounds, six-two, and I was benching 250 pounds," says Leo. Some of the prisoners, however, with nothing much else to do but lift weights, were benching far more and making their bitterness with their lot well known to Leo and other guards. After nine months, he quit, "because it was too dangerous."

I was a correctional officer, which is another name for guard, for a few months before I became a medical technician. I worked in a house where the inmates were locked up twenty-four hours a day. If they had to go to the hospital, I would take them out of the cells, handcuffed, and bring them back. I'd watch the trustees feed them. They were supposed to get showers once a week, but since they were under twenty-four hour lockup, they didn't get showers at all. You can't blame them for being really bitter. Many times I have walked on the gallery, and I've had piss and shit thrown at me. Once I almost got stabbed in the neck with a fluorescent light tube. I was told by them that if they took over the cell house, I'd be raped and murdered.

Anybody under thirty years of age is considered a kid. If they put him in a cell with three or four other guys, he's probably raped the first night, and there's nothing anyone can do about it. There are sometimes six prisoners in a cell, and a lot of them are gang members. You got guys in there who still think they're in the sixties—they call themselves by their gang name, and they run the prison. There are some real manipulators in there. They'd talk you out of your shoes and try to kill you besides.

A lot of the inmates would be changed around in the cells, and we couldn't get their medication to them. We had heart patients who were taking nitroglycerin, and some wouldn't get theirs. It was terrible. In three months as a technician, I never took a day off, because I felt I couldn't keep up with my job if I did. I could work all the overtime I wanted, so I'd work seven days a week, ten hours a day, just so I could make sure everybody got his medicine.

There was no such thing as rehabilitation there. They throw a twenty-one-year-old in a cell where he gets his ass kicked and raped every night—that ain't no rehabilitation. When he comes out of prison, he's going to be so bitter he'll probably kill the first person he sees.

One reason they were bitter was because they would get money from their relatives and they were supposed to get commissary slips that they could buy things with for the amount of money they had on the books. Somehow they never got their stuff—shaving cream, candy, whatever it was. If you were searching their cells, as you left they could drop their TV set on the floor and say you broke it. They could sue you for that, and I've seen it done. Guards will go right down to their level, and swear right back at the prisoners. You don't do that; you go up to them and ask what their problem is. Maybe the guy just got a letter from his wife, and she wants a divorce. It's bad enough that he's in prison without something like that.

The state just doesn't seem to care. If I got killed out there, what would they do? They'd just send my family a sympathy card and hire someone else. Money is so poor, the guys they hire aren't qualified. They're alcoholics, everything, and the administration is bad. You can't really blame the inmates, and you can't blame the guards. The whole system is messed up.   ✔

POLICE OFFICER

"When we talk about policemen and money, we all know what we're talking about." So says Jack C., who, after several years on a big city police force, decided he didn't want to be a cop after all. During his career, he scorned "the high-priced secretaries with guns and uniforms" who sat around all day at headquarters—Jack opted for the street instead. There he found temptations, though he says he never succumbed to the big ones. In any case, we're no longer talking about apples off the pushcart.

If you're talking about the streets and what's available to a police officer, you name it, and it will be available, from a free cup of coffee to maybe a $100,000 bribe. It's like a friendship, no big thing, but at the same time the guy is ripping you off. Me, I appreciate freebies every now and then. But I always have to keep in mind, "Why is he buying me that meal? What will I have to do for him in return?" You never ask somebody right out, especially if he has anything to do with attorneys. He indicates to you; he doesn't actually tell you. He might say, "A friend of mine is in trouble. Can you do anything for me?" And I say, "Sure, what did he do?" He says, "Well, it's three counts of armed home invasion." And I say, "What can I do?" Let's face it, police officers have a lot of contacts. If I can help out a guy—I

160

don't care who he is, I will try to. They know that with a badge I'm in a better position than they are.

But a patrol officer can't do very much. We're limited. People ask me if I was an honest cop, and I say, "I don't know." I never was really in a position where I could steal anything of value. Taking money is not the worst thing a police officer can do. Let's say a guy takes a $5 bribe from a traffic violator. I don't think a prison sentence is appropriate, because the guy in the car does all the work. Police morals are lower than other people's. They are cynical; they may eat or drink excessively. They are not accepted by anybody. They can't disguise their job. Who wants to talk to a copper? They don't enjoy a normal life.

You're always involved in your neighborhood. Somebody does something wrong, and they call you. This kid was all beaned out on pills, and he pulled a knife on his dad. His dad called me, and I asked why didn't he call the police? He said, "Well, what are you?" And I said, "Oh, wow." Technically, you're on duty twenty-four hours a day, but if you have your pajamas on or your're putting the finishing touches on some project, who needs it?

You can tell when a cop's no good, just by talking to him a little bit. When you're on the beat together, if he wants to drive first, that means you'll know where he's at within a couple of hours. If he says, you drive first, then you know he's lazy—but he might be all right anyway. A guy who's not on the hustle doesn't move too fast and watches the street real nice. You learn that if you want to make a million dollars you can. In your two hours together, the guy says, "I have to go see somebody." You say, Okay, you're driving. So you go there, and if you don't know the guy, he's going to get out and leave you in the car, and then you look around. What is it, a grocery store? Maybe the guy's an eater, maybe he wants to pick up some cigarettes, or maybe he stops in a place where you think there might be a little gambling going on. He doesn't tip you off right away. I made it my business not to know what somebody else does—even though I really do know. I know many guys I would bet my right arm on that they were pushing dope. From what you see as their associates, you can tell right away what kind of action they're in. You have to watch the sort of position you're placing yourself in. I know the street. I know murderers, robbers, dope pushers. I see them. I know the consequences.

For those who don't want to remain honest, it's horrible. If I wanted to, I could rob any bank, sell dope to whomever I wanted to. A street police officer could commit any crime—he could be a master criminal because he's sharp. The average simple police officer knows more about life; he becomes sharper than other people who have experienced life for a lot longer. You see ripoffs constantly, and you know where society is at. My chances of getting caught are far less than yours, because I know how to do the crime. If I were to commit a burglary, I could cover up my tracks well enough that even if I got caught, it would place me in a better position. I know what to say, what not to say. I know what makes them hot.

I used to work traffic. Since leaving the police department, I've been stopped twice. I did not mention I was a former police officer, and I talked my way out of both instances. First, I got out of my car and let him sit in his, real nice. I walked up to his car with my hands showing, so he knows I'm not going to pull a gun. Start out with a smile on your face. How are you doing, officer? You know. Just be nice to the guy. That used to work on me. I agreed with him 100 percent. I said, "I didn't look at my speedometer, but if you say I was speeding, then that means I was." He was a young guy, and I told him I was listening to a real nice song on the stereo, and maybe I was speeding. I said I was very sorry. He asked to see my license, and I said, "Yes sir." He gave me a pass. I said, "Can I do anything for you—have lunch or something?" And he said, "No, we don't take money anymore," and I said, "We don't!?" and he said, "What do you mean?" and I said, "Forget about it. . . ."

Traffic fixes are very hard now. The cops are afraid. Tickets are so much bullshit anyway. I used to fix a guy if I had to write a ticket, if I needed one, and if the guy was nice. I used to put Xs on his yellow copy; one X if he was bad, and if he was a real jag off, I didn't put anything. I said to this guy who was nice, now, when you come to court—because who can remember a traffic

162

signal eight weeks ago?—you say this, and I'll say this, and the judge will throw out your ticket. In court, I glanced at his ticket and I didn't see any Xs, so I said, "Yes, your honor, I remember the case. There was a woman with a child crossing the street, and this man swerved around her. . . ." And the guy stops me, and he elbows me, and he says real loud, "There are the Xs!" I said, "Your honor, wait. Now I really remember correctly. There was a truck in the way of the stop sign." So the guy got his ticket discharged. If he's nice, he gets a pass. That's common most of the time.

Say a guy I stop doesn't have his driver's license, and I say, well, you're going to have to go to the station and post bond. So he doesn't have bond money, and we're not going to take a check. What the fuck am I going to do? Bring him in and lock him up, or tell him to go home? So I save myself an hour's hassle and him a beating in the jail lockup and a big hassle with his wife, and I send him home. Technically, you know you're wrong, but sometimes a police officer has got to be a judge.

Each period of time has a new bag. Now if a guy wants to rip off, it would be drug dealing. There are these professional people; maybe some of them are prominent. It would wreck their reputations if they got caught selling a few ounces of tea. Pushers look good all the time. They're happy, and when they look happy, something's wrong. What normal man is always happy? They don't associate too much with anybody. They're doing fantastic financially. Who's going to stop them?

My precinct captain told me never to work vice, because everybody who does gets no fucking good. I listened to him, and I stayed out of trouble. If you work vice you'll either become an alcoholic or a sex degenerate, because if you work in the gutter, some of the shit's got to rub off on you. The horrible part about it is you start thinking there's nothing wrong with it. The only people you associate with deal in drugs. You stop them. You search them. You arrest them. You see this guy's got $20,000 on him. You start putting two and two together, and you say, hey, if I'm going to make a move, I'm not going to take a $10 bribe for a traffic violation.

If I wanted to make money, it's dope. I would work real

hard—be a dynamite vice dick. Make pinches, impound the heroin I would pinch. I would hit the papers, and people would say, wow, what a man. Then I would come in with, say, a ten-pounder, which is very easy to do. You have to work on it, but it's out there. Perhaps one-hundred pounds of heroin walks by my office in a couple of hours. They bring fifty pounds at a time—it's unreal. They take it to little places and they chop it up and sell it.

The only way you're going to find where the money is, is by working hard. Then you'll get to the bigger dope pushers. When you make bigger and bigger connections, there are two things you'll find: more dope and more money. If I arrest a kid with a nickel bag of marijuana, he may have a dollar in his pocket. If I pinch a guy who's selling a half-pound of heroin, he's definitely got $5,000 in his pocket.

So you work hard and find the right guy. Investigate him thoroughly. Because you're a hard worker, you will know this guy's character. Is he a stand-up guy? What do the other coppers say about him? Is he a stool pigeon like most junkies? Coppers respect guys who are not stool pigeons. When you get the big guy, you pinch him for everything—and you let him go. I'd never pinch him again. I'd go for one score. It's the modern times. The beauty part of it is you only have to make one move and you will make that $50,000. What more do you want? So then you take all that money and you go back in the blue. You work real nice—and nobody's going to bother you for the rest of your life. ✔

PORT SECURITY GUARD

Working with members of a special police department unit, Dennis O. was a civilian on the security force for the port authority in his home town. The port consisted of docking and warehouse facilities that accommodated ships that brought goods from around the world. Although he worked for the port authority and got paid by the police department, Dennis was very much a political employee of his own alderman. It was through the alderman that he got the job and lost it.

We ran patrols twenty-four hours a day, or we were supposed to, at least. Last Christmas, they had almost 200,000 cases of whiskey in the warehouses, and the alarms were going off a lot. I really don't know how it was ripped off, except having the police out there has cut down quite a bit of the employee ripoffs. My job specifically was to check the seals on the trucks when they left the port. Certain police officers were supposed to patrol the inside perimeter, checking containers, walking through the warehouses, checking the fences and the train gates. The day shift sometimes had eight guys. There was only one car, and the rest of us were on foot.

The cops they assigned out there were part of a special operations police unit, but they were the alcoholics, those who had had heart attacks, guys who'd been shot on duty, etc. It was unbelievable. The cops were earning $18,000 a year, and I was earning about $10,000. That's why they put me and other civilians out there—it was cheaper. A patrol consisted for one police officer and one civilian. Most of the civilians were political workers—I had a precinct job, and when my security job conflicted with that, the alderman I worked for made one call and got my schedule changed to days.

It was supposed to be our job to patrol the warehouses, but most of the police officers were bombed on alcohol from the time they got there to the time they left. They would bring their own, but sometimes, if cases of booze were damaged in the warehouses, they'd get the remainders to dispose of. On several occasions, I went with this one cop, who was an alcoholic, to a gas station to get wasted.

The police who were assigned to security duty, with a few exceptions, didn't do anything. A lot of the times they'd sleep in their cars. One time an officer and I went in the one patrol car we had to get cigarettes about ten miles away. Other times we'd

165

take off and get something to eat. I don't think I worked more than two hours a day. You could get there three hours late, and nothing was said. I would go to one of the nearby suburbs, where I had a girl friend, and spend two hours of my shift at her place. Her mother would cook me tacos and all that. We just signed in and out when we left, and if the sergeant came from headquarters to our office at the port and asked where we were, the others would just say we were taking our lunch break. Although we were supposed to be making the rounds all the time, we'd just sleep in the car, or do what we wanted. A couple of officers tried to do their job, but nobody was in charge. We were all our own bosses. I didn't have to take orders from the police. My boss was the alderman.

I finally quit because I had to pay so much money to the machine. It was unbelievable. You had no choice. Otherwise, you'd lose your job. All of us civilians at the port were under a CETA program. The mayor gets these jobs and passes them out to the aldermen as political patronage jobs. This is a ripoff right there. CETA jobs are for underprivileged people in the ghetto who need jobs. There were some blacks out at the port, but they got their jobs through political channels. But I wouldn't qualify for the CETA program. You have to be poor. My parents are earning over $40,000 a year. After I was forced out because I couldn't carry an election, I went down to the CETA program headquarters, which is in an all-black neighborhood, and tried to get my job back. They just laughed and said, "We can't control that. That's controlled in City Hall." I guess the federal government doesn't know that it's getting ripped off . . . that these people who need jobs aren't getting them. ✔

POSTAL WORKER

Though she was earning $15,000 a year sorting and delivering mail, Billie P. resigned after six years to pursue a more challenging career.

166

Even though she objected to the "silly little things," like uniform regulations, she enjoyed her five-day-a-week job and was aware that she was earning more than she would for sometime in her new field. In the time she worked for the postal service, Billie saw attitudes change considerably with a resulting loss of pride among the workers. "In the last few years," she says, "training of new employees has gone right down the hill." Billie's day started at 6:30 a.m., when she began sorting the mail she would deliver that day on her suburban route.

Once every year, route inspection goes on, which means that for five straight days carriers count every piece of mail they handle and record the time it takes them to sort, deliver, and do all their tasks around the post office. Then one of those days, picked at random, your supervisor will do all this recording, then go with you on the street and make sure you deliver properly, noting the times and everything.

They always do this in the spring or summer—never in the winter when there is snow on the ground—when the mail is the lightest. Nor do they take into account factors like mail being heavier around the first of the month because of bills, or the heavy Tuesday load of news magazines, etc.

This is just to determine what a good, average route should be. They take your figures for a week, using the supervisors' as a double check, and arrive at your average. The supervisors say they want all routes to be equal and that they are equal, but that is not true. There is a great variation in routes just as there is with the people who service them. Yet, they don't want the more productive people rewarded better.

Carriers are under no incentive to do the job fast. If you get your mail delivered early, you're supposed to come back to the post office and sort your mail and do little "good housekeeping" things to keep busy. If you want to go home after you finish your rounds early, you have to take either vacation or sick leave. The union's position is "Don't do any more than you have to." They never told me to slow down, but they would quietly make sarcastic remarks to other carriers who would do their routes in less than eight hours. The whole incentive is just to hit it on the money: eight hours exactly. Then you won't be in trouble for working too fast or too slow.

I was delighted to be paid $15,000 a year, but I don't think a majority of the people who worked with me were earning their money. Nor would they be making that kind of money on the outside. A lot of them wouldn't be able to hold a job on the outside because of tardiness or absenteeism. It's very hard to get rid of a postal employee. Certain carriers were known to call in sick quite often. We got thirteen days' sick leave a year, and if you didn't take them, they accumulated. If you retired before you used your sick leave, you would get paid for it in the form of a higher pension, but you couldn't collect for it until retirement. When I resigned, I had accumulated 170 hours of sick leave, but since I wasn't one of those who used all thirteen days every year, I never got anything for it.

A few months ago, there was a team of efficiency experts brought into our post office to watch our whole operation. It was a big joke to everyone—we were wondering what they were doing standing around with clipboards and pencils in their hands. There were about six or seven men, and they worked Monday through Friday, from nine to four, and took two-hour lunches. At the end of their six weeks, they came up with one suggestion on how to make things more efficient. We tried it for two days, and after they left, we went back to the old way, because it was more efficient. Instead of using pushcarts, which are sort of like big grocery carts, to pick up our mail for sorting, they wanted us to use plastic tubs because they thought the carts cluttered the aisles and were a safety hazard. Well, we had people trying to lift tubs with sixty pounds of flats (magazines and bulky items), and they couldn't do it. Real efficient!

No one is ever satisfied with our procedures, and the upper executives are always trying to get a little more productivity out of the carriers by thinking up new ways to do things. When I started work, we sorted everything together—except bulky items that couldn't or shouldn't be folded—by street numbers. Then they decided this was not efficient, so they decided we should keep the magazines separate. People who didn't were suspended without pay for insubordination. The old way was much more efficient; we'd have most of a person's mail right in our hand. Now we have a bundle of letters in our hand, and we have to keep going back and forth into the bag to make sure we're not forgetting any magazines.

Sometimes I think they don't want to call in real efficiency experts because they would uncover what really goes on. If the executives who sit around their air-conditioned offices devising new ways of delivering the mail would come out and do it for a week, they'd quit throwing down these ridiculous ideas and leave the carriers alone. We are the ones who have to do certain tasks, and we know the best way.

When I was new on the job, I was warned to avoid a couple of superfriendly young men, because they were being watched. About a month later, they were arrested for throwing away junk mail and stealing parcels—records, tapes, books, etc. Another carrier was caught taking money out of first-class mail, like birthday cards. I've heard this was common in the inner city, but this was about all we had where I worked.

Parcels tended to get damaged a lot the way they were sorted. The baskets were put in a semicircle, and there was a conveyor belt in the middle. The clerks were supposed to walk over to the baskets and put the parcels in, but they would stand in the middle and pitch them. Sometimes that didn't matter, unless it was a heavy box of books landing on a record. I got a package myself once that I was sure was damaged by a lazy clerk throwing it, but I got no satisfaction. They just said it was too bad it had happened. Parcels are a very low priority of the postal service.

I remember getting yelled at by supervisors, when I first started working, for doing things that carriers now do and which hardly raise an eyebrow anymore. Attitudes are slipping drastically in the postal service. I don't know why, but everyone has the attitude that certain things just cannot be changed. They don't appreciate the fact that they are getting very good wages, that they have good security. I mean, even if the postal service

169

goes under by $5 billion a year, it is still going to exist. Congress or someone will bail it out. There is a lack of pride because of the attitudes of the new people who are entering.

We had some people coming in who were awfully slow to catch onto a lot of things. You'd think that with the money they pay, the postal service could be pretty choosey about whom they hire. But I guess there are enough people who don't want to make $15,000 a year if there is no challenge. That's why I quit. I felt it was not challenging enough. And, of course, it is not a high-status job and never has been. You cannot hire an eighteen-year-old and promise much of a future. Delivering mail is always going to be delivering mail. ✔

HEALTH CARE

PATHOLOGIST

Well past normal retirement age, Dr. J. likes to say he can do anything he did when he was in his twenties, except better. He watches his diet carefully, he does not smoke, and he can still run five miles. Yet Dr. J., a pathologist, has never had a physical examination except when he was in the army or applying for an insurance policy that required it. "Believe me," he says, "if it would do me any good, I would sure have one—and I can get them free." Although he believes that the average American is greatly overexamined through routine medical tests, Dr. J. speaks from a minority viewpoint in his profession. "I am speaking from a purely humanistic point of view," he says, "from the point of view of statistics. I am talking about the health and welfare—the quality of life and the longevity and happiness—of the public. Anything that takes money away from them or worries them unnecessarily has to be counterproductive."

In the late 1940s and early 1950s, the idea that we could help people by diagnosing disease in the presymptomatic stage came into being. The idea that everyone should have an annual physical started to prevail about that time. It seemed simple and logical. If we could diagnose cancer before the person became aware of it and treat it, perhaps by an early operation, we could get a better cure rate. The same was thought true for diabetes, gout, heart disease, etc. So there was a great push by insurance companies, industry, and government agencies to have people get annual physicals. Let's take the components of this examination.

First of all the . . . I won't call them patients . . . the *examinees* fill in a little form—in the larger plans it is done by a computer—on family medical history, then on their own personal history: childhood diseases, adult diseases, fractures, operations—women give their menstrual and contraception history—then the examiners go over each organ asking if examinees had had any abnormal trouble, etc., etc. Then, blood is drawn for multiple laboratory tests, then vision, hearing, height and weight, skin-fold measurement, percentage of fat, etc., are checked. Then they get a thorough physical examination by an internist, who checks blood pressure, eyes, ears, nose, mouth, throat, neck, thyroid, chest, lungs, breasts, heart, abdomen, neurological apparatus, extremities and back, skin, lymph nodes, male genitalia, the prostate, etc. Women, of course, have a pelvic examination, urine analysis, Pap smear, blood test for syphilis, a stool test for blood, and a thermography and/or mamography, etc. All of this takes from two to four hours. The cost varies. At a certain resort clinic, people spend a few days playing golf while they are having their examinations, and the exams alone cost about $400.

Despite all this, we know that people who have these so-called executive annual physicals have no better chance of avoiding disease or living longer than people who don't have them. The Kaiser Permanente Foundation in California conducted a survey that had many, many thousands of participants—people who went through these examinations over approximately a fifteen-year period. They took a similar group of people who didn't have these examinations and found that there was no difference in the death rate. In the last years, we know that these examinations have done nothing to increase longevity and nothing to decrease the death rate from important diseases. For instance, in this country, cancer of the lung and of the bowel continue to increase, as does diabetes, in terms of incidence per thousand and death rate. Of course, heart disease is the greatest killer of all. But although the incidence increased during the first two-thirds of this century, it peaked out in 1968, and only in the last ten years has there been a definite decline in the death rate from arteriosclerotic heart disease. (I make no reference to heart disease in children or congenital heart disease.) This kills approximately 984,000 people a year with its complications—through strokes, etc.—which is almost three times as many as cancer

172

kills. We will not know the cause of the slight but definite drop in heart disease for some time. We can only surmise it. Is the drop due to better treatment, better diagnosis, or because for a number of years people have been living a more rational life? Most of the people I have visited think it is the latter, that it has something to do with our changing life-style. We are exercising more; we have bicycles, tennis, running. Sports' shoes are a multimillion-dollar industry. People are eating lighter, less fatty, less sugary foods. Some companies have exercise programs. Instead of sitting around having a three-martini lunch, the executives have a three-mile lunch.

Annual physicals have made people more dependent upon the doctor and the rest of the medical profession and less dependent on their own efforts to take care of themselves. A lot of people think that by coming in on their birthday for a good, thorough examination that may cost anywhere from $90 to $400, their troubles are over. This annual examination has become a religious routine. It is like going to mass—you have to do it. Among a group of doctors I know, only four out of 150 say they have physical examinations—and not necessarily annually. We know these tests are unproductive, and we also would rather not know that we are going to die of some incurable disease ten or fifteen years from now.

Take the Pap smear. Many women get Pap smears to test for cancer of the cervix several times a year, or at least twice: once by their regular gynecologist and one at their annual examination. In the first screening among women of the middle class, the rate of abnormality is generally about five per 1,000. But in the second screening, among those whose first screening was negative, the rate falls to about .5 of 1 percent, about a 1,000 percent drop. And, of course, an abnormality does not necessarily mean a malignancy. Probably only 1 in 5 or 1 in 10 of the abnormal smears would be malignant. It depends on the population, because cancer of the cervix is a socioeconomic disease; it is most common in young prostitutes who have had many exposures and multiple partners early in life.

Now Canada, a couple of years ago, had a nationwide survey of

173

all the Pap smears—this has never been done in America. Their conclusions were that a screening should not start until the first sex act, then a second smear would be taken about a year later to allow for the possibility of a misinterpretation of the first one. Thereafter, smears would be taken every three years until age 35, then every five years till the age of 60, and, if negative, they would drop out of the program. If a woman passes the first screening, then her chances of showing up with abnormalities later are much diminished, and so forth all the way down the line.

The middle-class woman who has had two negative smears does not need these tests more than once every five years. All of our attention is focused on women who just don't get much cancer of the cervix—and the women who should get the smears aren't getting them. This is a tremendous economic wastage. It has been estimated that if every woman in the country had a Pap smear every year after the age of twenty-two, it would cost almost a billion-and-a-half dollars. Still, you have middle-class women coming in once or twice a year for a Pap smear, and they are getting ripped off at $10 or $15 each time, because they don't need them.

It takes anywhere from two to twenty years for a dysplasia, a premalignant lesion, to become malignant. So you are not about to miss it if you do a Pap smear every three years. It still catches it. There are, however, certain rare ones that are so virulent, a woman could have a Pap smear and six months later have a malignancy that was not detected, and it could start spreading right away. But those are unusual, and chances are in those cases, nothing could be done anyway.

Just a few weeks ago I met a Jewish virgin, in her fifties, who had a hysterectomy fifteen years ago. Her uterus was taken out for a benign lesion, so there was no cervix. Yet, she is still getting Pap smears twice a year. Everyone knows she hasn't a chance of getting cancer of the cervix—she doesn't have a cervix to get a cancer of. So they are doing Pap smears of her vagina. Now, this particular hospital, in fifty years, has never had a cancer of the vagina of a Jewish woman. Same with another Jewish hospital.

174

Israel has never had a cancer of the vagina in a Jewish woman—
it does not happen. This is the way the Pap smear is. It has
become, in some people's hands, a racket.

Another thing to consider is the markup—here is the real
ripoff. Doctors are eager for women to come into their offices
for Pap smears because they can give them a pelvic or physical
examination and charge them $30 or $40 for it. A Pap smear is a
two-second procedure for the doctor. He just takes the sample,
puts it on a glass slide, and has his secretary drop it in a mailing
container. At the laboratory, it is examined by a trained technician. If it is positive, the technician turns it over to a pathologist
for diagnosis. The laboratory's charge to the doctor for a Pap
smear runs from $2.50 to $4, yet the doctor will charge the
patient $10 or $15—my patients have told me this—for the test,
unless he buries it in his normal office charges. It is common for
doctors to get their take off a patient's lab work. The ethical way
to do it is for the lab to bill the patient directly, and in the case of
Pap smears, that's what the College of American Pathologists
recommends. That way there is no chance for the doctor to make
a markup as a middleman. There is no justification for that other
than greed. When the money is around, someone is going to get
it.

The routine chest X-ray on the asymptomatic person does not
have enough findings to justify the juice. There was a pulmonary
neoplasm research project in which more than 6,000 people got
chest X-rays twice a year. A similar group got no chest X-rays. At
the end of fifteen years, there were five or six cancers that had
developed in each group. The survival rate was the same in each
group, whether they had X-rays or not. That pretty well knocked
out the idea that routine chest X-rays are needed. Doctors never
have these things done routinely on themselves or their
families—but they want the patients to do it, because that is the
way to generate business.

We don't need electrocardiograms on asymptomatic persons.
You get so many abnormal EKGs you have to tell the patient
about, that you make a cardiac cripple out of a perfectly well
person. There is no point in testing and screening for leukemia

175

in the adult because, in the adult, leukemia is incurable. There is absolutely no sense in the periodic prod that everyone should get a blood test for diabetes. If the only effect uncomplicated diabetes has is a little higher than normal blood sugar, then you forget about it until the patient has symptoms. If a person feels perfectly well, he's not losing weight, he's not getting blind, he's not getting gangrene, he doesn't have kidney problems— there's no point in treating elevated blood sugar. Doing so will not prevent the complications of diabetes. You watch the person, of course, but you forget about treatment until the patient has symptoms.

A test on one executive in his early forties found that he had elevated blood urea, which is an indication that there might be something wrong with the kidneys. They then decided to do an intravenous pyelogram, in which a dye is injected into a vein, and the kidney is outlined in X-rays. This showed a deformation of the right kidney, which meant he had to have an arteriogram. In this test a tube is inserted into the main kidney artery, a dye is injected, and the blood vessels of the kidney then outline the organ precisely. Well, this showed that he had an extra artery going to that kidney, which caused the malformation, but it was a barren thing; it was not pathological, and it had no effect. So he still continued to have a slightly elevated blood urea, which a lot people who exercise heavily do have.

What developed, because he hit the site of the insertion of this big needle into his leg artery, was an aneurysm, a breaking down of the wall of the artery causing it to swell. The aneurysm ruptured, and he could have bled to death. He didn't—he went to see a vascular surgeon for treatment. All of these complications came from one finding of a slightly elevated blood urea, which never did him any harm and to him was not abnormal. This led to what is called a iatrogenic situation. When you do these tests, something is going to go wrong in a certain number of people sooner or later. They are going to get an infection, they are going to get hepatitis. In this case, he had a destruction of his artery and ended up spending several thousand dollars and had several years of extreme worry over what was going to happen.

176

Just because he took one of these tests when there was no disease present at all.

There are a number of cases where the doctor, if he knows the patient really well, doesn't tell him what he has found. He doesn't want to worry him about an abnormal finding that he knows nothing is going to come of anyway. This is a mental health consideration. Of course, you must remember the problems we have now with malpractice, with defensive medicine. If, by some grace of God—and it could happen; you can get struck with lightning—a woman should get a cancer of the cervix while she is getting follow-up examinations, and if the Pap test is left out, the doctor is afraid he might get sued. So he does a lot of tests that ordinarily would never be done just to avoid the remote possibility of a lawsuit. Some doctors have to pay as much as $24,000 every year in malpractice insurance before they make a single buck for themselves. This is because of the wave of malpractice actions, and I think in the end the consumer pays for this.

Instead of really examining the patient carefully and taking a good, careful history and physical, the doctor does a battery of automated tests on a machine. This multiphasic screening, as it is called, has never been shown to change the prognosis of anything at all. It is the prevailing mood . . . we think technology will solve all our problems. The "cancer prevention centers," like all other multiphasic screening centers, use these. People are supposed to come to these places when they don't suspect that anything is wrong with them. But they're a waste of time. They're going to do a shotgun over the whole body, and they are not going to concentrate on what your trouble is. Of a group of executives who died—all of them had regular annual or semi-annual physicals—in only 51 percent of the cases was the disease that killed the patient found on their last examination. In the other half, it wasn't found in spite of all the tests, and even if it had been found, that would not have stopped it from killing the patient.

You don't have to have a complete physical examination every year. There are a few things that you should do, but not necessarily every year. In 1976, an economist estimated that individuals could save maybe $20 billion a year by not having unnecessary examinations. Of course, people's feelings are shaped by the way their ox is gored. If there is money in it, doctors naturally are in favor of it. They will think they are being perfectly objective—they will delude themselves into thinking that they have good and sufficient reasons—but it is simply because they can make a few bucks.

There are several tests that are valuable, depending upon one's age group. A blood-pressure and an eyeball tension (to test for glaucoma) should be taken every year. The test for occult blood, bleeding anywhere in the intestinal tract, should be done annually. Every five years, a cholesterol and triglyceride test should be taken. There is a little difference of opinion, but I will concede the point that after age forty, a sigmoidoscope should be done. The proctoscope looks at the rectum; the sigmoidoscope looks at the sigmoid—it goes up ten inches—and we do find cancer with it. * This is the only test that really has to be done by a doctor, so that should bring down the cost of the whole examination to maybe $20 or $30 at the most.

Cancer of the breast is one cancer that if it is discovered early, you can get a better salvage. The routine thermogram is, I think, useless or misleading. It starts with a touch-screening first, anyway. The way to lower the rate of death from breast cancer is for women to do a self-examination every month—not every year. It has been shown that those who do this have found their cancer, and they get about a 25 percent better salvage rate than

---

Dr. William Keith C. Morgan provides this vivid description of the sigmoidoscopic examination: "After further bouts of purging accompanied by the usual electrolytic disturbances, weakness and dehydration, a hollow steel bar is thrust up the executive's fundament, to the accompaniment of grunts and wheezes from both ends, a sort of synchronous combined concerto for trumpet and oboe." "The Annual Fiasco (American Style)," The Medical Journal of Australia, Nov. 1, 1969.

178

those who do not. So, whether it is the woman herself, or a doctor, or an ardent lover who finds this early lump, this screening is of some value.

Now in all of this I am talking about the asymptomatic patient. Patients who do have symptoms are a whole different ball game. Once you have a symptom, go to the doctor for a complete physical, and don't waste any time.

You know as well as I do how certain diseases can be avoided. We know how to avoid most of heart disease: through proper food, exercise, weight control, and high blood pressure control—we know how to do that. We know how to avoid 95 percent of lung cancer: the average person who smokes heavily lives ten years shorter than the person who doesn't smoke. We know how to avoid 90 percent of cirrhosis of the liver—the percentage that is due to alcohol.

Of course, doctors are human beings, and I have seen those who believe that high cholesterol in the blood contributes to a greater degree of arteriosclerotic heart disease—yet they, themselves, are greatly overweight because of what they eat. They smoke. They will tell their patients one thing, but they, themselves, will do something else, even though a good example is more important than anything.　　　　　✔

DENTAL HYGIENIST

Lisa R. works in a dentist's office as a hygienist, cleaning patients' teeth, taking X-rays, giving fluoride treatments, and instructing patients in proper brushing and flossing of their teeth. Though dental hygienists are not allowed to diagnose dental problems, they often act in an early warning capacity and set up the dentists' patient-recall system. Sometimes they are paid a salary by the dentist; sometimes they work on commission. Because they work under the professional guidance of dentists, their own sense of professionalism is sometimes focused on the quality of the work their employers turn out—especially when dentists do the work that hygienists consider their own.

Cleaning teeth involves instrument scaling first and polishing afterwards. Patients with quite a bit of tartar need very thorough scaling. Tartar usually forms on the upper parts of the teeth first, but then it goes down beneath the gums. Tartar is more or less a mineral deposit. If it is left on, patients will eventually lose their teeth. First, the gums start to swell, then they start bleeding. The inflammation can get so bad it turns into an infection. Then the bone starts receding, and the gums start going down with it.

Hygienists have been told that we do a better job of cleaning than dentists do, because dentists are interested in doing other work, like fillings. Instead of seeing how much tartar there is, they tend to just polish the teeth. Compensation is definitely a factor in explaining why a dentist doesn't do a full job. A dentist does not earn as much when functioning as a hygienist. I can't understand why dentists clean teeth at all. If they had a hygienist, there would be two people working at the same time earning money. We'll get patients in later—those who've never had any more than polishing from their dentists—and they'll have gum problems because of that.

There is teamwork between a dentist and a hygienist. Dentists who don't have hygienists generally tend to overlook things a little bit. I sometimes wonder if the reason they don't want hygienists is because they don't want their patients to find out that they haven't been doing such a good job. That might be a terrible thing to say, but . . .

Occasionally, dentists get so involved looking for cavities that that is all they do, and they just kind of leave everything else to the hygienist. They figure that if the patient has any gum problems or disease, the hygienist will instruct them and take care of it. We are not allowed to do diagnoses of any kind, even though we are taught to. We can tip off the dentist to problems, of course, and some dentists rely on their hygienist for this. Gum disease, however, shouldn't be the responsibility of the hygienist to diagnose, but a lot of times dentists do leave it to us, because it is our major field. Still, gum disease and even cleaning the teeth are the dentist's ultimate responsibility. I think sometimes dentists don't even realize the problems because it's easy for us to clean off the tartar on the outside, and the teeth appear clean. If the dentists don't check carefully, then they don't catch these things. And, of course, a lot of time patients don't want to hear about their problems from us—they want to hear from the doctor.

Hygienists working on commission get paid per patient, so the more people you see, the more money you make. If you're the type of person who is just out to make money, you're going to get a lot of patients in, and you may have to do a haphazard job just to get them all done. I've seen cases of dental hygienists not doing such a great job in cleaning teeth, either. The commission system leads to greater abuse than the salary system, at least in theory. But it depends on the person. They gave us an ethics class at school and taught us a very high level of honesty, but a lot of people just don't want to go through with that. We're taught to do our best—it's a pride type of thing.

A lot of patients can now tell if they're getting a good job done on them or not. They're beginning to get educated. If anyone says anything, it causes a hygienist to start thinking twice. In our office, if the work is not adequate, the doctor will send the patient back and have us rescale his teeth. But patients of dentists who don't check are really just stuck, unless they go to another dentist. There's really no way they can find out. Dentists are definitely reluctant to blow the whistle on their colleagues. And if I knew of a hygienist who did sloppy work . . . well, that's a touchy thing to tell that person, "Hey, I don't think you're doing such a great job."

People getting into dentistry just to make money and saying the heck with care is a growing problem, because hygienists do make pretty good money, and I think that's becoming pretty widely known. I know there are a few people who do go into it for the money. From what I've heard, a hygienist can make anywhere from $8,000 to $27,000 a year. I don't know anyone who has made either figure, and I would say the average is maybe $14,000 or $15,000 a year. But that's not bad for a two-year investment in college.

I don't think dentists take X-rays often enough. In most offices they do it every six months, but that varies. A lot of times a patient will come in with a problem with one tooth, and we'll take only one picture, and that's it—rather than looking at other teeth, too. And if a patient doesn't want an X-ray, a lot of times we'll just skip it rather than arguing.

I've seen dentists say, when a filling is broken a little bit, "Let's not try to refill it; let's just crown it." This costs the patient more, but in the long run, a crown is more durable. Many times when silver is adequate, like when there's a small section of a tooth broken, I've seen doctors talking the patient into getting a gold crown. There are also cases, especially when the patient can afford it, where it's better to choose gold. This is true when the teeth are deteriorating and are too brittle to hold silver.

There are cases where dentists try to push people too soon—not just into gold—but into caps, in general. A lot of it is just out of a cosmetic type of reasoning. Maybe it's a little bit of both the patient's wanting it and dentist persuading them. I saw a case where a child chipped a portion of a front tooth—they do have plastic fillings that are white and don't show—and the dentist talked the parents into having it capped instead, which involved cutting down the tooth.

There's a big difference in the money a dentist will charge for a gold crown or a cap—maybe $100 to $135—over a silver filling. It takes a little bit longer to do crown work, but per hour they still make more money off a crown. That's why they push people into crowns—they make more money. This is pretty widespread. I know there are quite a few dentists who, if they could, would go strictly into crown and bridgework.

Of course, quite a bit of dentistry is cosmetic in nature, and a lot of the motivation for capping comes from the patients themselves. The dentists, however, don't put up any resistance to it. They will give you what you want, except for extractions.

When people need false teeth, they will often try to bypass

dentists and go right to the labs. The labs know how to make them, but they don't know how to do all the preliminary work. I knew a neighbor who went to a lab and had some false teeth made. They didn't fit her at all, and, of course, the lab wouldn't do anything about it. They didn't even know how to make alterations afterward. But this is just ignorance on the part of people who don't realize that dentists are trained for this work, and the labs are not.

In some cases, doctors will try to help out patients on the insurance claim by saying something "really wasn't cosmetic," that they had to cap a tooth because they couldn't keep the filling in. Dentists try to side with the patient. Sometimes, patients will come in and say, "I want you to change your records and say I had this extracted last month instead of several years ago," but the dentists say "no," because if the insurance companies ever found out, it would put us in a lot of trouble. Dentists, however, do bend the rules a little bit.

We have a few deadbeats who go from dentist to dentist and run up a small bill at each one. Sometimes, they'll call in asking us to send their records or X-rays to another dentist. Our receptionist will call the new dentist and warn the office if the people are delinquent in their account with us. We try to stay one step ahead of them. ✔

MEDICAL SOCIAL WORKER

Divorced herself and working as a medical social worker in counseling therapy, Bonnie H. has dealt with vulnerability personally and in her clients. In both cases, she urges caution wherever sex is offered as part of the healing process.

A client generally comes to a counselor in a vulnerable condition and depends on the counselor's professionality in providing emotional support. Though professionality is usually maintained, I've heard of situations in which a male counselor offers to go beyond a typical relationship to meet a female client's affectional or sexual needs—and he justifies it as a necessary way of helping her.

This happens all the time to women going through a divorce, where their lawyers will have made advances to them. So this is a problem not just in counseling, but anywhere a man or woman is vulnerable and is dependent on a professional to do a job. Of course, a counselor has greater potential for doing emotional damage to a person, because there is an emotional tie there in the first place.

I feel, as a counselor, that it's never acceptable to get sexually involved with a client, although people in my field differ on that question. You must maintain your objectivity, and obviously you can't do that if you're involved with somebody. I've never heard of cases where a woman patient has benefited from sex with her counselor—but some professionals would probably disagree with me.

Unless a patient moves away from fantasy and handles reality, she or he doesn't grow. Even though there is a dependency implied in the whole counseling relationship, its purpose is to help the patient become independent. The conflict in my mind is that having sex with patients does not encourage their becoming independent. Dependency is a role one plays to get a lot of attention. Counselors in private practice are making money hand over fist; there's absolutely no shortage of clients. If they lose one today, it makes no difference. There are always ten more on the waiting list.

The biggest ripoff in the field of counseling is the wide variety of charges. I don't know what a fair charge is—it probably varies depending on the number of degrees you have after your name. If psychiatrists want $50 or $60 an hour, psychotherapists want $40, and psychiatric social workers want $25 or $30. But I am not convinced that having all those degrees gives you a better capability of helping people with their problems. ✔

184

INSTITUTIONAL HEALTH CARE

PSYCHIATRIC NURSE

"No one cares about crazy people unless they happen to have one in the family," says Susan B., a psychiatric nurse who worked in an intermediate care facility that houses about 160 chronic mental patients. Her job was attending to the welfare of the patients, most of whom were elderly and poor, and seeing that their medical, dietetic, and hygienic needs were taken care of. She has since joined another institution but says, in anger and despair, that conditions in mental care facilities "haven't changed much since the days of Dorothea Dix." Several years ago, the state began closing the mental wards in its big hospitals and setting up a program whereby mental patients would be treated in smaller facilities in established communities. The theory was that they would get less institutional treatment and better therapy, thereby hastening their rehabilitation and return to the community. Presumably, the patients were already integrated into the community. Unfortunately, says Susan, this didn't happen in the case of her patients, 95 percent of whom were burned-out schizophrenics. The privately owned, though state-funded, institutions are "just warehousing operations run by big rip-off artists." Her facility was a cockroach-ridden former hotel with no courtyard in a decaying urban neighborhood. "If the rest of the community knew what these places were like," she says, "if they spent a week in one, maybe things would be different. As far as nursing services go, the only thing we can do is try to give the patients a little love—that's all there is. They're very affectionate people, and some are very intelligent. They can be very rewarding to work with. But the people who exploit them, like the owners of these halfway houses, are absolutely going to go to hell."

The care facility I worked in before was run by a corporation; none of us knew the names of the owners. They tried to cut their costs to the bone. Some of the beds didn't have any sheets;

185

unless the patients could afford their own, they slept on mattresses. The place was very dirty, and the people lived in squalor. There were great big roaches all around. The kitchen help, which was untrained, would use their hands for things you shouldn't. The laundry would come back dirtier than when you sent it out. I had a very hard time giving treatment, because there were never clean towels or anything you'd want to use on yourself. I used to have to bring my own supplies—Band-Aids, cotton balls, paper towels, stethoscope, etc., because I got tired of not having them.

The place did not meet minimum state standards and was therefore illegally operated. They had building code violations, like some of the toilets were stopped up, and in six months they never had a fire drill. It got so cold in the winter—and I don't mean chilly—there was frost in some of the patients' rooms. I threatened to call the board of health. I had to move some of the patients downstairs every night for warmth. The administrator, who was also one of the owners, used to turn down the heat before he left at night to save money.

We violated the law in terms of staffing. We were supposed to have nurses in charge who had special knowledge in pharmacology and medication. There was also supposed to be a male on the staff at night for obvious reasons. The director of nursing would often have someone punch her in on the time clock when she wasn't there. On occasion, there would be 160 crazy people in the building with one semiliterate woman—an untrained nurse's aide they hired off the street—in charge.

One morning after it snowed, I was the only one who showed up for work. There were no aides, kitchen staff, maids, nobody. So I called the director and said she had better get over there because I quit. When she arrived, she discovered that most of the other staff people had been punched in by the night staff. They were all pissed at me, but nobody got fired, just warning letters. If you got three warning letters in one month, they'd fire you. If you didn't get three, nothing would happen, and the next month you'd start over with a clean slate.

State law requires that the patients get therapy. But they

didn't, and the state knew they didn't get it, and it did nothing about enforcing its own laws. The state specifies that patients will get social rehabilitation, such as relearning social skills. We had the staff, but they were just kids who had the title but no training in either psychology or sociology. If they had a degree, it would be in something like music. Many of them were lovely, well-meaning people; they just had no training. They didn't stay very long, so the patients didn't have any continuity of care.

Our psychiatrist—we just had one for 160 patients—hadn't finished her residency. She came in one day a week and spent a few minutes with each patient. For therapy, if she heard they'd caused any disruption, she would threaten them. She used to put the patients on tremendous amounts of psychotropic drugs to quiet them. In about 25 percent of the cases, the drugs can have very serious side effects, sometimes fatal.

Our doctor, who also came only once a week, was an out-and-out quack. The nurses got to the point where they would come right out and say so. He was an over-the-hill doctor who was a friend of the owner. I had a patient with pulmonary embolism and said I was going to transfer her to the hospital. Our doctor said, "Well, who's paying for it?" I told him I really didn't know, but it wasn't going to be him, and it wasn't going to be me, so I didn't think he should worry about it.

The narcotics cabinet didn't have a lock on it, and there wasn't any control over the tranquilizers. We had a lot of them. Because the patient's were defenseless, it was easy for the nurses to give them a pill, write on their charts that they had given them a controlled substance, then keep the downer for themselves. We had one nurse who was a junkie. She took all the controlled substances for herself exactly that way. Another nurse was caught after she passed out in the medicine room.

Drug addiction is an occupational hazard in nursing, but not as much as it is for doctors. (I've seen doctor junkies in hospitals where there was a large staff. They have stressful jobs, and it's easy for them to get drugs by writing themselves a prescription anytime they want to. Drug companies give them samples. I had a friend, a medical student, who overdosed. They found multi-

187

ple vials of morphine in his refrigerator when they discovered his body. Drugs are a major occupational problem.)

The owners were disgusting the way they preyed on one of the most defenseless elements of society. One Sunday morning I came in, and there were no insulin syringes, and this was a life-or-death situation, because I had twenty-one diabetics. I called the owner at his home in the suburbs, and he asked how long the diabetics could live without insulin. I said I'd have them go without breakfast, but I'd need the syringes within a couple of hours. He said he didn't think he could get them that fast, so I said, well, I'm going to take the patients and their charts over to the hospital emergency room, where there's a $30 minimum fee, and that's going to cost you several hundred dollars. Well, he called another nursing home he owned right away and had them send some syringes over from there. But running out of syringes is being more than miserly.

I had another critically ill patient with chronic mastoiditis, which is an infection of the middle ear and very painful. He'd walk around in such pain, he'd shake his head back and forth and moan. I told the owner that this man should go to a real doctor, not our quack, who didn't know what he was doing. And the owner said, "Aw, the guy's just crazy." After about a month of hassling, I finally threatened to call the board of health if he didn't do something about it, and so then he sent him to a clinic. In some cases, the board of health might help you, but, hell, you have to call them one-hundred times a day. It's like dealing with landlords.

Once, when the owner wasn't around, I sent an old lady to the hospital who had fallen down. She was hemorrhaging on the brain. He even screamed about that.

He did all his business with one pharmacy, a cut-rate drug outfit. I know he had to pay a fine of thousands of dollars, which was peanuts to him, for illegal kickbacks from the pharmacy. Afterwards, he was laughing about it, because he considered it a light slap, and he went right back to doing the same thing.

The owners were not around much. One of them would come in just once a week, on trust fund day. After medical expenses

188

were deducted, patients on disability or welfare had a little spending money left over, a few dollars that the owner would disburse to them one day a week. If he were busy and didn't come in, the patients couldn't get their money, and he would say that was tough.

The people in the neighborhood knew when trust fund day was, and they'd hang around outside and trick the patients out of their money. Sometimes, they'd just snatch a handbag and run. The kids threw rocks at the patients and yelled at them and teased them. There was a big saloon right across the street that closed at 4 a.m., and the patrons would hang around until my patients went out in the morning and snatch their purses. These folks are slow; there's nothing they can do about it. I'd report this sort of thing constantly, but the cops would come, make a report, and leave. One lady's purse was snatched, and I asked her what was in it. She said she had three Kennedy half-dollars, a peppermint stick, and a letter from her mother. Now what the hell are the cops going to do about that, laugh? But those things are important if that's all you have in the world.

The merchants will rip them off, too. These patients want to go out—they should go out—on a nice day, maybe to go down to the corner and buy some pop. They'll give the merchant a $5 bill, and the guy will give them change for $1. When they protest, the guy will say, go on, get out of here. You're crazy.

The point of having them in these facilities rather than state hospitals was to integrate them back into ordinary life. It isn't happening. Most neighborhoods have strong negative feelings against these centers, and those areas that have it more together won't allow that zoning. That's why, I'm sure, there are so many in run-down neighborhoods like ours.

We've had open houses, and they were very depressing, because just a handful of patients would get visitors. A lot of them have family nearby but rarely get visits from them. Sometimes the families, who are usually very poor, give up on them. Some of these patients were in state hospitals for twenty years, and they just don't get any better. Still, for most of them, it means a lot to have visitors. Many of them are very affectionate. They talk about their families all the time. Some of them will carry Christmas cards around all year in their handbags.

At Christmas, the nurses all pitched in and bought candy so we could give the patients a little treat. We wrapped the pieces individually—the center didn't have anything like that for them. The budget never even called for dessert, so the director of nursing would buy several gallons of ice cream once a month and bring it down on a Sunday. That may not sound like much, but the patients don't get much out of life.

We asked one of the owners if the patients could have a turkey dinner for Christmas, and he said, no, it would be too expensive. We had a staff meeting, and I said, look, my friend and I will buy a fucking turkey, and we'll all pitch in, and all you have to do is have your kitchen help cook it. He said, no, that was too much work for the kitchen help, and he wasn't going to have a turkey, because the patients didn't need it.

This work is frustrating if you're a moral person. You say to yourself, "I should get out and into a different line of work," but then you look at your patients and ask yourself, "What about them?"

Although Susan's patients all had chronic mental conditions, occasional breakdowns would require their being sent to a state hospital dealing with acute cases. Though it was not part of her job, she stayed in personal touch with them.

When my patients were transferred I've gone out to the hospital to take them their personal articles. The hospital doesn't like them to have anything there, and they'll keep them there up to three weeks in the clothes they were admitted in. I would try to take them a change of clothes, and the hospital people would say, no, they can wash out what they have on. But if they have psycho-motor retardation, they don't do it, and after awhile they start to stink. Their cleanliness is left up to them.

When they admitted another one of my patients, a doctor told him he had a right to refuse medication, which is true, even for a mental patient confined against his will. The next day, a nurse was going to give him some medication, which he refused, so she called three guards, and they held him down and administered it. He had a severe allergy to the medicine and was paralyzed for a time. When they saw what happened, they immediately discharged him. He said, "I can't go any place, because I'm sick and don't have any money and can't walk." Well, they discharged him anyway, in that condition, and acted as if it was something he should be grateful for.

NURSE'S AIDE

The patients' regimen was determined by our schedule. Food came to the rooms at 7:20 a.m., which meant each of us had to get our twenty-five patients propped up, wash their faces, try to brush their teeth, and get them ready for their trays. At least half of them couldn't feed themselves. We were allowed a half-hour to feed them, so we'd try to get a few sips of liquid and a little bit of cereal down them, then move onto the next person.

After breakfast, we tried to clean up the patients, tidy up their hair, put on a new nightgown (once a month we would shave the men), and check to see which beds were unbearable. When a patient fouled a bed, we were not allowed to change the sheets. The owners said absolutely no more than two sheets per patient a week. This was insane. You don't have time to take them to the toilet, and if they can't walk, they're going to dirty their beds. To make them sit there in their own filth is incredible. Most of us just went ahead and changed them, and that's why we had such a large staff turnover. Most of the patients fouled their beds frequently; we would take the bottom sheet off and put the top sheet, which was already dirty, on the bottom.

When patients became confused or troublesome, rather than talking to them or giving them physical therapy—of which we had none—they were strapped into orthopedic chairs. It's generally acknowledged that once you do this to them, you can

191

expect them to die within six months. When we didn't have enough orthopedic chairs, we tied them into the chairs next to their beds. Since these people could not use the toilet facilities, we put two layers of Pampers underneath them. They were expected to relieve themselves in the chairs.

We only had two large bathrooms with tubs for nonambulatory patients. Even with these, you needed a strong person to get them in. There were no male orderlies on the staff, and you couldn't waste the time to get two or three people to get the patients in the tub, so we'd just sort of wipe them off in their beds. On the average each patient got one bath a week. There's only so much time you could give each of your twenty-five patients in a day.

At noon they had lunch, and again we didn't have enough time to feed them. As for the food program—there wasn't any. All patients, regardless of their physical condition and whether they were constipated or not, were required to take a strong dose of laxative. People who sit for long periods of time tend to become constipated, so we'd just jam those laxatives down them. The diet was chiefly mashed potatoes, gruel, and sometimes eggs, which were powdered, I think. There were no such things as fresh fruit or fresh meat. They would say, "Well, those old people can't chew anyway, and we don't have time to put their dentures in," so they never got anything that wasn't liquefied or mashed. It wasn't a balanced diet; it was mostly starch. A typical dinner menu was creamed frozen spinach, mashed potatoes, and gelatin. Occasionally, they served cottage cheese or hamburger—the cheap kind that was hard to chew. They gave them no fruit juice or vitamins.

When the nurses were understaffed—which was most of the time—they would put prescribed medications in little cups and tell us to distribute them on a tray, even though by law we weren't authorized to dispense medicine. The head nurse, who was in charge of the nursing home, was an alcoholic. Most of the time she was on duty, she was unfit, falling down in corridors. She had to report to the accountant, who came twice a month to check the books.

192

One woman patient was in the terminal stages of syphilis—her mind was really gone. One day, I saw a totally uneducated and untrained aide slapping her around, and I reported it to the head nurse. She told me to shut my mouth. Later, when I was depositing dirty linens, the aide came at me with a straight-edge razor. The administration didn't want to know about any of the horrible things that happened.

The nursing home had to meet minimum state requirements. One was that each patient's attending physician had to visit the home once a month. They'd walk in and cluck to the nurses; occasionally they'd bring them chocolates. Then they'd pick up one chart after another and ask, "Are they having regular bowel movements?" Well, of course they were having regular bowel movements—everyone was on laxatives. They'd say, "Fine, dearie, keep up the good work," and then leave. Very seldom did a doctor ever go see the patient, most of whom were so senile they didn't even know who the doctors were.

Some of the patients had been there ten years. Many of them were dear, sweet people, and most of them had their minds to a great degree, even though they were forgetful. They had no contact with humans; they sat in their chairs or beds and didn't communicate at all. There were no recreational facilities, except for a television that was out of order 30 percent of the time. Once they are confined to these sort of surroundings, they go into oblivion very fast.

Their next of kin were never aware of any of this, I'm sure, because they never bothered to visit, even though most of them lived in the area. The only family member I ever saw there—and we had more than 200 patients in the home—was one man's wife. The patients were 100 percent neglected. Not even any service organizations came to visit on a regular basis. It's funny . . . those patients who could understand and communicate with you were so thankful you were sitting there talking with them for five minutes—I'm sure it never entered their minds to complain.

We had a great little old lady who was just like a mischievous kid. The nurses got so fed up they tied her in a chair, but she'd

193

pull herself along the walking bars of the corridor and visit the other patients. In a short period of time, a week or so, she became more and more quiet. I'm sure they were tranquilizing her. Finally, I could hardly get her out of bed. She died shortly afterward. They all do . . .

There's a sort of graveyard humor that's typical in all medicine, but at this nursing home it was gross. If someone were sitting and choking on saliva, they'd say, "Well, he was a pain in the ass anyway, so it's no big loss." They didn't care. That nursing home was just a final warehouse. You'd walk into the place, and all you'd smell was death. There was no hope for those people. The whole attitude of the medical care profession, the attitude a patient in a nursing home has, is ultimately the difference between their living and dying. There's nothing in the structure of a nursing home that promises the difference between the two.   ✔

AMBULANCE DRIVER

Trained as an emergency medical technician, Barrett T. has worked for three private ambulance companies as a driver and attendant. One of them was well run; the other two were not. The attitude of his last employer, says Barrett, was probably best summed up by a supervisor who told him, "You are not paid to care for the patient—you are paid to make runs."

Some outfits, like two of the ones I worked for, will advertise themselves as ambulance services, when all they provide in actuality is a van with a stretcher, an oxygen tank, and maybe some sheets. Sometimes we didn't even have that, and some of the vehicles were unsafe. There was no way they were meeting the standards the city required of private ambulances.* These are companies listed in the telephone book, and their vehicles are seen every day screaming up and down city streets. It's the old meat-packer bit: Somebody is hurt or feeling pain, and you just grab them, throw them in the back of the van, and go pedal-to-the-metal with lights and sirens to the nearest hospital.

Once, we got a call for a patient who was listed as unconscious and unresponsive. When we got to her apartment, my buddy immediately started doing one-person cardiopulmonary resuscitation, and I called the fire department paramedics. We had been sent out in an old beater that barely made it out of the garage. It had a stretcher, a couple of oxygen bottles, and some sheets. The fire department responded and brought up an ampul bag—it's like a little football with an oxygen mask on it; you squeeze the football container to deliver oxygen to the patient. They had that; we didn't. They helped us administer CPR and get the old lady down to our vehicle. They said that since we were the first on the scene and since the patient had requested a hospital out of her district, we would be the ones who took her in. This was a definite heart attack. And even though we didn't have adequate equipment, they were almost in the same situation we were in. We asked our dispatcher to phone ahead and alert the hospital's emergency room, and when we got there, there was just one nurse, who said: "Oh, I think Dr. So-and-so is in such-and-such a place. I'll see if I can get him." It took them about ten minutes to get all their people together.

---

*The city in which Barrett worked had two levels of private ambulance licensing. "Ambulances" carried basic equipment, including oxygen, and were operated by emergency medical technicians. "Mobil intensive care units" carried more sophisticated equipment, including telemetry, and were operated by paramedics, who have a higher degree of medical training. The city's regulations incorporated the standards set by federal and state authorities and professional medical groups. The fire department also operated both ambulances and mobile intensive care units.

Another time I remember when we started out on our shift we had to holler and scream at the dispatcher to get even an oxygen bottle in the van. These vehicles, of course, get constant use and abuse, maybe 100,000 miles a year of panic braking, rapid starting and stopping, ripping around corners, bouncing over chuckholes—you name it, and they've been through it. They have to have the vehicles inspected by the city, but after they've passed that, they can let them fall apart. We were expected to make runs in one junker that had no emergency lights, the brakes were going out, and the siren and horn were missing. In my mind, this made us somewhat worse than an average taxicab.

Of course, a lot of our work was just basic transfer. An indigent man will check into his local emergency room, and the hospital finds that he doesn't have any hospitalization insurance and he's on public aid, so they don't have any room for him. So, they'll call us and have us take him over to the municipal hospital. A lot of times, the patients are fully ambulatory. Maybe Mama brings her little one in, and the ER (emergency room) finds nothing seriously wrong, but they can't have her around because Mama does not have any money. If Mama had five bucks, she could take a taxi. Well, she doesn't have five bucks, but she does have a public aid green card, so, okay, call Fly-by-Night Ambulance Service—they will take her.

The people in the ER will fill out this form required by the public aid people, and they will check two boxes: Yes, the patient was bed-ridden, and yes, any other means of transportation would have harmed the patient's health. Our office told us that if the hospital staff wouldn't check those boxes, we were to hand the form back to them and tell them they didn't need an ambulance. In effect, we were telling them to falsify the reports. We would then submit these forms to public aid for reimbursement. It was a great ripoff of taxpayers' dollars.

We were actually put in the role of salesmen to get this sort of business for the company. They called all the crew together and said, "You talk to so-and-so at such-and-such a nursing home, and you talk to so-and-so at this hospital and tell them if they make so many patient calls to us, we will make it

196

worth their while." We were also supposed to make these contacts whenever we made actual working trips. After these contacts threw a certain amount of business our way, a representative of the company would go out with a few fives and tens and pay them off. "You sent us so many calls that we can put into public aid, to Medicare, and stuff like that—okay, you get like five bucks a head." We were under great pressure to hustle business.

Some smaller hospitals that operate on the fringes, the standing story goes, you wouldn't take your dying dog to. It takes them awhile to get their act together. Once we brought a patient in to an ER, and there was another patient lying there the fire department had brought in fifteen minutes earlier. The ER wasn't responding well, so I ended up doing CPR on him, and my buddy had to run out to our ambulance to get an ampul bag, because the ER didn't have one. When I am rushing a patient to a hospital, I mentally review comments I've heard from others in my field and my own experience, and from that I know which hospitals to avoid.

Many times we wondered about the qualifications of the dispatcher. We knew for a fact he was not medically trained, and he didn't even know the city very well. In some cases, his diagnosis would be grossly inflated, and other times it might be grossly understated, and the patient really required a mobile intensive care unit manned by paramedics. He would blow things out of proportions because he wanted us to make time. We never saw the owner, and everything about him was very secretive. I don't know how they got away with a lot of the stuff they did, unless they knew somebody and were paying him under the table. Those of us who asked questions got stomped on with, "Hey, what are you sweating it for? This is the way things are done around here." ✔

CONSUMER ADVOCATE,
HEALTH MAINTENANCE ORGANIZATION

Health maintenance organizations are a fairly recent medical innovation that provide comprehensive medical care and hospitalization for members at fixed rates. Eleanor G. works for an HMO as a consumer advocate, seeing that members get the services to which they are entitled.

One health maintenance organization in our area—they're no longer in existence—knew that when you have an unsophisticated clientele, you can cut corners and provide minimal and shoddy care. They made sure their patients bought lots of glasses, had lots of dental work done, and got lots of prescription drugs. Although it was a nonprofit corporation, the owners and trustees of the plan owned the optical shop, the drugstore, the X-ray facility, and so on. This really was a conflict of interest.

They didn't do physical examinations regularly on people who may have had a lot of things wrong with them and who probably should have had thorough checkups. People getting mental health treatment would be kind of warehoused in that department and never brought back for medical care, even though they had organic illnesses. They were mental health cases, and that's where they stayed. It was an assembly-line treatment of patients.

I'm preparing a list comparing the prices between generic drugs and those with brand names for a lot of common prescriptions. Our physicians almost never have that information, unless they buy prescriptions for themselves. They don't have the foggiest notion of what the brand names cost versus the generic. Their reference book, of course, is put out by the drug companies. ✔

INSURANCE

INSURANCE SALESMAN

In the years Aaron B. has been selling life insurance as a general agent of an insurance company, he, like his colleagues, has considered his primary mission to be selling himself. "Anything that comes out later—anything that is written on an application," he says, "is just an afterthought." In other words, being nice to people is where his money comes from. The people, in his particular situation, are blue-collar families, where he goes into homes on "a one-shot basis, and you make the sale the first time or forget it." Although insurance salesmen, says Aaron, do not flat-out lie to their prospective clients, they do leave substantial room for misunderstanding.

I have gone into homes of people that I am approaching about insurance, and I have seen policies they have. Comparing them to what they think they have, there's a world of difference. I can see where the misrepresentation comes in. Their policy is as good as the paper it is written on, but the difference lies in the presentation that the agents make when they originally sell them. A life insurance policy can be sold as many different things other than what it really is. And those sales pitches that have been proved to be the very best are just plain larcenous. The companies never encourage using them, but if you put ten salesmen in a room, the same common denominator will keep popping up: Every one of them is going to use the same type of misleading information in the pitch. Most agents, however, will never lie to prospective clients, because there is a satisfaction in knowing that you did not really misrepresent—you just made the people misunderstand. And I'm as guilty as all the rest.

One kind of policy I personally use is a twenty-one-year life insurance policy called a twenty-one-year payback. Let's say you are putting in $500 per year. At the end of twenty-one years you

199

have two options: You could take back every penny you ever put in—at that rate you'd have $10,500 coming back—but, of course, you would lose the insurance if you took the money. Or you could take a paid-up insurance. Let's say the initial coverage of the policy was $10,000—at the end of twenty-one years, it would be a paid-for life insurance of $20,500. Yet, as it is usually presented by the agent, customers think that they have $20,500 *cash* coming back, that they have doubled their money. In other words, the agent has misled them into believing that they could cash it in for $20,000, when, in fact, it is only a $20,000 *policy on their life*. Agents are using such terms as *cash value* instead of *cash*, or they'll use the term *estate* after the twenty-first year: "This is your estate," when actually the estate combines cash money with insurance.

I go into many homes, and the person will pull out a policy and say, "Well, this is not life insurance; it is a retirement policy," and they think it's going to give them back much more than they put into it. Ninety percent of these policies I've seen—whether they're from top-name companies or newer ones—are going to pay less than the person has paid in. They may have deposited $10,000 up until age sixty-five, at which time they believe they are going to get back possibly $30,000 or $40,000 in cash. In reality, they may get back less than they've paid in. From what the agent tells them, they are assuming the agent's talking about $30,000 or $40,000 in cash, instead of that amount of insurance on their life.

On that twenty-one-year payback, if a person asks me, "You mean I can take $20,500 cash after twenty-one years?" I kind of break out in a cold sweat. I try to shoot them more curves and avoid giving them a direct answer. If it eventually comes down to that, I will give a direct answer, and I think most agents will. But 99 percent of the people are not going to put you in that position, because they don't read the fine print.

On this policy, there is a feature that allows parties to quit paying at the end of eleven years and have the policy paid for. Naturally, since they didn't meet the full twenty-one-year requirement, they would have a lesser amount of cash coming back, or less paid-up insurance. But in the pitch, the agent will often present it as a retirement, and that in eleven years, the customer has a finished plan and can start drawing a monthly income. This is a little misleading.

Your two basic life insurance policies are whole life and term. Whole life maintains a cash value, whereas term insures you for a certain amount over a certain period of time, then it's gone. Agents will tell you they own term insurance. It's about the only thing they will buy, because whole life is a ripoff. What is better, to pay less or pay more? At a given age, a term policy might cost you $2 per thousand dollars of insurance, while a whole life might cost you $10. You are not going to get back that $8 difference unless you live to a very old age. The only benefit whole life has is that it is a forced savings. For the extra $8 a year people are paying, they might possibly get $4 of that back, but look what inflation does to that money they're putting into whole life. Even if inflation were nil, I definitely would not buy whole life. Selling it, however, is another thing.

Companies make whole life more desirable for agents to sell. You have to realize it is the company that prospers every time a whole life policy is sold. Because it is more expensive, the company has more money to play with, and they reward the agents with a higher rate of commission than they would receive on a term policy. So whole life is exactly what salesmen try to sell.

Of course, a lot of term insurance is sold through banks or savings and loans for specific purposes: mortgage insurance, any type of credit purchase, like when you buy a car. They'll usually try to sell term insurance to go with these so that in the event of your death, your mortgage is paid off, etc.

But I can't honestly recall the last time I wrote a term policy as straight term insurance. I would imagine that for every million dollars in premiums our company writes, I would be surprised if more than $25,000 of that was for term insurance. It just isn't written. Invariably, the agents will pitch people into whole life, because naturally they want to make a higher commission.

Lots of times, as a compromise, we will write a whole life and combine it with a little bit of term. Let's say you need $30,000 as mortgage insurance. I'll write $15,000 whole life and add on $15,000 in term as a rider. You have a $30,000 policy that eventually decreases to $15,000, and it has a cash value. Look how fantastic this deal is; it's not like regular term. Yet, you are paying two, three, possibly four times more for it than you should.

I can take damned near all life insurance other than term and pitch it as a retirement income. You can do this with any life insurance that has any form of cash value, even if people only have a 10 percent return on the premiums they paid. This is where customers often confuse the insurance value with the cash value. But even if they took it to court after twenty years, saying this is not what they were led to believe, the companies' out is this: The customers have had a document in their hands for a long time that explains everything fully, so it's their own damned fault if they didn't read the fine print. In very few of these cases does anything come out to the benefit of the policyholder. People should forget about all of the "retirement policies" and take care of retirement on their own. Just buy term for their specific needs.

When I am pitching, if people want term coverage—if they know what they are talking about—I am not going to mislead them any. I will write it for them. However, I do at least try to talk them into carrying enough insurance for burial and funeral expenses. In that case, a $5,000 whole-life policy that is paid up by age sixty-five is a good idea.

The annuity, which is a retirement type of policy, has its advantages, and it's basically an honest plan. There's not too much room for larceny in them, except in misquoting the rates. You pay a premium, say $500 a year, just like an insurance policy. A table shows you what you will have back at the end of each policy year. The break-even point on an annuity is usually about seven to ten years. That means if you only kept it five years, you'd lose; you'd get less back than you put in. Like I say, things like this are not that well-pointed-out in most cases.

One common practice of agents is to come into your house with a straight annuity, and say, "We are currently paying 7½ percent," then show you projections, based on 7½ percent, of how much money you'll get at age sixty-five, either per month or in a lump sum. It will say the policy is guaranteed to pay no lower than, say, 4 percent even if the bottom drops out of the economy. All the charts the company gives the agents to work with are based on the 7½ percent figure, but I would be damned surprised if they ever paid over the minimum guaranteed. The companies are going to put all the liability on the agent that they possibly can. So the brochure will say down at the bottom, "These figures are computed at 7½ percent." It doesn't say why 7½ percent; it just leaves it to the agent to say in the pitch, "Currently, we are paying 7½ percent." It's an outright lie. They just fish that out of the air.

The ones who would really benefit from annuities are those who want to hide money. If people put money in the bank toward retirement, they will pay taxes on their interest. But an annuity is between you and the insurance company, and it's left to the responsibility of the applicant to pay taxes or not. This has even been suggested to me by tax people to use in my pitch.

Because of the scare lately, a lot of companies are writing cancer policies like hotcakes. These are lopsided health policies—straight indemnity—that pay only if your illness is diagnosed as cancer. Naturally, the benefits are very small. Statistically, one out of four people will come down with cancer, which would mean 25 percent of the policyholders, if they kept the policy throughout their lifetime. But we know that eight years is the average life span of such a policy, so we're pretty safe in writing them.

I've seen claims come in where bills have gone into the tens of thousands of dollars, and the settlements have gone out for two or three thousand. Insurance is not total reimbursement, and people are not fully informed of this. Let's say a policy is for $25,000 in total coverage. If an agent wanted to do a half-assed job, and get out of there with a sale, he could show the people that the policy will pay up to $15,000 for hospital rooms—without going into detail that that is only at the rate of $25 a day. Well, everyone knows you are going to spend over $100 a day now in a hospital. If they press you on the $25 figure, you can side-step this by telling them that their group insurance plans will take care of the difference—this is just a little extra. Of course, the surgery schedule will be like those in all accident or health indemnity policies. They stick to an unrealistically low schedule with no regard for prevailing market rates. You may have surgery that runs into thousands of dollars, and according to the schedule, it's only worth $250.

Newspapers and other organizations used to offer gimmicky little accidental death policies. I have had people tell me they only pay $20 a year, and they'll collect $10,000 if they're killed on an expressway in a car. What percentage of the population does this happen to? Kind of small. I've even seen people carry policies on steamship accidents. It's unreal.

There are lots of family plans in life insurance that appear to be low cost—whole-life policies that cover wife and children with minimal insurance. By the time the policy is packaged as one plan, the people are paying one hell of a lot more money than they would if they bought separate policies. I have found this to be true in every packaging system I have run into.

Some companies will use endorsements of unions, churches, veterans organizations, etc., to sell insurance. The people will assume it's being sold through their church, or whatever, and they will go ahead and hear the person out and buy the policy from him. They assume, what could possibly be wrong with it? It's pitched to them as if they were getting a break, because they are a member of a large group. It turns out to be something like one of those lopsided cancer policies.

One group packages a plan that incorporates life insurance for the whole family, disability income, and all kinds of options. They also have a home, and people are told that if they die, their children will at least be well taken care of in the home. However, one clause in the policy I like to point out to people is that they've already signed over their estate to the company to allow their children to go to the home. People bow their heads when they say the name of the company. It is very well respected.

One very common hustle among a certain group of life

204

insurance companies might be called "employment donations." They hire agents right out of college and pay them maybe $200 or $250-a-week salary. They generally put them through a two-month training period, after which they help them get their licenses. But during that time they furnish absolutely no leads. They use an expression, "Create a center of influence," which means: Sell your friends and relatives. By the end of two months, they have brought the company a considerable amount of business, selling little policies to Uncle Bob and whomever. But eventually they will run out of contacts and maybe stay on another two or three weeks before they get fed up and move on to another occupation. That is why a lot of people will say, "Yeah, I used to sell insurance, but I got the hell out of it."

Well, in that two or three months, the company may have paid an agent $3,000 in salary, but the agent has brought in ten times that amount in insurance. Most of the companies have what they call a vested renewal, where an agent gets part of the commissions when the policies are renewed. But these agents don't get a penny of that because of their training status. So the big companies are getting these people in, bleeding them, and discarding them. ✔

INSURANCE INSPECTOR

When people apply for either home or automobile insurance, companies send out inspectors to check on what they are insuring and to verify the details on the application. At least, that's how it works in theory. Mitch D. applied for a job as insurance inspector after seeing a classified ad in a newspaper. The employer was an inspector, himself, one who operated independently doing inspections for forty or fifty different-sized insurance companies. Mitch was told he'd earn $200 a week. He ended up earning $25, but as he says, he was not the only participant who got ripped off.

I'd get two or three pages of information pertaining to an applicant's homeowner's policy. I would have to drive out to the suburbs and find the place, interview the applicant, photograph the house or car, and go down a checklist to determine whether the house or car was safe or not. It it were a house, I'd measure the whole place and figure out the square footage on paper. To do one house, all this takes you a good hour. Well, this guy was paying me $3 for each house, and $1.50 for cars, so at that rate, there was no way I was going to make $200 a week like he said I would. Originally he told me I would make as much money as I felt like working.

At first, I tried to do it conscientiously, but it took a lot of time finding some of those houses in the hills and then there was always something on the forms I couldn't fill in—the homeowner didn't know, or something—and so I'd take them back to the office. Whenever I didn't have the proper information, my boss would just fake it, and he'd tell me he was faking it. So I asked him, "If you're faking it anyway, then why do I have to bother getting everything perfect?" And he said, "You're learning. After you learn how to do them properly, you can forget all this baloney and do them sitting at your desk."

Well, this guy is getting maybe $8 or $10 from the insurance company to do each of these, and he's paying some slob like me almost nothing to do the work for him. He was just ripping off the insurance companies. He had a bona fide company in a high-rise building in a wealthy suburb, and he was doing business with a lot of reputable companies.

I talked to another guy I knew doing the same thing. He said that since the insurance companies knew we were doing this anyway, there wasn't any point in doing any more than going through the motions. "They throw this pile at you in the morning," he said. "You don't drive everywhere the way you're supposed to. You fill them in by guesswork and go watch the ball game." I can't figure out how they got away with doing this, unless there's some sort of kickback system between the insurance companies and the inspectors. This other guy said the insurance companies are using it as a tax write-off. They do it so they can transfer money among executives and pull the wool over the IRS's eyes. All I know is that if you do the job right, you're not going to make any money. ✔

PERSONNEL DIRECTOR

Peggy E. started out as an assistant in the personnel office of a manufacturing corporation. While working on her master's degree, she was promoted to personnel director and given the responsibilities of salary administration and employee relations and benefits. Peggy enjoyed her work, but in the process of dealing with insurance claim abuse and meddlesome government officials, she said, "A lot of my idealism got knocked around."

There was a lot of hanky-panky in workmen's compensation claims—it was widespread after awhile, and there wasn't much we could do about it. The state has requirements in terms of the amount of insurance you have to carry and the minimum payments, but it's a private deal you have between your company and the insurance company that writes the policy. As claims went up, we'd have to keep paying higher premiums. Now, companies are being forced out of business because the cost of insurance is so exorbitant—it's like the malpractice situation. We would try to fight the phony claims, but it was very difficult. We were in a union setting, and the whole legal situation consisted of your word against theirs, and there was no evidence one way or the other. If people claim their back hurts, there is not a damned way you can prove otherwise. The inclination of the insurance company is to pay off right away.

One of our older managers had an accident while playing squash on his own time. It was a severe muscle or tendon problem, and he was laid up for a while. He had to walk with a cane, and there was the possibility of some permanent damage. He

207

filed a workmen's compensation suit, saying that the work he was doing—walking around, getting in and out of cars—was aggravating his injury. If what you do on the job aggravates your injuries, regardless of where you got injured, the company is liable. He was trying to get a fairly substantial settlement, claiming that he was partially and permanently disabled. I left before it was settled, but they probably just bought him off. Rather than fighting it, which would cost them a lot of money, insurance companies will just make the settlement and raise our rates.

There were numerous workmen's compensation cases in the production area. One woman slipped on a step and fell and complained of low back pains. The doctor didn't even take an X-ray and charged her $60 or $70 for treating a simple contusion. He knew he was making a deal with her. She continued to complain of low back pains, so we sent her to a clinic, and they diagnosed an intestinal infection, which they said was causing her back pain. She just dragged it on and on, and finally the insurance company paid her off, acknowledging that the back pains were due to the fall.

Another person had a nice three-week vacation out by his swimming pool, because his doctor said he needed a rest. It's very easy to tell a doctor you're on the verge of collapse. They'll just say, "Stay home and rest." Knowing the individual involved, I knew this was a total ripoff letting him collect disability insurance. I had a heated correspondence with the insurance company about a man who was claiming his heart attack was job-related but who had quit the company before it happened. The insurance company was too lazy to fight it. They just paid out. Once, a union steward accidentally lost the nail of his index finger in a machine—a legitimate accidental injury—and collected several hundred dollars for it. Another guy, a week later, showed up with the same injury, and it was my suspicion he did it deliberately.

I used to have job applicants coming in and telling me they didn't want the job, and would I sign their forms so the unemployment office could see they had applied. Our own workers came in and asked how they could get fired so they could go back

208

to school and collect unemployment. Just not showing up for work was the easiest way to get fired. If they applied for unemployment benefits, we would challenge the claim, unless they were legitimately laid off. One guy who had lied on his form at the UC office came into our building and threatened us after we'd stopped his claim. If they are discharged for cause, like theft or absenteeism, they cannot collect. But if they're discharged because they are unable to perform the job, then they can collect. Of course, our rates go up as the claims go up.

This whole syndrome was contagious. When people found they could collect a couple of hundred dollars for slipping and falling, they would do it. The righteous people thought, "Goddamn it, why should they get it and not us?" The first- and second-generation middle-European immigrants were at work every day, and we would have to tell them they could file an insurance claim. They'd say, "No, no, it's all right." I hate to say it, but percentage-wise, blacks were the worst offenders. In age groups, the young were worse than the old, except in the case of union members, where the senior ones were the primary abusers, because they knew they were safe. Of course, the clerical women had their own way of pulling shit, too.

Before I took the job there was a lot of discrimination there. The whites hated the blacks, the blacks hated the Latinos, and everybody hated women, round and round. But I thought the government programs, in the cases I saw, did irreparable damage. I was truly trying to be as fair as possible and, beyond that, actively encourage change and improve attitudes.

One woman complained that she had not been hired because she was a woman. The crux of the federal case was the fact that as a technician, she had been asked if she minded working in her "grubbies"—or work clothes. If she had been a man, the question wouldn't have been asked. The government felt that we were ruling her out because we didn't think she'd want to work in grubbies. The case never went to final hearing because we bought her off. Companies are under so much pressure from the government, they don't want to get involved in a full audit.

The government was so absurd with its quota and reporting

systems that we were forced to hire people who were not qualified. They stuck out like sore thumbs, and everybody said, "See, I told you so," or "Look what she's allowed to get away with." This did long-range attitudinal damage, whereas before, we had been making some progress. Thank God I never had to encounter OSHA people.

Speaking as an individual, I'm glad that if I'm being discriminated against, there is some place where I can go to complain. But from the point of view of personnel directors, all the equal opportunity people did was to make life miserable. The compliance officer was a real sweetheart. He ignored all our progress and advised us to pirate blacks from other companies. He said we should get to know the minority agencies and take them out to football games. ✔

LETTERS/MEDIA

NEWSPAPER EDITOR

In his two major jobs as a senior editor of a newspaper, Murray E. had the good fortune to work for papers with integrity and editorial independence. He was not subjected to the interference that many financially starving papers or controlling monopolies in smaller cities and towns often put upon their editors. And, as he says, times have brought a higher grade of professionalism to most newsrooms. I can remember, ten or more years ago, seeing a story of mine killed before publication, because it dealt with a competitor of a good advertiser, and we chose to knuckle under to the ensuing pressure from our "business side." I have either written or edited numerous "please use" stories, the sort of crap that enhances the stature of some high official in my company. I have worked for a paper that studiously avoided good local coverage on its front page on the theory that playing foreign and Washington stories made the paper look more like the *New York Times* and avoided potential hassles with the City Fathers, who disliked interference from the press in their affairs. I have made up news sections in which I was told to honor the edict laid down by a prominent advertiser that "no nigger news" would be printed within three pages of his ads, despite the fact that a substantial portion of his customers were, indeed, "niggers." But that was ten or more years ago, and forgive my digression, Murray, things have changed. Newspapers, however, are still not black and white and read all over. There are still perceptible shades of gray.

One of the real ripoffs in newspapers is the so-called special section that is put out—not by the editorial department—but either by the advertising or the promotion department, or even some outside contractor. I remember one real estate section that was put out at the *Bugle*. There was an article that dealt with the pros and cons of buying a house now. Well, there *were* no cons. I went through the whole article, and there wasn't a single con. That was the kind of copy that the editors of the paper would not have put in had they been putting out the section. So readers of such a section have to be on guard and not be conned into thinking that this is the staff of the newspaper they know and love giving them unbiased advice. I have had people, intelligent people, calling up and complaining about sections like these and saying, "Why is the *Bugle* saying this?" They were taken in by it.

The way papers get around this—or the way they *think* they get around it—is by using a different kind of headline and body type and saying, "The reader is going to know that this is not an editorial product—it is something else." Also, they might put a little line at the top saying "An Advertising Supplement" or something like that. We'd put out seasonal automobile sections when the new cars came out, camera sections, etc., and because we used a different headline typeface, we'd say, "Okay, now the reader knows." Well, I don't think the reader does know.

As for the regular sections of the paper, the real estate, food, and travel sections are good examples of sections that would not exist if it weren't for the fact that advertising requires them to exist. Therefore, they often—not in all papers, but in many of them—reflect not what the consumer or reader should know, or even what the editors think they should know, but what the advertisers want them to know. This probably varies in proportion to the success and financial solidity of the paper. The paper that is in a precarious financial position is more likely to have bad special sections than the paper that can be independent of its advertisers. For example, we are consumer-oriented and frequently print articles that must send the advertisers right up a wall. When I was at another paper I also had a consumer-oriented food editor, and I had to walk a tightrope, trying to get the stuff she wrote into the paper and, at the same time, fighting off the screams from the advertising department.

Advertisers, of course, aren't in there because they like the paper. They advertise because they have to, and they make money by advertising. I know a number of occasions when they have pulled out—for example, car dealers have a tendency to pull out their ads when you say something nasty about used-car dealers, or something like that—but they come back.

While food and travel sections would not exist apart from their advertising base, there still would be reporting on food and travel. I'm not knocking them; they can still be great service sections. Real estate sections, however, are one of the most blatant examples of dictation by the advertising that supports them. We will sometimes run multiple sections, and obviously the real estate news for our area doesn't require multiple sections every week. The real estate sections in our paper and others still clearly reflect the point of view and the interest of the real estate groups who advertise.

I was never told by anyone that I must put in editorial material pertaining to the advertising in those sections. On the other hand, I never tried to put "hard" news in them because they were special sections that had come into existence before my time and that was just the prevailing policy. ✔

FREE-LANCE WRITER

A former wire-service writer and editor, Perry M. has been working for the last eight years as a free-lance journalist, specializing in personality profiles. He sells his pieces to both newspapers and magazines. When he first begins researching his subjects, Perry becomes intensely aware of how much recycling of information goes on in the popular print media.

To research a piece, serious journalists are going to go to the clip files and look up a subject before they interview the person. By clips files, I mean the "morgues" that newspapers and magazines maintain of clippings from their own publications and others, filed by subject. First, journalists want to familiarize themselves with the background, but what's more important to

213

writers who want to do an original piece, is they want to see
what to avoid so they don't repeat a lot of previously used quotes.
However, in looking through the clips, you can see who has
already ripped off whom. You notice certain things that are consistently repeated from article to article to article: choice quotes,
interesting pieces of information, choice phrases, etc. In some
cases, you can see wholesale lifting of material—entire para-
graphs. A lot of this picking up is presumably done by newspaper and magazine rewrite people when they are put into a com-
petitive, deadline situation. Certainly, I could sit down right
now and write a 5,000-word piece on any major figure if you gave
me enough clips.

I don't see this as a problem of copyright infringement; it's
more a minor but persistent flaw in the system. If I'm doing a
piece on an oft-interviewed subject, I want to protect myself
from repeating a lot of crap that has been reported before. The
clips tell me what a subject has said to my colleagues previously.
I remember spending eight hours with one man, and he still did
not give me anything he hadn't already given everyone else—I
learned that from the clips.

A few years ago, I was going to a story conference with a
national magazine that had ripped off two fabulous, raunchy
quotes I had used in a personality piece for a newspaper magazine a few months before. They just lifted two of the strongest
quotes I had without crediting either me or the newspaper. I
had every intention of reading them out for this, until I walked
into the editor's office, and the first thing that came out of his
mouth was, "Well, how many times have we ripped you off?"
This magazine consistently rips off like crazy.

I don't want to rip off anybody, and I don't pick up quotes
unless I have to. If I've interviewed someone for five hours, and
I just forgot to go into an area I should have, and I find someone
else's quote helpful, I generally write, "He has said." That, to
me, is enough to tell the reader that it's not my quote. If it's a
longer quote, I would credit it: "He told the *New York Sun*,"
"He said on national television," etc. Paradoxically, I truly be-

lieve readers want to read things they've read before. It makes for a comfort, an ease, a previous association with the material. A reader wants to read a piece of information about the subject that is well known. But how it is phrased is something else.

The ripping off of ideas is much more subtle, and I know of no legal remedy when someone steals your ideas. All newspapers and magazines read their competitors carefully. They all get ideas from one another. When I was working for a feature service, at least one out of every ten of our ideas was a direct steal from one newspaper. Of course, we did our own version, but we still took the ideas. *Everyone* steals ideas.   ✔

BOOK EDITOR

When he went to work as an editor for a book publishing house, Edgar F. was almost solely responsible for "establishing the level of excellence" for more than 100 books every year. He set out doing structural and organizational work on the manuscripts. He made sure the grammar and the spelling were correct and the facts were accurate. He tried to improve the authors' style. All that, he thought, was the job of a diligent editor. It turned out they didn't want that at all.

As a book editor, my main job was to acquire manuscripts, which was kind of like being a salesman. In a way, I had to sell in order to interest agents and authors into writing for me. Of course, two-thirds of the books any company publishes are books that it is anticipated they will lose money on. But you don't know which ones they are ahead of time—not for sure. Some of the rest of them will either break even or maybe one or two will make a lot of money—that is always the hope. Because we were a medium-sized company and paid fairly low advances, we couldn't expect many people to come to us and offer us books—unless they had already tried all the hot publishers, which generally meant that their books weren't first-string. So this mostly defined the nature of my job.

However, I discovered this only gradually. It took me a year to discover it and another six months to turn my head around. I knew that I was a pretty good editor and could work with authors, and I loved books. Well, I edited like hell, and I would work from nine in the morning till ten at night and on most weekends, beating my brains out trying to edit these reasonably good books and make them better. At the end of the first year, my boss came in and said, "Every time I see you in there editing, it makes me mad." So I redoubled my efforts! I thought he meant that I was not editing hard enough, or something. What he wanted me to do was get the hell out of the office and sell.

On a sales trip, I was talking with a magazine editor, and quite abruptly in the conversation he said, "Well, you know that books aren't edited anymore." He pointed to a new one and said, "Now, there is a book that wasn't edited at all." I had just read an excerpt in a magazine, and I had noticed the same thing. I thought they had gotten a bad chapter, but he said the whole book was like that. "Editors are not editing, because the publishers don't give them the time," he said, "and what's more, the readers don't really care anymore."

I had been trying to do everything, because I thought good editing was essential in producing a book that would sell. As a matter of fact, it probably has nothing to do with it. Still, poorly edited books are not as readable as well-edited books. Mainly, it amounts to style. Either you had a foreign-born author who just wrote strange English, or you had a relatively young inexperienced author who was an awkward writer. The author would patch sentences together and expect the publishing house to fix up the book. But I suppose how a book comes out stylistically does not matter—the buying public is none the wiser.

I was never held accountable for lack of editing. The authors were expected to make their books factually correct, and we did little checking on that. Most authors who sold books to publishers repeatedly were able to do so not so much by their writing ability, but by the fact that they sat down and kept churning the stuff out. Magazines, for instance, were, by and large, much, much better written and more tightly and more skillfully edited than books.

I heard recently that some big outfit was getting rid of those editors who had been hired specifically to work with writers to develop and improve their work and instead was hiring more acquisition people who could get stuff in and out quickly. It is a matter of profit. Forty-thousand books a year are written, and the trend of not editing books is sweeping the industry—and it will get worse. I consider this the prime ripoff in the publishing field. ✔

TELEVISION PRODUCER

Milt J. had been a television producer for five years for major network stations when a job opening listed in a national broadcasting journal caught his eye. Even though he didn't get the job, Milt learned that the station had at least valued his services as an unpaid consultant.

I researched for twelve to sixteen hours preparing for that interview, studying the station's programming, its weaknesses, etc. When I went in, I had an hour-and-forty-five-minute interview with the program manager. The average interview for a job of that nature would be about a half-hour, and the three finalists would come back for a second, longer interview. It was an important job; it was a producer's job involving an aspect of program management. In this interview, he asked me how I would attack every imaginable problem in programming and all about what my experience was where I had worked before. He was positively pumping me for inside information, because some of my experience was with his competitors. His line of questioning was: What would you do if you were in that chair? He pumped me for ideas that would translate into programming, like, "How would you improve public awareness through public affairs pro-gramming? How would you get the community more involved?" One idea I gave him for a segment of programming appeared on his station less than six weeks later. They used everything I'd given them but the titles. I had an hour-and-forty-five minutes of getting my brain milked.

Now I know they had no intention of hiring anyone from the outside. Several months later, they announced in the same trade journal that they had moved someone up from inside the station to that position. There was no way they could tell me this person didn't exist before, and that they were only looking for ideas. I knew how to do that job. Right now my job is doing that, plus one-hundred other things. After all that, I don't think I ever even received a letter from them. There are a lot of schlocky people in the electronics media.   ✔

MISCELLANEOUS

STOREFRONT MINISTER

During the time he was undergoing training for his ordination, Howard A. assisted a once-influential minister who was then running a Christian denominational storefront church. Howard knew the work well, since many of his acquaintances are or were storefront ministers themselves. He also knew the man he worked for well; in addition to helping him raise funds, he also took care of some of the books. Eventually, he left both the storefront church and the ministry itself: "Not so much because of the ripoffs," he says, "I just didn't like the whole show."

The man I worked for was once a legitimate, straight minister for a big church in a wealthy parish; yet he never made much money, and he had a big family. He had tremendous expenses, because a minister has to live like his parishioners, but, of course, on much less salary. This guy was deeply in debt when he had a fight with his parishioners and was fired. Five years later, after starting his storefront church, he was living high on the hog. He lived in a gorgeous house, had a maid and a gardener, he traveled to foreign countries, and he put on a big wedding for his daughter and wrote it off as a church dinner. He made a hell of a lot of money.

In his storefront, he had a congregation of about twenty people. This gave him something to do. It was good for his conscience, and it was a good show for the government, since he was licensed to run a church. Of course, he didn't want to get money from his parishioners. They'd send it, but he would discourage them. Their donations were just small money to him.

The storefront was in a bad neighborhood, and he couldn't have paid much rent for it. I worked for him running his bingo operation, and I was paid under the table. In our city, bingo was

219

allowed only in churches. He had a sisterhood and other fake clubs set up so we could run separate bingo games—we had six different games going, and he didn't report any of the money on his books. Later, he staged Las Vegas nights in an old catering hall, where people could play baccarat, roulette, etc. He'd gross $7,000 or $8,000 a night on this and pocket the take. Technically, Las Vegas nights were illegal, but the police would just wink their eyes at it since he was a minister. After I left, I heard he was making $100,000 a year just having Las Vegas nights once a week. His storefront was just that: a front.

He would deal in real estate, using the church as a front. By keeping the property in the name of the church, he didn't have to pay real estate taxes or capital gains taxes on it when he sold it. He'd keep the property a few years, rent it out, then sell it at a profit, and he faked the whole transaction as a fund-raising for the church. He'd write off his vacation travel as an educational experience for the church. He once got a $5,000 donation and gave the donor a receipt for $25,000. Of course ministers frequently get a lot of gifts they don't report, like when they perform a wedding ceremony for wealthy members of their congregation.

The majority of storefront churches are legitimate, but there are a lot of others run for the personal benefit of the minister. If a storefront minister wants to be unscrupulous, he can make a hell of a lot of money, a lot more than he could as head minister in a traditional, wealthy parish. And, of course, the government is nice to churches in America, although I don't know why. Maybe because they fight communism or something.

Lunch programs are another favorite fund-raising tool. The government gives money to run lunch programs for the poor during the summer, and they get nonprofit organizations to sponsor them supposedly so no one rips off the recipients. I've never been involved in these programs, but my family has. It's a big business. The government usually pays them $2 a meal, and they spend only 50 cents making it up. They end up with $1.50 profit. They'll use inferior foods and also claim that there are three times as many people in the program as there are. The inspectors rarely inspect, but if they do, you slip them $20.

Some people I know are in this for personal gain, but most of them do it for legitimate purposes. But even legitimate organizations rip off, because that's the only way they can raise funds in a tight money market. Some are doing illegal things, but they're very moral people. It depends on what you mean by being legitimate. A preacher could do it for his own good *and* for the good of the church. Not all of them interpret Jesus as saying not to steal. Some of them interpret Jesus as saying: Be moral. ✒

PARALEGAL

For a few years, Norma N. worked as a paralegal for a nonprofit corporation whose mission was to provide legal services to poor people. As a paralegal, Norma did "the nitty-gritty work" of researching cases and writing briefs, supposedly under the guidance of a lawyer. She had no formal legal training as such, and now that her work in this field is over, she has no desire to go back into the law.

Our funds were allocated by the government on the basis of about $7 for every poor person living in our area. The funding we got was determined by the number of welfare recipients or the number of people receiving disability, Aid to Dependent Children, or whatever from the government. With this money, we set up a legal-service center with a staff of about twenty-seven. Our program was in a depressed area, and we had a budget of about a half-million dollars. From my experience, it didn't seem that the service was set up for poor people at all—it was to educate young lawyers coming out of law school. I was in the admissions end of it, and I was in a position to know which clients were accepted. They only interviewed 5 percent of the population eligible for our legal services, and of that group, they actually helped only 3 percent.

All of our lawyers were from out-of-state and right out of law school without any experience. They didn't know the state and local laws, nor did they know the local problems. They had no overseers who were experienced attorneys. The turnover was high. Once they got the experience they wanted, in contract law, or whatever, they went back to where they wanted to go and went into private practice. If they wanted to become political, this was a great thing to have on their records.

If lawyers wanted to take a case, if it were something they were interested in, they would take it. If it didn't interest them, they wouldn't. The lawyers would go to court on behalf of their chosen clients, when they wanted the experience. But I can remember cases in which people went in with problems, and they were simply dumped. They accepted a lot of cases, but they didn't help them—they would let them go. After a few weeks, they would tell the people that they couldn't help them, for one reason or another, without doing any adequate research to see if they could. Many times I would do all the work on a case, and it would be dropped. Maybe it was not the way the lawyers wanted it done, but then they would never tell me how they wanted it done. Their mandate was to help everyone who came in, but I think they were sitting on their asses. They never had to face these people again, and they had no intention of staying—they were there strictly for the experience and the credentials it gave them. They just came and went as they pleased and did exactly what they wanted to do. They were too engrossed in their own personal achievements.

Most of our clients were white and really poor and ignorant. Most of them didn't even have a sixth-grade education. When they came in with one problem, you'd find they really had ten or twelve. And when you took care of one problem, you were only treating the symptoms. I would talk to the clients after they walked in and get the gist of their problem, then explain it to one of the attorneys. If they didn't want to take it, they wouldn't.

The administrative situation in the office was totally screwed up, because there was no direction. On paper, everything was fine. The director was supposed to say, "We've got 100 cases this week, and each attorney will take ten." But the attorneys would say, "That is too much for me. I am ethically bound to refuse this case, because if I were to prosecute it effectively, this would take me away from cases I have already taken." But the director wasn't telling them what to do. I was supposed to have a supervisor, but I never really had one. I was left more or less on my own. And that doesn't make sense for a paralegal not to be working under a lawyer's direction. It was against the ethics of the bar. There were regulations we were supposed to follow but never did—you can do anything you want with figures. We would report the number of people we had seen rather than the number we had helped. We would record that we had given them the right advice, patted them on the back, and that solved their problems. The board of directors was kept in the dark by our reporting system.

I worked on some pension cases on my own, because I knew that several old miners who were entitled to a pension were destitute without it. They weren't getting their pension, because of corruption in the union. I won a couple of cases on my own just by going down to the union and raising hell. But the lawyers in our office didn't want to handle the cases. They simply said that they were too much work. Or adoptions. In some cases, where grandparents were supporting kids and barely able to make ends meet, and adoptions would allow them to receive some assistance, the lawyers' principles always came before the people. "We don't do adoptions for financial purposes," they would say.

I remember one flood case in which a man lost his house and everything, and his brother, whom he had been real close to, drowned. The city wanted to condemn a huge part of his land and have the corps of engineers come in and dredge it for flood control. Well, this man appealed to us for help, because he didn't want his land taken away, and our lawyers turned him down, saying, we don't do property cases. He told me that he had already lost everything he was going to lose, and I knew that

223

if anybody came in and started messing with his land, he would shoot them. That case was only going to get a lot worse, because we didn't take it.

The lawyers, of course, would take divorce cases before they would do anything else. Two-thirds of our cases, at least, were divorces. The thrust there was simple dissolution and maybe child support evasion. There were maybe ten or eleven different procedures, and it was just a matter of zipping through them, depending on the complaints. Divorces are simple. You cannot mess them up, unless you are a total idiot.

I think this whole program is a ripoff. I was really upset to see such a small percentage of people helped, and all these lawyers getting credit for being saviors of poor people, when they really didn't give a damn about them. One lawyer told me, "You know, it does something for poor people to be able to say, 'I am going to go and see my lawyer.' " Oh, sure. They don't know they're getting screwed. They think they are getting the best service available, because before they had no service at all. The law is not to help people. It is strictly designed to maintain the status quo. The world is more complicated now, and you go by the rules, or you don't play. The trouble is, the rules are not fit for anybody who is not already winning.   ✔

PSYCHIC

"If people didn't want psychics, there wouldn't be any," says Rudolph C., a psychic who says he served a two-year prison term for interstate transportation of stolen securities. Psychics, who claim to have a sensitivity to forces beyond the physical world, have been around for centuries in the form of prophets and seers. Now, by getting paid for what they feel, as opposed to what they think, they have become, says Rudolph, a $300 million annual business. He has charged as much as $300 for readings when he knew the person was writing it off as a business deduction. "You can pick up the *National Enquirer* every week, and there will be something on psychics," he says. "Why? Because people are curious about the unknown, and they feel a psychic can explain some of it." Why do some people enlist the aid of psychics rather than psychiatrists? "When they come to me," he says, "they don't have the stigma that they're crazy."

People pay psychics for what we feel, for our impressions. A psychic must have the ability of disassociation and the ability to tune into an energy flow. Some psychics will completely blow you away, and you'll say, "Gee! How did they know that?" They'll give you sensations up and down your spine. This leaves a tremendous amount of openings for us. It opens people up when you tell them about themselves, because they feel no one else knows them. This puts people off guard, and they become enamored of their psychic.

Sometimes, we work in an office atmosphere; sometimes we have to build one. People like to deal with a mystique—crystal balls, palmistry, cards, numerology, astrology—all these are what I'd call openers. I don't even have to be right; I just have to be honest. I deal with a person's energy flow and build a momentum from that. Once you hit them with four or five things that are definite, they will agree with you on everything else, even though they'll only remember the four or five things. The person will let a psychic know whether he is successful.

I've known spiritual advisers who will scare the shit out of somebody so that the person has got to put out $2,000 or $3,000 to get rid of a curse. They create a thought form and put it into a person's mind; then they work on it and work on it. They'll say, in effect, "I'm warning you ahead of time what's happening, and you have to make a sacrifice."

It's playing on people's fears. The IRS works on people's fears. The church works on people's fears. People always work on fear if they want something—it's our one common denominator. Fear creates respect; so people tend to respect the mystics and the prophets for that simple reason. They fear that we can create something against them or take something away. Often, the people who come to us are desperate, and they'd try anything. Then the adviser will say, "I'll burn candles for you." It'll be $75 a shot, and before long you've got a $300 bill. I've seen people pay as much as $50,000 to get a curse off their family. Something was definitely wrong, and after they paid the money, whatever was bothering them seemed to go away. They could have been guilty about their money, and knowing someone was working on their problem took the pressure off.

A woman who has a sick husband will come in and want to know when he is going to die. These people you start charging. The ripoffs you pull depend upon your needs at the time. A woman in that situation came to me, and while I knew what I was doing wasn't right, I did it anyway. I knew something was going to happen from that, so when she gave me the first check for $100, my show was on the road. I needed the money so I took it.

She wanted information on her husband. She was worried about her security and wanted to buy more insurance on his life and things like that. So I just kept taking, taking, taking. I ended up charging her over $25,000. When he finally died, she came into a lot of money. But she thought I'd overcharged her and took me to court. She had paid me as we went along over about a nine-month period, $75 or $100 a shot. A couple of times she gave me $1,000. At the time, she didn't protest. She didn't protest until everything was over. She contended that I had misrepresented myself, as far as being who I said I was. The state felt I hadn't given her anything in return. The checks I got from her, they said were obtained through fraud, so they were in effect stolen securities. They gave me two years in prison.

With some psychics, it's strictly a con game. I wasn't exactly a con artist. It was that one instance when it became a ripoff for me. You could go to five different psychics and get five different readings, and all of them could be right. Who can say what percentage of people are ripped off by psychics? Only you can be the judge. If you have peace of mind, then maybe the psychic has helped you.

FUND RAISER

Donald L. was in charge of raising funds for a private agency that dealt with developmentally disabled adults. He was always told by his director that the money should be put into a general fund and that the donors should be discouraged from attaching strings to their gifts. This, he suspects, was to allow her to "feather her own nest."

When service agencies raise money, they always turn in exaggerated reports to the United Fund. There are two budgets: The one you live by and the one you turn in to get a larger share of the money. Our budget was overstated $85,000, and the extra didn't go through. Since agencies know their needs and automatically pad them, there's really no falsification of records. Sometimes we will raise funds for the same need or for something we've just purchased, like an air conditioner. And, even if the money has been earmarked, it usually goes into a general fund anyway.

Donors seldom follow up and want to see the equipment they have helped buy. They don't demand invoices before they give money, and they should. There's no accountability to the United Fund.

I finally resented the fact that the money was going into a general fund. The board didn't have the control it should have. Our agency hired people right off the street for $2.75 an hour—people who were not qualified to work with the handicapped. Then the agency would use the money for the executives. The director brought in a friend to a $19,000 assistant's job, but a woman who had the highest rate of placement for our clients was paid almost nothing.

In another job, working under a government program, Donald acted as a consultant to the same sort of agency for which he had been a fund raiser. He said he and his colleagues were soon spoiled by their five-hour work days.

The agency had a workshop in which disabled adults were given work in a sheltered environment. One man got contracts for the clients to work on, and another man was in charge of placing them in jobs. The state and federal governments funded the program, and the clients paid a token amount. The agency had a blind woman as a client, and on another consultant's advice, I sent her to a facility for the blind for free treatment. Well, the agency got very upset and said I should have asked permission. They didn't want this blind student to leave, because when they lose a client, they lose their funding money for that client.

This happened many times. The agency had a sign saying it had placed so many people, but then I realized the sign hadn't been changed in a year. It was a sham. The agency doesn't measure its success by the number of people it places in jobs. What incentive do they have to place clients, when placement means they'll lose their revenue? ✔

ACCOUNTANT

Merlin L. has been a bookkeeper and accountant for a variety of firms, many of which were small businesses. The accounting field, he says, "is pretty clean. It's the guys you work for who pull the tricks."

Owners of businesses use charge accounts illegally all the time. I ran across a case recently where the guy turned in a charge for $50 from a restaurant. Well, you don't take clients out and spend $50 to eat—at least he doesn't. You take the family out and spend $50 on them. These guys throw that into sales and promotion, or maybe advertising or travel expense—they just bury it somewhere. Common sense tells an accountant when something isn't bona fide entertainment. When this guy goes into a catalog store and buys merchandise, then puts it down as sales promotion, it's unlikely that he's buying a gift for a prospective client.

One place I worked, the owner didn't draw much salary, but he drew a hell of a lot on his charge card. I think he was living off that money and treating it like an expense account, charging things off to travel, sales promotion, etc. He wasn't paying any taxes on the money he was drawing, and he was beating down the corporation's profits so the company didn't pay any taxes, either. A company is allowed a reasonable percentage for expense, but it all depends on the volume of business. Sometimes in a merchandise operation, they'll pull shenanigans with the inventory, if they find they're going to make more profit than they expected. They'll understate the inventory, which has the effect of reducing the profits by the same amount.

If the owners of a business are skimming off earnings or trying to bury expenses, they generally hide the true nature of what they're doing from the accountant, too. All an accountant can do is handle it and forget about it. If you know what the story is, you don't want to stick your neck out, because your reputation is at stake, too. I suppose you could report these things to the IRS, but you hate to be a stool pigeon and bite the hand that feeds you.

PUBLIC TRANSPORTATION

FLIGHT ATTENDANT

Though many people in the airline industry have responsibilities of greater weight, the flight attendant is the employee most in the public eye—the one passengers remember for good or merely passable service. Flight attendants, of course, serve food and drink and attend to the passengers' comfort. They are also responsible for the passengers' safety and evacuation in case of emergency. Chris Y. is a flight attendant for a charter airline.

Drinking is a natural thing to do in this job. You spend a lot of time away from home, and little plastic hotel rooms get on your nerves. You're stuck out at airports where the most natural place to go is the bar or club. Flight crews, in general, drink quite a bit.

I'd say 15 or 20 percent of our crew members are alcoholics. * Of course, some guys can slosh them down night after night on the road, but they won't come close to violating the rules—the FAA regulations say you can't drink within twelve hours before your flight.† I've been in bars with crew members who will look

---

The definition of alcoholism is admittedly not precise and has a certain amount of subjective content. Another flight attendant on the same airline estimated that of cockpit crew members, 25 percent were "heavy drinkers."

†*A spokesman for the Federal Aviation Administration says that Federal Aviation Regulation (91.11) governs the use of liquor and drugs by crew members on commercial aircraft: "A) No person may act as a crew member of a civil aircraft (1) within eight hours after the consumption of any alcoholic beverage, (2) while under the influence of alcohol, or (3) while using any drug that affects his faculties in any way contrary to safety."*

231

at their watches and say, "Uh, twelve hours," and up and out of their seats. There are a substantial number, however, who break the twelve-hour rule, but in terms of getting on a plane with abilities completely or partially impaired, there aren't that many. In terms of gross neglect of the rules, I'd say 10 percent or fewer of the cockpit (pilot, copilot, engineer) people are involved, but those who are, are habitual.

One person hides miniature liquor bottles in the lavatories, and in midflight, he slips in to get them. These bottles have popped up in the supply areas or have been hidden behind the paper towels and toilet paper. I can't be positive they are put there by him, but I've been told by other flight attendants it probably was this particular person. In any company there are guys who get caught—everybody knows who they are.

I've seen some copilots on flights who may not have been drunk but were really hung over. And I've seen flight engineers whom I don't even know how they got up the steps to the aircraft. Flight engineers break the rules a lot more, perhaps because they never fly the aircrafts. Yet, just the same, if their judgment isn't sharp, it could endanger the ship.

There's a story about a captain (pilot), a known alcoholic, who was coming in for a final approach. He was doing everything completely wrong, and the copilot had to take over. The pilot got fired. The guy who relieved him is now a captain so he tells the story every chance he gets. He's also an alcoholic and has been known to get on a plane completely gone.

Once, the company called early to get a plane out of an airport where the ground crews were going on strike, and this guy was completely smashed. We were at a crew party, and everybody knew how blasted he was. But the company said we want you to get the plane out now, and he said, okay. In a case like that, when they changed the schedule and bumped the flight time up, the captain should admit he's in no shape to fly. There's nothing the company can say. There wouldn't be any penalty to him, because the schedule had been changed, and his agreement with the FAA supersedes any company policy, and if they ever tried to fire him, the FAA would back him up.

The thing that makes my job the most difficult is how the ground crews and sales agents out-and-out lie to people. Once they've sold the trip, they tell people things you wouldn't believe. They'll rush us out to the airport, then we'll find out the plane we're waiting for just left Paris, and we'll have a seven- or eight-hour wait. Meanwhile, they're telling the passengers it'll only be another hour. So the people say, an hour's not so bad, and in fifty minutes, everybody's collecting possessions ready to get on the plane. Then the guy comes out and tells them it will be another hour, and they replay that scene six more times. By the time the passengers get on the aircraft, they're not passengers anymore—they're vicious, brutal animals. Leveling is not part of our operating procedure. They even lie to us. If we have to sit in an airport for, I think, eight hours, we have a right to opt to go back to a hotel. So headquarters, in the interest of saving money, may know it'll be an eight-hour delay, but they'll tell you it's four, so you can't get the hotel room. They can make you sit in an airport for about eight hours; then if it's an international flight, they can fly you for fifteen more hours—that's a twenty-three-hour day. ✔

TAXI DRIVER, CITY

One morning, after ten years on the road as a traveling salesman, Lou S. woke up and decided he no longer liked what he was doing. He decided to trade that life for driving a cab, which he now does fifteen to nineteen hours a day for the sake of $25,000 a year, only some of which he reports to the IRS. Meanwhile, he's biding his time and paying off his mortgage. Though he likes the daily contact with people, Lou rarely associates with other cab drivers and prefers to think of himself as a "transportation engineer."

I lease my cab from the company twenty-four hours a day. The company furnishes liability insurance, but I have to post a

$100 bond to cover the deductible. A few weeks ago another driver sideswiped me. My passenger, who was an attorney, said he would testify that I had been cut off by the other driver. Our supervisor, however, came out and wrote a check to the other driver, and I was charged $75. Today, an uninsured driver with no driver's license ran a red light and hit my door. That's going to cost me $100. When my bond is forfeited after an accident, I can't lease another cab until I post another $100. If I contested an accident in which I was not at fault, they wouldn't give me another lease.

Although they charged me $75 for the first accident, the cab was never repaired. You've ridden in enough cabs to know there's not a one without a dent in it. So if I, or anyone else who got this same cab, happened to get hit in the same place there was a dent before, they'd charge us for the same dent again and again. I would like to earn in a year what my company earns off of unrepaired damages. We have several supervisors who drive around with checks in case of an accident, and they try to get a release from the other motorists, like the guy who sideswiped me. The company feels it's better to get a release on-the-spot rather than going through attorneys. I've heard of cases where the supervisor and the other motorists kind of split: "I'll give you a check for $500 if you give me $250 back." Of course, the same thing goes on inside the company. I pay the mechanic to work on my cab right away instead of keeping me waiting four hours, and if you need another cab, you slip the dispatcher a buck, too. When new cabs come in, the managers will take $100 under the table from someone who wants a brand new one. I think management knows what's going on—I'm sure they underpay some of their key people because they know they make it up on pay-offs.

There are a lot of animals who work the airport at night after the starters leave. They'll give their passengers special rates of $25 or $35 to the city, when the meter rate is about $11. The other day I saw a driver with his meter already running—he had a newspaper over it—picking up a passenger, and who knows what was already registered?

I've had passengers who ask me where they can get laid, and I tell them right away I'm a cab driver, not a pimp. There's one place, a night club, that pays a taxi driver $8 for every person he delivers to their door who comes in. I was approached by some girls with matches from the place who told me that. I told them to keep their matches.

Once, I drove a couple to a bad area, and he got out one side and she got out the other. He said to her, "Be sure to give him a good tip, because he was nice enough to bring us here." It was just $1.25 on the meter, and she gave me $2.50, and he kept saying, "Give him more, give him more." I just wanted to get out of there, so I drove away and looked down and saw that my change purse was gone. He'd reached through the window and taken it while I was talking to her.

Another time I picked up two couples, who were going to a bad neighborhood, and while we were driving along one guy opened a door and threatened to throw his girl out the cab, then the other guy took out his knife and threatened to shove it up his girl's rear end. When I pulled up to a red light, a driver from another cab company pulled up alongside, and I waved to him. Then the passengers told me to pull into a driveway, and I stopped and said, "That will be $5.15." One guy said, "I didn't order the cab," and the other one said, "Neither did I." Doors opened on either side, and through the rear-view mirror I saw the girls looking right and left, and I knew something was going to happen. All of a sudden, one guy asked how much they owed, and he paid me. I looked in my rear-view mirror again, and there was the other cab behind me. I went over to thank him, and he said he was worried about me and thought he'd follow me. Overall, cab drivers are a good group of people.

Legally, I have no right to refuse a passenger going to a bad area of the city. Some drivers will say, "I'm sorry, but I don't work that area." But the people who would complain are intelligent people who know their rights and would get on the phone, so I run with the fare and hope for the best. I won't say I've never refused a fare, however. I will look people over, and if they look legitimate, I'll pick them up, otherwise I don't even see them.

Police tend to look at cab drivers as a bunch of animals, and as a result, they are more stringent with them, and for good reason. Cab drivers consider themselves above the law, and they will take risks that are out of line—U-turns, pulling out into traffic—because they are so hungry to get the meter running.

My tips run, on the average, about 30 percent—nine out of ten of my passengers will tip me. That's higher than normal, I'm sure. But I know the city, I have experienced it, and I try to be helpful by telling out-of-towners what's going on and keeping them company—and they tip me for this. A tip, however, is a gratuity for something above normal service, and I really believe the only obligation a passenger has is to pay the meter. ✔

TAXI DRIVER, SUBURBS

Mary Lou H. cruised the suburbs as a taxi driver and found the fares much harder to come by, and the tips not so high. With relatively few cabs serving a sprawling area, service was erratic and customers impatient. "A lot of times," says Mary Lou, "we'd answer a call and wouldn't find anyone there. That's what we called a deadhead." It didn't take many deadheads in a shift to reduce her earnings drastically. "I figured that anything I made over $20 was a good day." Despite her relatively meager income, at least she had the shelter provided by skimming off some, but not all of her earnings, as tax-free. "You do report a certain amount," she says, "otherwise the IRS will know."

Our cab company used to be run by a guy who had a quaint trick. If you ever were in an accident, your $100 bond would be automatically forfeited. No matter how much the repairs cost—even if you could pull the dent out of the side of the car with your hands, which you could do with most of his cabs—he would get the $100. Then, because he didn't carry adequate insurance, he'd also charge you for the repairs, sometimes $200 or $300 for a $50 job.

A lot of the drivers were inexperienced, but those of us with experience just told him off and quit, like I did. He lost out on me, because I never turned in my last fare envelope. But that was the bad thing about posting the $100 bond. If you ever left the company, you had a big hassle getting it back. Nobody ever got their full $100 back. He'd get us in other ways, too. When they'd take your cab in for repairs, he'd say yours had extra mileage on it that you hadn't reported. Even if it didn't, you'd have to take his word for it, and he'd charge you for it.

I didn't expect much in the way of tips from customers. Most people tipped me a quarter, regardless of what the meter read. It was a rare case when someone tipped me over 50 cents. I would take people to the airport and carry their luggage for them, and most of the time I only got a dollar.

Once I got an early morning call from the dispatcher to pick up someone fifteen miles from where I was—only ten minutes before I was due. After I found his place and picked him up, he said he had only fifteen minutes to make his plane and was bitching about how late I was. My company was given the order to pick him up because the one he had called couldn't make it. Well, we were fifteen miles from the airport, and I was going 70 m.p.h. down the freeway. Of course, I had to pay any traffic tickets I got. Well, I later heard from the dispatcher that he did make his plane, but he never even tipped me.

A lot of times customers will get out of the cab without paying you, although most people are good about paying. Sometimes drunks will stiff you, but sometimes they'll give you more than they owe—and you never say a word about that. They'll give you $20.50 when the meter says $2.50.

I'll have people say, "wait," and they'll say they have to go in and get change. Sometimes they'll even leave stuff in the cab— like empty boxes, or something—as security. Most of the time they go in their house, then out the back way. Sometimes they'll give you an address close to their own. There's nothing you can do about it other than tell the dispatcher. We have a long list of people we won't pick up because they've done it before.

RETAIL SALES

JEWELRY MAKER

Since her childhood, Sybil L. has made jewelry and found it fascinating. Over a twelve year period she has sold various pieces at art fairs and at parties in private homes. In the last year, she has worked in the jewelry department of a retail chain store. Her craft primarily involves working with semiprecious stones. Diamonds, says Sybil, is one field she wouldn't get into. "I'm afraid of it," she says. "I don't have anyone dealing in precious stones whom I trust." Even among lower priced stones, ripoffs are not uncommon.

Unscrupulous suppliers will come up for the show circuit—the arts and crafts shows—from May through September and try to take advantage of someone just getting into the business. They'll offer a junky jade that comes from Wyoming and sell it as Burmese jade. You could get a four-by-four inch slab of Wyoming jade for maybe fifty cents, but a piece of Burmese jade like that would cost you $75 or $100, depending on the grade. Burmese jade is much harder. It looks like hardened milk with a little bit of food coloring and has a soft look. Wyoming jade is just a blotchy, mottled, pale green stone; it's almost always bad. They'll also sell black onyx as black jade, and there again, there's a great difference in the price.

A lot of these people are what they call "rock hounds." They will pick up the stuff on vacation, cut it and grind it, and sell it at art fairs as something it is not. I've dealt with people who sell a stone called sodalite as lapis lazuli. A four-by-four-inch slab of lapis sells for about $75; the same piece of sodalite you might get $2 or $3 for. Turquoise is another stone that is unbelievable in terms of ripoffs.

They will take a piece of halite (rock salt) that's absolute garbage and dye it to look like turquoise. It does hold the dye for awhile, and it even mimics turquoise. Like turquoise, when it picks up some of your perspiration it will turn a little bit green. Or people will get a cheaper soft piece of turquoise and coat it with dyed lacquer. It will be so heavily processed that it is really a piece of lacquer with a lot of pigment. They will sell it in jewelry or paperweights as turquoise.

Actually, the softer turquoise also requires dyeing and stabilizing with lacquer to prevent the stone from being dissolved by perspiration or from changing in any way. You use the same dye and lacquer you use with halite, but an experienced person can easily tell the difference between the two stones. Turquoise comes in grades, ranging from a soft stone that is almost like sandstone or soapstone all the way up to one similar to malachite. You can run a little test by running a pocket knife over the surface and looking at it with a magnifying glass. Good turquoise won't scratch. If you see a little whitish material around the edges of a knife mark, it's probably the lacquer on a softer piece of turquoise that's been scratched. If it leaves an absolute rut, with white powder deep down, it's probably halite. It's a simple test. Otherwise, you can take the stone to a jeweler or lapidary shop you trust and have it appraised. It may cost you $10, but if it saves you a $50 mistake, it's worth it.

There are unscrupulous dealers who will sell 14-karat gold-filled jewelry as 14-karat gold.* I had a friend who went to a suburban jeweler and said she wanted a 14-karat gold cross without the chain. She asked whether it was gold-filled or not, and he said, "It is 14-karat—solid 14 karats." She said, "Would you mind if I looked at it with your magnifying glass?" and he refused. Finally, he let her, although he wasn't happy about it. Sure enough, it was marked on the back of the cross: 1/20th

---

*Karat designations refer to gold's percentage of purity. Pure gold is 24 karats. When gold is mixed with other metals for durability, it's karat-rating decreases (12-karat gold is half pure). A range of from 8 to 24 karats is common in jewelry. Gold-filled means that the piece just has an outer layer of gold, generally 1/10th or 1/20th the thickness of the total piece.

gold-filled. He didn't say much, just, "Well, I must have made a mistake."

A certain retail chain department store has been burning people left and right. They have displays of gold-filled mixed with 14-karat gold wedding bands that do not specify which is which. The salespeople are impatient and don't take the time to help you. In retail accessory stores in the inner city, I've seen where stores have intentionally had their people put gold-filled earrings on 14-karat cards.

Something you have to look out for on rings is the mark H.G.E., which means "heavy gold electroplate." Over a period of time, depending on your skin's acidity, the gold will come off like little flakes of mica. It also depends on what you work with: A beautician friend of mine who works with hair spray can wear gold-plated jewelry, because the lacquer in the spray seals in the gold. My husband, however, can't wear it, because he works with solvents, which dissolve it. You can tell plated from solid gold by the darkening on the plating, or there may be a few bubbles where air pockets developed when the metal was solidifying. A lot of times, under a magnifying glass, you will see little seams or imperfections or a certain blotchiness in gold-plated jewelry.

For their own protection, most jewelers and gold manufacturers insist that when a piece is 14-karat gold it should be stamped on it. But when it is not, they are somewhat lax about it. The important thing to do before you go to a jewelry store is determine its reputation, and after you ask what kind of guarantees they offer, get them in writing. It may seem like a big rigamarole for buying a $20 pair of earrings, but you will feel better.

There are so many wholesalers around now who will get stolen rings in and try to fence them. If the rings can't be fenced, they will destroy the settings and try to sell the stones. I really got stung once but good. I went out to this guy I'd heard was a wholesaler and told him I needed a certain piece to match another one a woman had ordered from me. I described it, and he said, "Fine, I'll have it for you Tuesday." Normally, it takes three or four weeks to get something like that, so I thought something was funny. Anyway, I got it, and when I took it to the woman, I thought she was going to have a stroke. She said, look inside that band and see if there is a K.D.R. in there. I looked, and there was. I'd almost sold her back her own ring. She'd been robbed in a parking lot, and the stupid jerk fenced it in his own area. I'd paid $650 for the piece, but I let her have it after the police arrested me on suspicion. I got off, and the woman was nice enough to give me $300 for helping her get the piece back. It really irritated me, though, that I'd been so dumb to deal with that guy and hurt my reputation.

People who don't tell customers what they should know and those who don't know what they are doing are sometimes just as bad, from the customers' standpoint, as those who purposely rip them off. Customers should be told not to use paste metal cleaners on jewelry, because many times the paste deteriorates the stone itself. A jeweler's cloth will clean the metal without affecting the stone.

People just starting to make jewelry may attempt to do repairs on gold jewelry with diamonds. They don't realize that heat is one of the few things that can ruin a diamond as far as looks. When you drill or solder, you have to use water cooling. I had a blue diamond a friend of mine offered to fix, and unfortunately he didn't know what he was doing. When I got the stone back it had turned yellow. It looked almost like a topaz.

Many times customers are not told when they bring their old rings in to get the stones reset that the old settings are going to be completely ruined. Many people want the old band for sentimental reasons, and they aren't told the shank will be bent or the prongs broken off. ✔

CLOTHING STORE MANAGER

Willie A. worked a brief stint in sales as a manager trainee in a large retail men's clothing store chain. After learning sales, inventory, shipping, and receiving, he worked his way up in several months to first assistant manager, then manager. By then it was apparent that his career, at least with this particular chain, would be short-lived, because at that time they were proceeding to go out of business. The resulting confusion, however, at least proved to be personally profitable to Willie.

"Shrinkage" is the term stores use for losing merchandise. We had a large store, and we would lose maybe a couple thousand dollars a week in shrinkage. Maybe eight or so of our suits would just walk out the door. Well, when I was put in charge of the store, I felt like I cut down shrinkage by 90 percent. I knew the people who came in the store, and I knew the habitual shoplifters. I would tell them, "Where I am at, don't come anymore. You take and you steal from me. You can't do that." I made them understand, and they would go peacefully and leave me alone.

Well, I just stopped the shrinkage from going out the front door. The shrinkage stayed the same, but the merchandise became mine. I had a security guard there, but he was working with me. Every time an employee went out with a bag, he had to check with me. But it was no trick for me to walk out with suits and put them in the trunk of my car.

When we got the notice from headquarters that we were going out of business, I had a field day. Shipping mistakes were big in the company. Maybe we had 200 suits in the back, and we got a request to send 100 of them to our store in say, Indianapolis. The suits they wanted would be $195 retail. But I would send them $125 suits with $195 price tags on them. I knew they were going out of business and they were all jumbled up, and the other store knew I was slipping them $125 suits and billing them $195, but it was just a mistake, the kind that happened from time to time. Or I'd send them suits you couldn't sell—they were going out of season or out of style. I jumbled around with receiving. I wouldn't receive merchandise that I did receive. When I received eighty suits, there would only be seventy marked as received. There would be a miscount. The main thing I was doing with all this juggling was just covering up for the shrink-age.

I was taking the suits and selling them on the street. I'd take about ten suits a week—they wouldn't miss that—and I would get about half their price, unless, of course, I did a little jug-gling. I could take a $125 suit, put a $195 price tag on it, and get $100 for it.

It's not very difficult to rip off a company; there is always a way, but it takes time. What I was doing was really short-lived, just making a little extra money by way of inventory control. I stopped one form of shrinkage from going out the store. I knew in my heart that our chain would rather I had the money than anyone else. ✔

CLOTHING STORE SALESMAN

Neal P. worked as a salesman in a clothing store that was part of a chain. Although the stores, many of which were in shopping malls, looked fine from the outside, they employed practices, says Neal, that were "really shoddy." The salespeople were courteous, but once cus-tomers paid their money, the store didn't care about them anymore.

When people didn't have enough money to pay for a coat, they would put some money down, and we would put the coat on layaway. In the meantime, if someone else came in the store and wanted that coat and we didn't have it on the racks, the manager would say, "Oh, we have that," and he would go get the layaway coat and sell it to the guy. When people came back for their layaways, we wouldn't have the coat they had planned on get-ting. We would give them their money back and come up with some excuse, like our back room was flooded.

Once this did happen to the coats on layaway—they were actually under water. The store didn't do anything to them other than brushing them off and hanging them up to dry. They didn't even send them to the cleaners. I'm sure the insides were ruined, but the store sold them anyway.

There were instances on cash sales where advertising would be worded very cleverly, like on refunds. If customers were Christmas shopping, the salespeople would tell them anything they wanted to hear. "Oh, yes, no problem. Seven-day refund," they'd say. What they didn't say was that it was not seven days after Christmas, it was seven days after the date of sale. So, if someone bought a Christmas present on Dec. 12 and came back after Christmas, there was no refund. They could only exchange it—and on that day only. But if it had come from one of our franchised stores, one that was not company-owned, then we wouldn't refund it or exchange it—they'd have to go back to the original store.

There were times when the managers would take damaged merchandise and mingle it with the good stock trying to sell it at the regular price. This was their own stuff that maybe had been on display and was a little faded. If someone brought it back and complained, the manager would say, "Well, it wasn't like that when you got it." They were not nice.

When they hired me, the manager told me that in addition to my salary, I would be earning a 6 percent commission on all sales I made. I'd keep asking, but I never got it. Finally, I quit and took it to court, and the company denied that they ever had a policy of paying sales commissions. Finally they blamed it all on my manager, who had been fired by then. They said he was under indictment for stealing several thousand dollars worth of stuff. ✒

CASHIER/SHOPLIFTER

In the few months she worked as a cashier in a small variety store, Janet J. said she was able to steal about $1,500 in both cash and merchandise before she was caught by a spotter. Janet says she began stealing as a child, and eventually it got to be a habit she enjoyed, much like smoking. On the eve of her taking a new job as a cashier, however, Janet says she has finally reformed.

I would get to the store before my shift began and spend the time "shopping." I'd put away a few bags of stuff for myself on the side, then at quitting time, I'd just tell the owner, if he asked, that I'd already put money in the register, even though I hadn't. Sometimes my mother would come in and pick up the stuff, and I'd ring her out with a small purchase of forty-two cents, or something.

At the register, when a customer bought something and left exact change, I would put the money in the register but not ring it up. I'd already taken maybe $20 out of the register, and I'd do that with all the exact-change purchases, until they added up to what I'd taken out. When people left their change, I would just pocket it.

After I was caught, they wanted me to take a lie-detector test, but I figured the job wasn't worth it, and I called up and quit. My boss gave me $25 extra in my last check because I had been a good worker. I was on time, and I never missed a day.

When I was six, I was in a candy store, and everybody was in back. The money was kept underneath the counter, and I leaned over and grabbed a handful and put it in my pocket. Then when the girl came up front, I bought a whole bunch of candy with it. In my teens I shoplifted a lot, and I never got caught. I'd try on a pair of pants I liked and put my old ones back on the rack and wear the new ones out of the store. I'd change price tags a lot—put a $3 tag on a $10 item—especially at Christmas, when nobody notices that much. If they told me at the cash register that that was the wrong price, I'd just say I didn't want it then. Once, I went to buy a christening blanket, and I put an extra one in the box. They just bagged it, and I paid for the one. Some of the stuff I had put lower price tags on I would take back to the store and get a full refund on them.

246

After taking stuff for awhile on my last job, I started feeling guilty about it. I knew it had gotten to be a habit I had to break. I've got a son, and I would never want people to say to him, "I wouldn't trust your mother." ✔

SERVICE BUSINESSES

BANK CLERK

In the public view, the lobby is where most of a bank's business is done. Velma A., however, is a bank clerk never seen by her customers, and her daily transactions dwarf the sort of dealings to which most depositors are accustomed. She works for a large city bank, and her job involves the transfer of millions of dollars to and from the accounts of the thousands of corporations her bank serves. Velma sees neither the public nor the money, some of which moves by wire, some by telephone, and some which is picked up at the bank when she instructs other clerks to "pay on proper I.D." But though she doesn't physically touch the money, she has it at her command. "I've handled somewhere near $500 million in four hours," she says. "When one transfer alone might be $40 million, a million dollars looks quite small."

I could arrange a fictitious transfer, because I have access to all the account numbers. There are code numbers banks use, (XX) and five other numbers—we all know them; they're no big secret. You're not supposed to take the forms used for transfer out of the bank, but I've written things on them and taken them, and there's nothing to keep me from copying down the account numbers.

When I'm called, I don't know for sure whether the callers are who they're supposed to be. So if nothing is wrong with the name or the account number, I'll go ahead and transfer the money without double-checking. When I say "transfer," it's transferred. I could sit here and write you one. We'd eventually get caught but you could slow them down a lot. There are a lot of incompetent people who screw up transfers so badly it takes the bank months to straighten them out. I've thought about transferring money to some country they can't come and get you from.

That could be done. I've sent money all over the world. If they can't get you, you're cool.

We screw up money amounts and account numbers sometimes just for the hell of it—just because someone raised a voice or didn't talk nice, or used foul language. When it's hectic, someone is usually pissed off. If you phone us and wanted to transfer some money, and I didn't like the sound of your voice, I'd put you on hold or cut you off. We do business with a certain foreign bank, and we can't understand the way the guy talks when he calls, so we'll put him on hold. If I'm pissed off, I may not give customers as much as they ask for—or maybe I'll send more. Maybe they asked for $2,000, but they'll only get $1,000, and they'll have to send that back before they can get the $2,000.

We all cheat with time. This morning I was an hour or so late. Most people usually come in that late, and nobody ever says anything about it, because the supervisors are usually late, too. Our supervisor's office is in our area, but he's never there. If he's not in the cafeteria, then I'm not sure where he is. When he hired me, he said, "I'm not going to watch you. I'll leave it up to you to do your work." So if we have any questions on anything that's complicated, we just ask each other. I'd say I see the supervisor about two hours a week.

When we're hired, we don't have a supervisor training us; we just listen to the other clerks for a couple of days, and then we're into it. We have a new girl who's been here a month, and she's still screwing up everything. Usually someone covers for her, but sometimes we just let her sit there filing her nails or singing. I try to ignore her; maybe she'll go away. I know of people with the bank who have police records. They say on your application that if you have a police record and withhold information, you can be fired. But they never told them, and they're still working. I don't think the bank is checking.

It is easy to get into the vault, even if you don't know anybody there or even work in the bank. I've been in the vault area by accident. I just stepped into the wrong elevator, and I wasn't challenged and didn't have to show any I.D. I don't know how much money is lying around in the vault, but it's a lot. It's just on

250

shelves out in the open. There were a lot of security guards, but that doesn't give you any sense of having the money protected. It didn't feel the same as walking off to county jail.

My attitude would improve if they paid me more money. It's not the time, but the attitudes you deal with. When a person calls and doesn't know the account number and expects you to know it and wants $5,000 transferred, it makes you wonder. Take the amount of money that goes through us every day, like $25 million transfers, then your supervisor brings you your check . . . it's like a drop in the bucket.　　　　　　　　　　　ﬞ

WATCH REPAIRMAN

As an independent watch repairman, Clifford S. took pride in how he serviced his customers' watches. He ensured that they were cleaned properly, by dipping them in three different solutions; benzene for cleaning, another dip for rinsing, and a lubricant for oiling the parts. Often, he had to disassemble the watches partially to facilitate cleaning. As an independent, he would clean no more than ten or fifteen watches a day, because "It takes thirty minutes to clean and dry a watch properly." With the nature of the watch business changing dramatically, Clifford gave up his independence and took a job in a mass-production repair facility of a large manufacturer. There he found they used shortcuts that greatly increased production, but which, he says, did not clean the watches effectively and also required the use of chemicals that he directly attributes to his own failing health. After three months, he left in a storm of protest and once again is self-employed.

There were thirty of us working in that basement room for eight hours a day. There was no ventilation, and a lot of people were smoking. I'd worked there two weeks, when I started getting nauseated. I felt hyperactive, and I kept sneezing. I had a fever of 101°, and my eyes started to hurt. I asked some of the

251

others if they felt sick, and they said, yes, they had stomach problems and pains in the eyes and in the back of the neck. But nobody would attribute it to the solution we were using, and nobody would complain, because they knew they'd get fired if they did. My symptoms came on after I started with this company. I had had a physical examination just before, and I was in good shape. My lungs were excellent, and I'd never missed a day of work because of sickness before.

Originally, watch repairmen used benzene, which was recently banned by the government, to clean the watches. That ban was ridiculous because I've never heard of a watchmaker getting ill from benzene. So at this repair shop we used a chemical called ----, which they'd get in gallon cans and which we'd pour into small, open containers and keep at our benches. The label clearly said: "Caution—prolonged or repeated breathing of this vapor can be harmful. Use only with adequate ventilation. Do not transfer liquid to another container. Do not take internally. Causes toxic gases when in contact with flame." It's a strong hydrocarbon solvent. Well, here they've got bottles of this stuff open all over the room, people smoking, and no ventilation. You have to dip the watch into it, then blow on it to dry it. So the chemical is close to your eyes, and it gets in your nostrils, and you're doing this thirty-five or forty times a day. This is a great disservice to the manufacturers of this chemical, because it's meant to be used for short periods, then capped. It's being misused.

This solution that made me sick doesn't clean the watches either. You can't dip a watch in once and blow it off—the parts inside don't get clean. All it does is clean the hairspring. If the watch stops during the warranty, they don't care if it comes back. They'll just dip it again.

My doctor said he had never seen me so sick and put me in the hospital. I stayed for two days at a cost of $625. I paid my doctor $125 and only saw him once. I called work, and they told me to come in, or I was terminated. They said I'd have to see the company doctor, but he told me, "Don't come in. If you can't stand the fumes, quit your job." He wouldn't send the chemical out for testing—he didn't want to get involved. I finally went to an eye doctor, who said I had an infection in both eyes and was convinced that the chemical was causing my problem. Now it's in the hands of my lawyer.

All along, I told the union steward we needed air conditioning, but he said he didn't want to get involved and not to use his name. He wouldn't do anything, so then I went to the business agent, and he was hostile to me. Our contract with the company was a sellout anyway. They have complete control over the methods and processes of production and allow no interference from the union. A "real" union wouldn't allow conditions that endanger the health of its members.

It's all different these days, anyway. They hire inexperienced people and train them in watch repairing. The parts are now replaced instead of repaired, because repair would call for experienced watchmakers. Most of the employees are cheap labor from minorities. When companies are forced to report illegal aliens, it will empty them out. It's a lot better now that I'm self-employed again. Now I can breathe.   ✔

OFFICE EQUIPMENT REPAIRMAN

Working as an office equipment repairman, where his labor is billed at $26 an hour, yet he doesn't even see $6 per hour, Greg K. figures he's learning his trade and paying his tuition toward the day when he can go out on his own. The shop he works for both sells and repairs office equipment, about 80 percent of which are typewriters. As for the customers, says Greg, "They do and they don't get a fair shake."

We charge a minimum of one hour's work, even if we correct the problem in about ten minutes. The minimum charge is $26 an hour. No one expects to get out for any less than $26, or, on rare occasions, $15, which doesn't cover much more than blowing the dust out of the thing. It is geared to the individual. If it is a business that is doing pretty well, I guess the explanation is that they can afford it, so we charge what we can get away with. If it's a little old woman who brings in a machine in her shopping bag and explains that she can't afford much, we're not going to charge her that much.

Say, a job honestly takes three hours, then the customer would be charged at least four-and-a-half hours, which is inflating it about 50 percent. But this is only if they look as if they can pay it, or if they have given us a hard time. It might even be drawn to a level of personality conflict. In dealing with a business, the question of charges rarely comes up. It's more like, "This purchase order will take care of it, just bill us." If it's tough work, we increase the time we charge for. The boss will ask, "Was it an older model?" or "Did it require a little more work?" Well, I had to pop a couple of screws off first. "Well, that was extra work. Charge them an extra hour-and-a-half." That doesn't correlate at all with the work I put in, which might have been ten or fifteen minutes. But they're billed at $26 an hour. If somebody yells, then we have the flexibility to back off a little. Give an inch rather than lose a customer.

Out of all the parts that are put in, I would say that 50 percent are not needed, but this varies among servicemen. Of what some put in, 75 percent might be unnecessary. Often, the people you work for will suggest that you add phantom parts to the repair order just to make your work look a little more legitimate. Our prices for parts, however, are pretty fair. We will charge regular customers our cost, simply because we know we can make up for it in our labor charges.

Once, one of our customers had a typewriter fastened to a desk top to prevent theft, and somebody tried to steal it one night, and it came to us for repair. This was like a $900 machine. The repairman gave an estimate of $350 just to cover us in case there was a lot of work in it. The machine wasn't working at all and appeared to be badly damaged. Our best repairman looked at it back in the shop and determined that the problem was that the frame had been bent a little. He whacked it on the bottom

254

about ten times with a hammer and got it working. All the systems were fine, and there was no replacement of any parts. He said, "We gave them an estimate of $350. We'll give them a break and only charge them $300."

I don't like things like that to happen. A business has to make up for its new people who spend more time on repairs than we can legitimately charge, or novice technicians who might break things, or warranty work, which we don't make any money on. But still customers pay inordinately large sums of money for people who have expertise in special technical areas. What the hell does the average customer know about the inside of a typewriter? I've talked with guys in other shops about this, but they seem pretty closed-mouthed about it. It is kind of like an understanding that it's not something we talk about because everybody does it, as the cliché goes. Nobody, I hope, is proud of it. I'm certainly not particularly proud of my job. ✒

HAIRSTYLIST

"The people who make money in the beauty business are the big names," says Sally I., who cuts men's and women's hair for a living. She learned her trade as a stylist by working for a big-name salon for several years. Sally regards the experience as priceless, though she did feel ripped off in terms of the pay, a situation she shrugs off as paying her dues. Under the commission system, by which she is paid, a typical stylist, she says, can earn up to $45,000 a year (including 10 percent tips), though some might make $60,000. The biggest ripoff in the hair industry, she says, is the customer's not getting what he or she wants.

There's a great difference between what people think hairstylists get and what they really take home. I worked at a well-known salon for five years, and we were paid the least amount of commission possible. The usual commission for a stylist ranges from 30 to 70 percent of what the customer pays. Yet I cut $180,000 worth of hair and took home only about 10 percent of that. They would take our weekly totals, which was the record of how many clients we'd had, and screw them up. We never got paid for the total amount of work we did. When I kept my own records, they told me I was crazy when I handed them in.

We had to keep assistants, who would shampoo and blow-dry the customers' hair as well as perform other services, on our personal payroll. We had to pay anywhere from half to all of their $50-to $150-a-week salaries. So that's where a lot of our tips went. Our tips might range up to $5, but the average would be about $2 on a $20 haircut, or about 10 percent.

When we would do shows for one of the trade conventions, we had to kick back 50 percent of what we made to the salons we worked for, even though we were not at the show under the salon's name. We were doing it on our own, and the convention was our employer. This was just the salon's way of collecting more commissions. They would say they had trained us even though they never had.

Back at the salon, they would skim $2.50 off the top of, say, a $20 haircut for the manager's traveling and training fund, then the stylists would be paid their commission on the remainder, or $17.50. I don't know how much they collected that way, and I didn't mind as long as I knew it was going toward good publicity for the salon and toward the best possible facilities for my clients—both of which helped me make money. But when they take 60 or 70 percent of your intake and don't spend it wisely to promote the business and make it grow, that is shoddy. So they keep you in this stringent bracket of being underpaid. There's nothing you can do about it, because the big-name salons would fire you immediately for taking down a client's telephone number. So if you try to go out on your own, you'd lose your whole clientele.

If a stylist doesn't take the time to comprehend what the customer really expects, that is the biggest ripoff you can pay for. Some stylists feel that they are so artistic that they know what is right for you and don't want to listen. There's a fine balance

256

between knowing how to change a person and knowing, if they don't like the change, how to go back to their old style with few problems. If you give a customer something she didn't want or cut her hair too short, that, to her, is the second worst thing to rape.

Razor cuts are not that good for the hair, and with them your hair has to be cut more often. Also, the person cutting the hair doesn't have to be as highly skilled to do them. If you want good hairstyling, go to someone who is on his toes, someone who attends seminars and learns new techniques. A lot of barbers aren't very progressive and are not interested in going back to school. The difference between a styling and a haircut is that the stylist usually has spent a year or two learning how to cut hair a lot better. A haircut may last four or five weeks, but a good styling can last up to three months. So even though you're paying more for it, it's more economical.

I became a hairstylist, because I was ripped off plenty of times as a customer. I said I wanted a specific length or a specific style and got nowhere near it. I would say that happens 50 percent of the time. My advice to customers would be to go into a salon and see how it is run. Have something as simple as a manicure. If the hairstylist doesn't have enough time to speak to you and tell you what he can and can't do with your hair, get the hell out of there. Now, if I were sitting in a chair and the stylist were doing something drastically wrong to me, I would let him finish, but I definitely would not pay my bill. If it's a big thing, don't let it pass. There are a lot of people who don't deserve to be in this business. ✔

WAREHOUSING/SHIPPING

TRUCKING DOCK SUPERVISOR

Wendell M. lost a lot of money trying to start his own business, and when he had to give it up, rather than declaring bankruptcy, he worked out a plan to pay off his creditors over a period of several years. Because he needed the money, he took on three jobs. As a trucking dock supervisor, he worked seven days straight, thirteen hours a day, then got the next week off, which he spent working in a factory and pumping gas. In two years time, he had paid off his debt, but not without being hospitalized twice for exhaustion. After five years, he decided the grueling pace of the trucking terminal was no longer for him.

As a supervisor you are going all the time. I have supervised as many as eighty dockworkers at one time by myself, and these are hard-core, tough men. My responsibilities included making sure the paperwork was properly filled out—the manifests that went with the trailers, the freight bills, etc.—the proper checking of freight, taking care of problems that came up, like broken cartons, and, of course, supervising the crews. I was on the outbound end of the dock. They usually put the tougher, more aggressive guys there, because they had to move at a faster pace; there was so much more outbound freight. During one of my shifts, we broke a terminal record—which has since been broken—of moving about 1½ million pounds in a twelve-hour period.

Supervisors work seven days in a row, say, from midnight to noon. They wanted us in at 11:15 for a proper relief, then, of course, the person going home wouldn't get out of the terminal till 12:30 or 12:45 by the time we figured up our reports. Sometimes, it was closer to a fourteen-hour day, which gets rough in midwinter. It takes it out of you when you're walking around with all the extra clothes on. In five years, there never once was

259

a scheduled break or a lunch hour for the supervisors. It's an unbelievably hectic job. Guys drop out of there constantly. Fistfights break out all the time, because the pressure is unrelenting. We would fight over men: "Damn it, he is mine. I'm taking him." "No, I need him." I had to be carried out twice after I was beaten up by dockworkers. They were very flip and there was no backing whenever a supervisor got in trouble with the men. The guys who beat me up didn't get canned or anything.

On one of our days off, it was mandatory that we come back to the terminal to attend a meeting, which might be thirty minutes or four hours. We weren't paid for it. I don't think a month went by without my being called into work for someone—thirteen hours extra with no compensation.. They were known for going through management people like crazy. They'd wake you up at 1 a.m. and say, "Look we just fired so-and-so, and we need you in here." You would say, "Hey look, I just went to bed at eleven," and they would say, "Do you want the job next week, or don't you?" I was losing weight working those long hours, and they kept saying, "We're going to promote you, we're going to promote you," but they didn't like to promote good people on the dock, because they desperately needed people out there who knew how to make the place run. Right now they probably pay a guy doing what I was doing about $350 a week.

You hear a lot about security in the trucking industry, because the thefts go on continuously. One box of calculators was worth a fortune. This was before you could buy a calculator for $7—they were going for $300 and $400 apiece. We were self-insured, and losing a box of calculators could completely wipe out the profit of the next ten freight movements.

What would happen is, dockworkers would go out to a loading area that had these calculators. But for any given trailer load you might have 100 different freight bills and a whole mixture of anything you can think of from nuts to lampshades. The first step is to make sure that the freight was sorted properly. The workers would have to take four pieces of this order going to this com-

260

pany, and hold it on the side waiting for the fifth piece to show up. It was their responsibility not to send the order out to the loading trailer until all five pieces were accounted for. The loading area is eight-feet wide and forty-two-feet long, so there is a lot of room, and a dockworker can literally build a wall of freight outside the trailer while sorting the freight. Even though dockworkers would find the pieces they needed to send the order out, they would hold them on the side in another area—and unless you handled freight for awhile, you wouldn't know what they were doing.

So now that they've got a camouflage, they find the box with the calculators—it says right on the freight bill: calculators—and they open up the box and stuff their pockets with whatever they can fit in without getting caught, which is quite a bit in the wintertime with all the extra clothing. They can get away with opening a box, because it is their job to recoup or repair freight that is damaged. If a box of undershirts falls and ruptures, they are compelled by union rules to restack all those undershirts carefully in the box, get masking tape from a supervisor, and tape the box up. They are supposed to report that immediately, but that falls by the wayside, because the supervisor is so damned busy moving trailers and watching all the other guys, he just tells the guy to put it back together. You are not going to go by an old-timer's trailer that does not give you trouble. You see him with his hands on the freight, recouping a cardboard box, and you're not going to jump him for it. Hell, you are glad that he has recouped the box, even though he may be filling his pockets.

The big problem is where you get a lot of freight of anything small and expensive—wristwatches, soldering guns, calculators—anything that can be moved quickly at a flea market or some low-quality retail outlet. After a dockworker working the inbound area builds his wall of freight, he drops a box off the dock, down underneath the trailer. After his shift ends he walks around, gets the box, puts it in his car, and takes off. Now, although he has to account for shortages in his trailer, this is only

261

when the trailer is completely unloaded, and this is the problem.

Let's say he works in that trailer for four hours, and it gets real busy on the outbound end of the dock, and they need every man available. So he gets a brand new job assignment, and that trailer is going to sit there untouched. That's what gets him off the hook: He did not finish working that trailer. If one guy does the first half of a trailer and another guy does the second, if things are missing, then nobody gets blamed. When you have a poor terminal manager who bounces guys back and forth, you can have eight guys working on a trailer before it is empty. You lose control.

This is one reason why claims are a multibillion dollar industry. I was in charge of settling claims for another trucking company. Some companies will do anything to get out of a claim. "We don't have a driver with a signature like that," they'll say. "You didn't give that to us." They'll say, "That is not a seven, it is a two," and that sort of thing when examining the original bill of lading. Or, when a stationery store opens the box that looks like it hadn't been opened when they signed for it, and it is filled with bricks, not calculators, the trucking company says, "Hey, you signed for the boxes—they're no longer insured by us." There are people who ship empty boxes, saying they are calculators and try to get away with false claims. Shippers and consignees, the persons the freight is destined to, get together. People claim false values: Even if they only get 10 percent, that's 10 percent more than they had when they started. Claims against some trucking companies amount to 10 percent of their business. Generally, the industry regards 3.5 percent as tolerable.

Of course, shippers are not always honest on the matter of what is called weight and rate. A rate is the dollar amount charged per hundred pounds of any given freight. This is a tariff schedule put out by the government, and everyone in the shipping business will abide by these rules, period. It looks like twenty sets of encyclopedias, there are so many volumes involved. The rates take weight and volume into consideration, as well as the value of some items where a higher risk is involved. It may cost a lot more to ship a twenty-pound box of lampshades than, say, a twenty-pound box of steel washers, which don't take up so much room. These rates establish a reasonable profit margin for the trucking company for hauling whatever kind of freight it is.

I once caught a big sporting goods firm trying to save $300 on the charge for shipping basketballs. On their freight bill, they claimed they were sending deflated basketballs, when, in fact, they were sending inflated ones. You can imagine the size difference between the cartons you'd need for 3,000 flat basketballs and 3,000 inflated ones. A deflated basketball goes for, say, eighty cents a hundred pounds, but an inflated one, because it takes up so much more volume, might cost $1.80 a hundred. The shippers knew what they were doing. The company I worked for ran a survey and figured they were losing something like $5 million a year just because of crooked shippers misdeclaring their goods. We hired a man who does nothing but spot-check shipments for rate and weight corrections, and he is picking up almost $2,000 a week in extra revenue.

Or let's say a man ships a skid of books that may cost $1 a hundred. He says his pallet weighs 500 pounds, but when it gets to the terminal and we put it on our scale, we find it weighs 1,000. Well, we've doubled the revenue we're entitled to charge. He may have made an honest mistake, or maybe he didn't have a scale. But when you start dealing with the bigger boys, the guys who do know what they are doing and do have scales, you've got a problem. If a company ships a million pounds of true weight a month and only pays for 700,000 pounds, we've moved 300,000 pounds of their freight free—and it is on a scale like that with some big outfits.

Now, the trucking companies are starting to pool their information so they can identify the chronic offenders. We can go to the ICC with copies of every corrected freight bill and tell them to jump on those guys. But even then, it's like anything you put into the government—it can be disallowed for any reason. So even if you really build a case, you can't convict the violators.

You can just hope the government says, well, you guys better straighten out.

Truck drivers, themselves, pull a lot of shenanigans. Say a driver goes to a company shipping calculators, and they have twenty shipments going to twenty different places. Maybe the shipping manager gets confused, and the driver just takes one of the twenty bills of lading and doesn't sign it. That's how he gets off scott-free, because the shipper doesn't have any record that he made that particular shipment. The driver leaves, and there is no way of stopping him from pulling up to another warehouse—there's nothing suspicious about that. So if he's in cahoots with a dockworker at that warehouse, he takes the cartons for that particular shipment off the truck and destroys all the paperwork pertaining to that shipment. Or he doesn't even have to go to a warehouse. He can act on his own and fence the goods. There is no signed document that says his firm ever picked up the freight, and they're going to fight like crazy to say that they never got it.

On deliveries downtown, drivers will have to go into the store or office and leave their trucks unattended. The delivery will be for fifty boxes, and the consignee will say, "Okay, we want them on the third floor." Well, the driver has to wait for elevators and everything. He may get tired of jumping up on his trailer, getting five boxes, then locking the door, so he may take his fifty boxes and set them right in the alley. On one of his trips up, he gets ripped off by someone in the alley. He calls the company and tells them what happened, and they can't do anything to him. But maybe that never happened; maybe he took forty-five boxes and dropped them off first, then went to the place he was delivering to and told them he had fifty boxes for them. Well, those people are all busy; they're not going to come out and watch the guy, so he'll bring five boxes in, and he says, "Holy cow, they took forty-five boxes on me"—and they will all substantiate his story.

The contracts with our drivers make it next to impossible to fire people for ripping off their employers. They are sort of tacit acknowledgment that the union is full of pretty crooked people.

I'm in the union, and I know they're crooked. This stuff goes on all the time, and they are blatant in their disregard for what's right. They are just loaded to the teeth with righteous indignation whenever you think you have caught them, and they stand behind their people. A guy has to be worthless before you even try to fire him. Of course, if it's not justified and you say, "He's not coming back to work," the union will say, "Fine, nobody is going to work," and there you have a strike. Or if you want to enforce some regulation, they'll start driving slower or walking slower. They are paid on an hourly salary, and slowdowns are very much a part of their operating methods.

When I was a dock supervisor, the union organizers used to come around on Saturdays and try to collect dues from brand new employees and sign them up. They would get five or six older union guys talking to them, so I'd go back as a supervisor and try to break it up and get them back to work. They would just casually scratch their back, or pull their coat back or something, and show me the butt of a .44 sticking out under their arm. Every time I tried to break up these gatherings, I was reminded they had plenty of muscle.

Back when I was working as a dockworker, I needed the job, and I wasn't going to get fired for standing around. One night this big dockworker—he was probably close to 300 pounds, a stereotype with tatoos, stubby cigar, the whole bit—told me that if I didn't slow down, there might be an accident, where a fork-lift broke my legs. He said people who hurry on the docks get hurt, and that accidents even happen in the parking lot— they'll slip and fall, and they'll break both arms, both legs, and their jaw. He was the union steward, so I accepted that as the official union point of view.

The union will look the other way when a guy really hustles during the first thirty days when he's trying to get into the union. On the thirty-first day, he'll be admitted into the union and given the same privileges as someone who has been there ten years. But then they'll say, "Okay, you've put on your show, and everyone is impressed. Now slow down, or you're going to get hurt." It was an unwritten rule that you would always leave

265

work for the next guy so he could support his family. Most of the dockworkers I ever talked to looked upon working slowly as a patriotic gesture. They were creating jobs. ✔

RECEIVING CLERK

In a recent study of workplace crime,* it was estimated that dishonest employees in cargo transportation cost the economy $2.5 billion a year, nearly half of which was attributable to trucking ($1.2 billion). In the same study, a security expert placed a $3.3 billion price tag on employee theft in the retail sector—a loss greater than that caused by shoplifting.

These two sectors, transportation and retailing, intersect on a loading dock where Ben G. worked as a receiving clerk for a large department store chain. There, goods came in by truck to the company's warehouse, where they were sorted and priced before distribution to the retail shelves. The receiving clerks were there to ensure that the goods the truckers said they were delivering were, in fact, delivered and safely stowed inside the warehouse. Ben and the others quickly learned that whenever shortages were discovered, just like water seeking its lowest level, it was the receiving clerks who got the blame.

When a truck comes in, you sign for what you receive. Some drivers say, "Gee, it won't matter to you—you're receiving 200 cartons; let me keep twenty and don't put any exception in, and I'll take care of you." A couple of our people will do that, but I don't because it's not worth it. The truck driver will take it someplace and drop it off or exchange merchandise with other drivers. He's got a clear bill and nothing to worry about. Eventually, they'll notice the shortage, and the receiving clerk will

---

*"*Stealing from the Company: A Fact Booklet on Workplace Crime*," (*March 1978*), *National Council on Crime and Delinquency.*

say he had them all; then he might get fired. The guy who signs the bills gets fired when a shortage is discovered. But he was taken care of by the driver. He'll give the driver his number, and the driver will call him, and they'll go out for a couple of drinks, and he'll pay him off—a couple-thousand bucks, or whatever.

One time I was listening to a driver tell another receiving clerk there were about 180 cartons of Levis, and he wanted to keep about twenty, worth about $10,000. He told the kid he'd give him 20 percent. The kid knew I was listening and said, not this time—maybe some other time. These are drivers from big trucking companies. I'd say about 10 percent of them do it. I used to hear one of our guys tell drivers that if they'd give him a few bucks, he'd let them take off with a couple of cartons and sign a clear bill.

Once, a driver delivered about twenty-four cartons of small calculators—at the time the calculators were worth about $180 apiece—and unloaded the truck himself, which they usually do when there are under twenty-five pieces. It was really busy, and the supervisor told a receiving clerk to go sign for the cartons. He did, and after the driver had left, he discovered the middle ones were all empty. Only ten cartons were full. The clerk got screwed, because he was told to sign. Even though they were unloaded, he should have checked the cartons for his own protection. There are more supervisors there than people working—and the supervisors never take the blame.

Sometimes a driver unloads twenty cartons, and the receiving clerk goes into the office for a minute. Then the driver throws a couple of cartons back onto the truck, then closes the doors. The clerk has already counted the cartons, so the shortage won't get noticed until the merchandise gets up on the storage floors.

Drivers sometimes ask us to unload and pay us a couple of bucks if we do. We could put a couple of cartons away and say they were short, and they can't say anything. But eventually, the guy who first loaded the truck would get in trouble. The blame eventually goes to some low person—not the dispatchers, or the supervisors, or the truck drivers—but to whomever loads or unloads the truck. They're the ones who get in trouble.

About six years ago, we were missing a lot of TVs, and they couldn't figure out how they were getting out. Well, when they delivered a new appliance to a customer, they'd bring the old one back to the warehouse as a trade-in. They'd store the old appliances in a little room, and every week a junkman came in to pick them up. Well, somebody was putting new TVs inside the old refrigerators, and nobody knew. The junkman said, "I just pick 'em up and drop 'em off," but he was probably involved with someone in the warehouse. Still, they never could prove anything.

After they mark the clothes, they bring them down to the docks on trolleys and truck them to the stores. I knew a guy who every day for about a month would take dresses from the trolley, go into the bathroom, and put them on under his clothes. He used to sell them on the outside or give them to his girlfriend. One day I saw him, and he quit.

The computer is the best way to get merchandise out of the building. Let's say I put on the computer that we received 150 cartons. I could go to the computer and change it to 130 and take twenty cartons home. They may compare freight bills against the computer, but they always believe the computer. There are about nine of us with access to the computer. I could use somebody else's code, and there's no way they can tell who changed the figures. If I ripped up the freight bill, they couldn't double-check it.

Many people can get hold of sales tickets—what they use to write up a customer's order. They could just write up a tag with their own address, and the driver would deliver it. The driver may have a connection with someone upstairs, and after he delivers the merchandise, he won't bring the paperwork back with him. It's got to be teamwork between a driver, a guy loading, and the guy upstairs.

You've got access to anything in the warehouse. They log merchandise out, but the place is so big they can't get control of it at all times. You could pull a TV out and put your neighbor's name on it, and they wouldn't know you're stealing it. All of this goes on right in front of everyone's eyes. It's tough to know if somebody is legitimate or not.

Management is so stupid—they don't know what to do about all the theft. I was going to tell them how I think it's being done, but if I did, they might think I had something to do with it—so I stay back. They have a suggestion box, but it's always empty. Nobody wants to give them suggestions, because they'll think you have something to do with the problem. If you try to help them, they think you're trying to screw them up, so it's not worth stepping forward. ✔

PAPER WAREHOUSEMAN

As a paper warehouseman, Fred S. is responsible for receiving and checking the grade of the rolls or paper that come by boxcars into the printing company for which he works. He deals with diversity—the paper comes from Canadian as well as European mills—and he deals with quantity: His firm prints catalogs and magazines for national accounts. As is so often the case, when numbers are involved, confusion can't be far behind.

Sometimes we get the proper grade of paper, and sometimes we don't. Paper grades go by poundage, 28, 32, 40, 50, 55, and the higher the grade, the better the paper. The poundage refers to the pounds of tension per square inch. The lighter tension paper rips on the press quicker, and that screws up the operation and causes a lot of lost time. The mills are responsible for slipping us the lower grades. They are just trying to see if we are on our toes. Well, we're a big operation, and whatever you can get away with, you do. Some may be carelessness on their part, but a lot of it is intentional. All the mills we deal with do it; one or two try to keep it to a minimum, but the rest of the mills go right down the drain. Percentage-wise, about 25 percent of the paper we get is the wrong grade. This creates real problems with advertisers, who are paying for a certain grade of paper— they are selling visual appeal. So, if their ads are printed on lower grade paper, you have to make some allowance on what you bill them. This keeps a lot of people busy checking and creates work where there should not be any.

On any printing job there is waste, and you can tell the customer that this went wrong and that went wrong, and there was waste, waste, waste. If a job is being done right they expect to pay no more than 5 or 10 percent for waste, but we have billed as high as 25 percent. There are forty to forty-eight rolls of paper in a boxcar, and on a national magazine run of several million, I would guess our company is overcharging for waste by a couple of boxcars, at least. That could be almost 100 rolls of paper at, say, $500 a roll. That is $50,000, which is quite a bit. Customers can't verify this, unless they have someone there twenty-four hours a day, but still, that's only one person. One person can't watch everything. If people ask to see the two boxcars of waste, they are there, but the waste may not be from their job. It is shredded and compressed into bales, so there is no way of figuring out whose product it was. I have worked in several printing plants, and this happens all over.

I've even worked for daily newspapers, and they do it well. There the newsprint comes into the warehouse, and they can take it and hide it all over the place. There are a few guys who want to make a buck on the side, usually the foremen, and if they can control what goes in and what goes out, they can sell it. I worked for a big city newspaper, where the foreman sold rolls of newsprint to the suburban papers. The suburban paper's truck would come up in the dead of night to pick up the paper. You could get twenty-five to fifty rolls on it, and away it went. You'd do what the foreman told you. Those guys have come up through the ranks, and they know everyone in the trade. So, all they have to do is pick up a telephone and say, "Do you need some stuff?" All of us knew that he was selling it. He covered up for it at inventory time as waste or bad rolls. When this sort of thing

270

happened, all I got out of it was four hours or so of overtime. Nobody ever tried to blow the whistle on him, because that would have meant good-bye job, good-bye union card, good-bye everything. These guys have come up through the union, and they would have you blacklisted. They even did this in broad daylight, because some guys are always loading or unloading paper—who is to know?

When the newsprint comes in by boat, the longshoremen unload them, and you don't fool with them—you let them do whatever they want to do. They could take the boat with them, and I would not say a word. They are responsible for unloading the boat, and we are paid to watch them unload. They put it in the warehouse, and although we don't touch it, there must be a crew of warehousemen there. I've seen that when the longshoremen unloaded the boat, not all of the paper came off—it just stayed on the boat. There would be a manifest or something, and when the paper was supposedly all off the boat, they'd say, here, sign it, and even if the paper wasn't all there, the foreman would still sign it. Just before the river freezes, you have to get in as much as you can. Well, hell, you can get away with murder, because you are working, working, working, and the warehouse is bulging it's so full. You know damned well part of it is just walking away.   ✔

STOCK HANDLER

In three years as a stock handler, Jon W. saw a lot of corn snacks coming into his branch plant, which was a storage facility for the manufacturer. The corn snacks came into the branch by semitrailer load, and they went out on the trucks of the wholesale route drivers. As it turned out, the distribution system was a bit more complex than the home office ever realized.

My job was unloading the trailers and loading the little baby trucks in which the wholesale route drivers made their rounds. The dispatcher at the plant knew how many corn snacks they were supposed to be shipping to this branch, but he didn't know that each trailer was overloaded at the factory by 25 percent and that that portion of each load was not accounted for. Our branch manager was keeping separate books on them. He was crooked as hell and must have been paying off the people on the dock at the plant. We kept this hot stuff all by itself.

Every night, about four or five of our route drivers would get as much of it onto their regular truckloads as they could. The next day on the street, they would sell it to the merchants, little stores and tavern owners, at half-price. Say, a box of snacks the tavern guy would normally pay $7.30 for, here he was paying $3.40. Instead of a $2 profit, he was making $5. A tavern owner of course, had to buy some corn snacks at the regular price to get in on this. I would guess that this hot stuff amounted to thousands of dollars a week. Each of the drivers got a share, and so did the manager. I only loaded the trucks; I didn't get anything out of it. I just got fired for knowing about it.

WINING AND DINING OUT

CATERING MANAGER

"I got a better position than a busboy by keeping my eyes and ears open," says Burt M., who a few years ago was a high school dropout and now is a catering manager in a country club. He is responsible for providing food and beverage service to the various groups who book his public rooms for wedding parties, bar mitzvahs, institutional gatherings, etc. He has waitresses, busboys, cooks, and bartenders working for him, and Burt, himself, works for a management company that runs that club and others. As the day of the party approaches, Burt's preparations begin when he checks his stock and orders the necessary provisions.

I deal with wholesale purveyors for our food. You start ordering the bulk of your food from them, and they will take care of you. You can work out a deal where you can fill up your own refrigerator at home. Sometimes they offer you a box of food, sometimes you tell them, "I need some steaks, couple heads of lettuce, ten pounds of potatoes, etc." and they will take care of you. It will come in a separate box with your name and no price on it. The same thing with liquor—it may be their house brand, but it's still booze. What I'm saying is, you'll never go hungry.

I'm feeding my family on what I get. To get that, I'm throwing the purveyor about $1,000 a week in business. What they give me in return would probably cost $70 in a supermarket. The companies that don't give rebates don't do a lot of business. They are run down, and they are the ones that will give you a poor quality of meat. You don't want to deal with someone who's giving you crap—you've got to think of quality—so the best places to go to are the ones that are giving kickbacks. I'm getting about $300 worth of free food a month that doesn't show up on my income tax. But I have no fears about that; I'm just living life one day at a time.

Everyone above me knows about it because they are in on it, too. The home office of the management firm gives us a list, and we're told, "These are the people you are going to buy from," so you know they are getting their share, too. They tell us what to do, but they don't check up on us. All they look at are the bottom-line figures. The people in the club getting kickbacks, are me, the bartender, the dining room manager, and the general manager himself. The ringleader is older and has been in the business for a number of years. So if he holds up his hand, all of us take what we can get, and if he says no, we cool it. Of course, he has to cut the general manager in, because he could pull the whole plug on us and really mess us up. Flowers, wedding cakes, you name it. There are always kickbacks. A lot of this job is: You just have to bullshit a lot of people. If you can't bullshit them, you're not going to go anywhere.

The other day we had a wedding party, and the gentleman who was paying for the liquor was told to bring in cash, because we did not have time to run a check on his credit. Well, the bill came to $400, he paid us, and the four of us each made off with $90 apiece. There was no written contract for the party, and nothing was reported to the accounting office, because we didn't mark the party down as having a bar. Well, there are lots of dry weddings—so we just put down $20 for a couple-gallons of punch.

Sure, that's ripping off the company. But I guess you can say that we feel that we are not making enough money—that's what it boils down to. We get a percentage of all the parties, so if the season is dead, we're not making any money. This was during a time when everyone was hurting.

The client does not know it, but we have a 17 percent gratuity charge on top of the price of the food and everything they have, and this is divided among all the help on a percentage basis. I get gratuities as a manager from all the parties. In a good year it adds to my regular earnings from $5,000 to $7,000. I never keep track of all I pocket, but my kickbacks must amount to at least what my gratuity is. Combined, that's $12,000 or so a year tax-free.

Unless clients specify call brands of liquor, we buy the cheap stuff. So they're paying $18 a bottle, plus tax and gratuity, and I think the highest we pay for, say, a bottle of house-brand bourbon is $3.72. There are a lot of ways of making money. Or, if they specify a call brand, say, they want a certain Scotch, we charge them for that Scotch, but we don't give it to them. There are different brands that are technically the same as the expensive brand. The difference is that they are sent over to the United States in drums from Scotland and bottled here. But our cost is $2.50 or $3 cheaper, so that's what we give them. We recently had to change our bourbon, because the gut-rot stuff we were getting was beginning to taste it. We've changed back to better stuff now.

It's illegal, but we will pour the cheap stuff into bottles of call brands. It's called marrying. You just take a funnel, lock yourself in the storage room and pour the booze from one bottle to another. Most of the marrying we do is with the vodka we buy, which is a diluted, 60-proof booze. It says "60 proof" in big letters right on the label, and we don't want people seeing that. It's a no-name brand that I've never seen in liquor stores—I think it's for bar use only. There is low-proof booze in all descriptions available—bourbon, Scotch, you name it—and it's bought by bars and catering people. We figure this is the way for us to make ourselves look good when they check the figures at the end of the month—and nobody notices the difference. That 60-proof vodka runs us less than $3 a bottle.

The management company audits our food and booze operation, but we give them all the figures. Most of the time I phony the inventory. Once they ran a spot inventory on us, and it was funny because the accountant came in and said, "Okay, this month let's take an honest inventory." Well, I'd already taken it, and it was strange because it was the first month I'd done an honest inventory. I don't know why—it was just a slow month. If I'd done it the way I normally do it, I would have been in trouble. This guy's an accountant for the company, and it never seems like he could give a shit either.

Of course, you teach your bartenders to short-pour—I mean

give the customers less than a shot. This is when the host is paying by the drink. For the first hour of cocktails, you tell them to pour away; let the people know they are having something; let them taste the booze. But then, after dinner, boom, you hit them with nothing. They don't know the difference. If it has the smell of booze, they can't tell. You normally get thirty shots out of a quart bottle. When you short-pour, you can get as many as forty-five.

When they are paying by the drink, after the bar closes, we measure the bottles with our eyes. There are ten tenths to a bottle—a bottle half-full has five tenths gone. We figure three drinks to a tenth, so if half a bottle were used, that is fifteen drinks. At the end of the party, we count how many empties we have and how many tenths were used out of the others and multiply those figures by three. Of course, we always go higher. Say they used up eighteen bottles; you know that's a lot of drinks, and we can inflate the total by maybe fifty drinks, which would be another $50 or $60. You can inflate your estimate by about 10 percent. The clients don't know, and they are not going to check.

When they're paying by the bottle, you pour away. Or, if bartenders are working for themselves, going for good tips, they may only get 20 shots out of a bottle. You want to show as many empty bottles at the end as you can, so the client pays for more—and, of course, that raises the gratuity, too. Smart bartenders will empty a bottle of booze into a soda bottle or something and put it on the side. If I see them doing it, I might stop them and I might not—it depends on the people. As a manager, I don't encourage them to do that, but I will tell them when I want them to short-pour.

The only time we count drinks is when there is a cash bar, and the customers are given tickets for their drinks. We will inflate the count of the tickets only if our cashiers handle the dispensing of the tickets. We don't inflate heavily, only, say, 10 percent. They're not going to count them. We only had that happen once, and that was the one time we were doing it straight. It was an organization helping the handicapped.

When people ask for a spiked punch at a party, we'll give them a rum punch for $20 a gallon, but we don't put any rum in it. We use a rum extract for cooking that has 25 percent alcohol in it. We pour in maybe a quarter of a cup, and it tastes just like there's a bottle or two of rum in there. It costs us less to serve, and they can't tell the difference.

For a champagne punch, we pour in a bottle of $1.97 champagne, a little soda, a little Seven-Up, and some cherry juice. I don't even know the recipe for a proper champagne punch, but I imagine it would call for a couple more bottles of champagne. If people want an orange punch spiked with vodka, we use half a bottle of the married stuff, which is enough because you can't taste the vodka anyway. We will get compliments on the punches, because a lot of our clients are nice old ladies who do not want to get blitzed anyway.

We only play a few games in the food service end of it, mostly in meats. If people can't meet our price, we'll say, "Well, we'll try to work something out for you." We'll buy second-rate meat—the inside, the top rounds—which, if it is cooked right, can taste the same as the better cuts. If the chefs know what they are doing, the clients won't catch it at all. Or sometimes on a lunch, we'll say we are serving seven-ounce portions of something like chicken, but we'll go out and buy six- or five-ounce cans. They really can't tell the difference of one or two ounces—they don't have scales at the table. We do a little substitution, like in the meat, but as far as food goes, we're pretty decent. It's the food that brings customers back.

The waitresses and busboys don't get in on any of the free stuff, but sometimes clients will give you money to pass out to them, and we give it to them. We're not going to cheat them because they're workers. Usually, we won't try to rip off a client representing a good cause, like a charity, even though they might be ripping off people who have donated money to them. If they are good people and are really straight with you and say, "We don't have a lot of money to spend on the party," then you

277

wouldn't do it. We just sort of base our thinking on how much money we've made for the week and how much the guy's able to pay. ✒

COCKTAIL WAITRESS

Georgia N. "didn't know vodka from Scotch" when she began the first of three jobs she had as a cocktail waitress. A divorcee, she worked the trade for several years while waiting to get a job in her chosen profession. During this time, she got hardened to some of the practices that go on in suburban cocktail lounges, and she learned a lot about the business by dating a bartender. "A lot of waitresses would make fun of you if you were honest," says Georgia. "Eventually, I got to the point where I would not feel bad padding a customer's bill." Nevertheless, it was neither a satisfying nor a particularly lucrative occupation, and finally she was glad to get out of "this flow of cheating people."

Customers are easily ripped off by waitresses. The easiest way is simply to overestimate the bill. In a couple of places I worked, it was the waitress's responsibility to call out the prices to the bartender, who would ring up the bill. The bartender is usually so busy, he doesn't have time to add the drinks up himself, so the waitress can just add in $2 or $3 more than the customer ordered. The house benefits from the overcharge, but the waitress gets a bigger tip, since the bill is inflated.

I worked with a girl named Maggie, and there was always a controversy around her. She was experienced at waitressing and good at ripping off customers and the joint as well. We ran tabs all evening, and each waitress kept her own checks for each of her tables in a little divider thing at the bar. Of course, I would write down the table number and everything I could think of to help me remember which table it belonged to so the drinks were

278

right, and so forth. Maggie never wrote down any names or table numbers on the tabs she kept—just whatever the bartender put on for each round of drinks—$13.50, or whatever.

She would then mix up the checks, and if there was a group of people who looked like they didn't know how much their bill was, she would present them with a larger bill when they were paying. Say their bill was $26. She would show them another table's bill, which was, say $40. The guy would ask, "Are you sure?" and then she would vaguely go down the line and say, "Remember, you had this . . . and this . . . etc." And the guy would shake his head and say, "Oh well, I guess it's all here on the bill," and he'd pay up. She'd then pay the bartender the $26 bill and pocket the rest. And there I was trying so hard to keep all my tabs straight. She was incredible.

Some of the waitresses were so hardened they would rip off change from your tip jar. We each had our own jars because we wore little skirts and couldn't carry the change with us. Maggie, however, was very careful to keep in good with the other waitresses, because she knew that anyone watching her too closely could tell on her.

In one place I worked, where we usually just told customers what they owed without presenting a bill, I would tell people their bill was more than it was and pocket the difference. The bills there were smaller, $10 or $12, and it didn't bother me to add $1 or so onto a bill. The only ones I would rip off were the ones who had been mean. Often, they're the worst ones to do it to, because they would ask to see the bill and go over it. If you were caught, you'd correct your mistake and be a little apologetic, and everything was all right.

In another place, we carried cash in our pocket, gave out our own change, and bought our own drinks. The bartender was so old he couldn't add anything, so, since that was our responsibility, we would simply not pay him for all the drinks (I did this only occasionally). Let's say there were sixteen drinks on the tray, four of which were $2.50 each, and the rest were $2 each. I would just multiply sixteen by $2 when I was paying the bartender for them, and he would never remember that he had poured more expensive liquor into those four glasses. I probably made $4 a round at the most doing that.

The last place I worked I really did it up good, because I was dating a bartender. That's where I made a whole $20 on a tab, because he didn't ring it up at all. I just pocketed the customers' money. Of course, he could have gotten in trouble if there were spotters around. The owner of a place, especially one who is losing money, will hire spotters to come in and sit at the bar and watch the numbers on the register, the number of drinks, etc.

Sometimes bartenders would not make me pay if I had lost a tab or if customers had walked out on me without paying. It was the waitress's responsibility to pay a tab anytime there was a walkout—and this happened maybe once a night. These were usually small tabs, $12 or so, and usually involved college students. I've had to run across the parking lot to catch a walkout. They'd say, "Oh, I forgot."

Despite the fact that I dated one, I would never trust most of the bartenders. Most of the ones I saw hired were pretty questionable. It was their whole life-style—dealing with people all night long, people who are really not themselves, is kind of unrealistic. Most of the honest ones I knew were working full-time at something else and just moonlighting at the bar.

People who deal in stolen credit cards sometimes either work in conjunction with bartenders, or they'll use them to see if the cards are still good. Bars, of course, if they accept credit cards, get the hot-card lists. I've seen customers asking the bartender to check to see if a credit card was good, then, if it was, paying and leaving right away. Probably to purchase all they could elsewhere.

When an owner was losing money, he would start doing more inventories and have more spotters come in. But the minute that everything loosened up, the bartenders would take advantage of it. They would bring their tennis stuff in, then when the bar was empty during a slow time, they'd put a bottle in their carrying bag.

I didn't see any drink-watering, although I was told by a bartender they had refilled certain wine bottles. They would substitute hard liquors, if the house brand was the same quality as the more expensive one—mostly because it was right in front of them and so much handier. The owner would set the standards for the amount of liquor in a drink, although usually the bartenders poured more, because it gave them better tips. They'd generally give regular customers a free drink for every tenth one they served them, and the owners went along with that. Actually, it was no big deal—the cost of the liquor in a drink, I've heard, is something like ten cents, and the labor is not that much, since the waitress is working mostly for tips. Most of the cost is the overhead.

Waitresses' salaries are almost nothing. We worked for $1 an hour at the most, and in some big places you just work for tips only. That's why you get hardened to it and why waitresses rip off people. You're not treated in a very businesslike way. They would make you come in and do all kinds of work: Scrubbing up tables and trimming candles and wicks, and then they'd tease you about your short dress. Once, they told me to get a different bra. I depended on tips almost entirely. Sometimes a customer would not leave a tip, but generally I found people were pretty good about it. We averaged about 15 percent.

It's the customers who are trying to make a big impression on the people they are taking out who are ripped off. Maggie used to short-change them. She'd just put their change on the table without counting it out, and because they were trying to be cordial, they'd put it into their pocket without counting it, either. Couples who come in only occasionally are seldom ripped off, because they are higher risks. Very often I'd hear waitresses talking about the wife complaining about a bill. The husband was not going to question it, but then the wife got angry and did. If it's a husband and wife, it's always the wife who brings up the question.

We could tell instantly which customers were out on business entertainment where the company was paying the bill. They were usually big tippers, because all their business associates were watching them pay or sign their credit card ticket. We would all fight over those tables, because often they made the difference between a profitable and unprofitable evening. Expense account people drank a lot more and faster—because it was all on the company. You could usually recognize a business group, because there was not an equal number of men and women. You usually know the story of half your customers, and I often saw guys I knew who were married taking out a couple of their secretaries for $20 worth of cocktails.

At one place I worked, if a woman was drunk, they would ask her to leave, saying, "I really think you have had enough." They were honest enough to do everything possible to keep her from getting another drink. At another place, though, it was just the opposite. We would never tell anyone they couldn't order another drink—instead the bartender just gave her the mixer, and she was so drunk she could not tell the difference. The people were throwing around their money so fast that I don't think we felt any pity. 🖊

TAVERN KEEPER

As the keeper of a small, neighborhood tavern, Walt A. is fortunate to have the sort of people tending bar whom he can trust when he's not there. He's also blessed with a good accountant, who tells him just how much income he can get away with skimming.

When the percentage is down, any tavern owner can siphon off some income. We all do. We just have to be sure and siphon no more than looks reasonable. Normally, you buy all your beer and booze from a distributor, and the bills go in, and you pay taxes on that. But if you buy booze from a liquor store, there is no bill, and that's our main way of doing it. Especially when booze is on sale, the liquor stores are selling it cheaper than the tavern keeper can buy it through the normal channels. You can buy a quart of whiskey for $5, and at seventy-five cents a shot, you're going to get about $25 selling it across the bar. So that's $20 you can put in your pocket. You'll ring up the sales, but no one's going to see the tape, other than the bookkeeper.

If you don't skim 10 percent of your gross, then you are crazy. The danger limit depends completely on your volume and how much was reported before you bought the place. You have to be careful, but hell, your CPA or bookkeeper will tell you what you can and can't do. Every CPA I ever knew gladly told me to skim. They even keep two sets of books for you: One they give to you, and one they turn in. They'll come right out and tell you, "Hey, dummy, don't send in more than . . ." I'd say a good minimum average in the trade is 10 percent, but in many cases, it's probably higher than that. I know a guy who's ridiculous. His wife is driving a new Caddie, he was in Florida last week, he went to Hawaii, he took his mother to Europe, and he was in Vegas and Acapulco, and he isn't making any money, officially. ✔

FAST-FOOD WORKER

It would come as no surprise to most Americans that the hamburger outlet Rosette G. worked for kept her hustling most of the time. As a new employee, she looked forward to earning the minimum wage while grilling hamburgers, frying potatoes, making shakes, and working the counter. Once aboard, she found the manager ran a tight ship, though not one without leaks. Rosette is no longer employed by this massive purveyor of fast foods, nor does she eat there anymore.

I have seen hamburgers sit out on the warming tray for forty-five minutes to an hour—you could just see the grease coming out of the package. It is company procedure that if they've been out there more than ten minutes, you throw them away, but the manager will not allow this. He'll say, "Look, they'll eventually sell," and hopefully someone will come in with a big order, and they will. But by then the whole bun will be soggy. The same thing applied to french fries, and once, I scooped up a bunch of soggy ones and threw them away. The manager told me to stop throwing them away, or I would be charged for them.

One day, this girl made about twenty-five shakes, and the manager came up and said, "You made too many—you'll have to pay for them." The same thing happens with hamburgers. Nobody tells us how many we have to make, but if we don't make enough, we get chewed out. There's no procedure for this, you just have to look at the crowd and judge how many you need. Then the crowd may suddenly dissolve, and there you are sitting there with thirty-six hamburgers. That girl had to pay for the shakes, and the manager pocketed the money. He would either demand cash on the spot or tell you it would be deducted out of your check. Usually, it was for cash, because if it were deducted out of your check, he couldn't pocket it. If you didn't have the cash, he would tell you to bring it in tomorrow or when you cashed your check, or else you would get fired. All of this, of course, had nothing to do with company procedure. He'd just end up putting the shakes in another freezer. The food he charged you for he usually sold, anyway, so it made his report look better at the end of the week.

If a piece of meat fell on the floor, we were told to pick it back up and put it on the grill. You didn't even put it under the faucet. The sanitation is pretty good, but the floor still has grease and a lot of bun crumbs, and people are walking all over it. Once we had a whole box spill in the freezer, and there were about seventy-five all over the floor. The manager said, "We're wasting money, cook them anyway."

The managers would give hundreds of dollars of food away to their friends, yet we would get fired if we ever did it. They would get a bag and start stuffing it, or they would come to one of us and pull us over to the side and say, "Fix a bag of a couple of hamburgers and some fries and hand it to that guy over there."

You'd hand it to them and not go to the register at all. They were just friends of theirs who'd wandered in and wanted food.

One night, several hundred dollars was missing. They said it was missing from the registers, but it wasn't, because none of them had that much money, and they are changed every hour. They called my whole shift in, and nobody said anything, so they suspended the whole shift one week without pay. If something like a box of cookies was stolen, they would accuse somebody they just wanted to get rid of and fire them. You had to be screwing the manager to get along. If a girl were going with him and he liked her, he'd take her out for pizza for an hour and leave the whole crew on the floor unattended.

On an eight-hour shift, we only got a twenty-minute break, and if you cursed on the floor, they would take your break away. Well, if you burn the hell out of your hand—cooking fries in all that grease—what are you supposed to say, "Oh, my, I burned my hand"? One girl had a whole basket of hot fries fall on her arm—she had marks and stuff—and they just put some burn ointment on and made her go back to work. They don't even pay any damages. One guy got burned, and they took him to the hospital. They found the burns weren't serious, and the guy had to pay the hospital bill himself. If you say, "Hey, I would like to see a doctor," they'll tell you, "See him on your own time."

When you're scheduled for closing, you have to stay and clean up, even scrubbing the baseboards on your knees. You get paid until a half-hour after closing, but if it takes an hour or hour-and-a-half to clean up, you don't get paid at all for your overtime. They have tried to unionize us, but the company fights it. They have stacks and stacks of applications—and a lot of kids in my neighborhood need that job, so they are not ready to cause a bunch of static to get unionized. If all the employees in one particular shop said, "we have unionized," they would just fire all of us.   ✔